Worship Matters

A United Methodist Guide to Worship Work

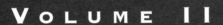

WITHDRAWN

Volume II

Edited by
E. Byron Anderson

DISCIPLESHIP RESOURCES

P.O. BOX 840 • NASHVILLE, TENNESSEE 37202-0840

www.discipleshipresources.org

Cover design by Sharon Anderson

Book design by Kym Whitley

Illustrations on pages 137–39 by Susan Harrison

ISBN 0-88177-280-1

Library of Congress Catalog Card No. 98-96831

DR280

Contents

ABBREVIATIONS

All references to the official resources of The United Methodist Church listed below appear in parentheses in the articles.

BOD	=	The Book of Discipline of The United Methodist Church—1996
MV	=	Mil Voces Para Celebrar: Himnario Metodista
UMBOW	=	The United Methodist Book of Worship
UMH	=	The United Methodist Hymnal

Introduction

E. Byron Anderson

Assistant Professor of Worship, Christian Theological Seminary, Indianapolis, Indiana

THE UNITED METHODIST CHURCH FACES MANY CHALLENGES today. The shape, practice, and style of worship ranks high on the list of our concerns, because worship is the single most public event in the church's life. The church expresses these concerns in the form of various polarizations. We express and create tensions between those perceived to be "high church sacramentalists" over against "low church preachers." There are conflicts between "traditionalists" and advocates of "contemporary" liturgical and musical styles, as well as between those concerned with theological orthodoxy and those more concerned with social-cultural relevance. There is stress between growth experts who argue for a communal homogeneity—whether of age, musical taste, economic status, or personal need—and those who call our attention to the increasing racial diversification and globalization of our churches. The list continues to grow. As it does so, United Methodist pastors, preachers, worship leaders and planners find cause to explore the particular gifts and graces of United Methodist worship, particularly as represented in the basic worship resources of the church: *The United Methodist Hymnal* and *The United Methodist Book of Worship.*

These conflicts are not the only reasons to give renewed attention to United Methodist worship. For more than half a century, we could safely assume a stable, relatively homogeneous, church community, with churches planted at every crossroad or train stop across the country. We could also assume that our churches would continue to grow as our children grew, married, joined the church, had their own children (in some order of these events), and as their children repeated the pattern. For a variety of reasons, this is not the case today in many of our churches. The church has changed, as has the religious sensibility of the country. We know that today the largest number of unchurched people is not across either ocean but in our own back yards. The mission field is on our doorsteps. We also know that many people of all ages, but especially youth and young to middle-aged adults, are seeking places and practices that will give meaning to their lives. North-American Christianity today, especially United Methodism, provides a quickly changing landscape in which to explore a tradition of worship.

In many ways, it is our very awareness of this changing landscape and of the missionary context in which we live that places the questions of the shape, practice, and style of worship before us. Although the mission field in North America has always been with us, the shape and context of that field has changed. This creates new questions for the practice of worship:

- Can we create worship that is open and inviting to the unchurched? What does this mean and look like?
- Can we also create worship that nurtures and sustains the existing Christian community? What does this mean and look like?

Some insist that invitation and nurture are, by necessity, conflicting goals, but we need not let them be. Rather, they create an opportunity inviting us to a new creativity and exploration of the ways we worship. In the midst of this exploration, we know that no single book, not even the two volumes of *Worship Matters,* can definitively describe or define a final answer to our questions. Nevertheless, we can attempt to clear away some of the underbrush that clutters the landscape, preventing us from visiting or revisiting what should be familiar territory. In these volumes, we hope to keep these questions, conflicts, and tensions before us, using them to dig deep and to think hard about the work of worship in The United Methodist Church.

As we dig and think and question, we do so with specific reference to the official worship resources of The United Methodist Church that were approved or authorized by action of the General Conference and defined in the *Book of Discipline:*

> The hymnals of The United Methodist Church are *The United Methodist Hymnal* (1989) and *Mil Voces Para Celebrar: Himnario Metodista* (1996). The ritual of the Church is that contained in *The United Methodist Hymnal* (1989), *The United Methodist Book of Worship* (1992), and *Mil Voces Para Celebrar: Himnario Metodista* (1996).
>
> (*BOD,* ¶1112.3)[1]

As we give our attention to these resources, we also are attempting to take seriously the charge laid upon deacons and elders in their ordinations to receive the "order, liturgy, doctrine, and discipline" of the church (*UMBOW,* p. 690).[2] We also are attempting to take seriously the truth that there are numerous gifts in United Methodist worship, but only one Spirit through whom God's love is expressed in a variety of ways. That is, while we are *united* as a Christian people and church in worship and praise of the triune God, our worship and praise are not *uniform*—as the English and Spanish titles of our worship resources and their diverse contents make clear.

WORSHIP AS LITURGY/LITURGY AS WORSHIP

As we begin to reflect on the work of planning worship, it may be helpful to think about what it is we think we are doing in worship. What do we mean by *worship?* For some, worship is primarily the sermon. For others, worship refers to the activities of song and prayer that build toward the sermon. For still others, worship primarily is gathering about the Lord's Table with thanksgiving for the sharing of bread and cup. For some, worship is a duty; for others, it is a delight. For some, it is the means by which people are brought to new life in Christ; for others, it is the primary means for sustaining and renewing that life—a kind of weekly "filling station." What becomes clear is that, to some extent, worship is all of these things.

Even so, there is also a sense in which we have lost sight of what worship is. Arguments about style and form have turned us away from the intent of worship. *How* we worship—formally or informally, with traditional or contemporary music—is not *what* worship is. Nevertheless, *how* and *what* are related. When our attention turns more and more to those who come or those we hope will come to worship and, therefore, to how we worship, worship becomes more what is done to us or for us and less what we do for another. When this happens, regardless of how we worship, we miss what matters most about worship.

Worship, at its most basic meaning, is "to give worth or respect to something or someone."³ Worship, therefore, is something we do; no one can worship for us. Why? While communities and groups may define what is worthy of our respect, our individual response is required. This response of worship recognizes the presence and worthiness of the other. In worship we place ourselves in the presence of that other. In worship we express a desire for and place ourselves in relationship to that other. So the psalmist sings:

> O come, let us sing to the LORD;
>   let us make a joyful noise to the
>   rock of our salvation!…
> O come, let us worship and bow down,
>   let us kneel before the LORD, our Maker!
>   (Psalm 95:1, 6)

Or as John records in Revelation 5:13-14:

> "To the one seated on the throne
>   and to the Lamb
> be blessing and honor and glory and might
> forever and ever!"
> And the four living creatures said, "Amen!"
> And the elders fell down and worshiped.

In duty and delight, with lamentation and praise, in recognition of and response to the presence of God, we worship so that we may be joined to the holiness of God. Worship is something we *do*, joined in community with others who have recognized and responded to the presence of God. It is in this sense that we can talk about worship as *liturgy*. It is unfortunate that most of us on hearing the word *liturgy* think of printed texts and orders of worship. By doing so, we set up some of the perceived tensions between "high" and "low" and "formal" and "free" styles of worship. When we reclaim the basic understanding of *worship* as "giving worth to God," we must also reclaim the root understanding of *liturgy*. The word *liturgy* is a combination of the Greek words *laos*, meaning "people," and *ergos*, meaning "work"—thus, "people's work." *Liturgy* is "work undertaken by or on behalf of people."

In the secular world at the time of early Christianity, *liturgy* referred to what we today would call "public service"—projects undertaken by individuals or communities for the good of a community. New Testament writers used this understanding as well. The connection between *liturgy* and *service* is hard to see in English translations; so in each of the following biblical references, I have placed in bold the word or words that translate *liturgy* or *liturgist*. In the Gospel of Luke, Zechariah's **"time of service"** in the Temple is his liturgy (1:23). In the Letter to the Romans, Paul describes the civic authorities who collect taxes as God's **"servants,"** that is, as God's liturgists (13:6). Paul speaks of himself as a liturgist when he describes himself as "a **minister** of Christ Jesus…in the priestly service of the gospel of God" (Romans 15:16). Paul also describes the collection for the church in Jerusalem as a liturgy: "The rendering of this **ministry** not only supplies the needs of the saints but also overflows with many

Worship is something we *do*, joined in community with others who have recognized and responded to the presence of God. It is in this sense that we can talk about worship as *liturgy.*

thanksgivings to God" (2 Corinthians 9:12). The Letter to the Hebrews not only describes Jesus as a "liturgist of God" but also describes his work as a liturgy: Christ seated at the throne of God is "a **minister** in the sanctuary and the true tent that the Lord, and not any mortal, has set up" (Hebrews 8:2). "But Jesus has now obtained a more excellent **ministry,** and to that degree he is the mediator of a better covenant, which has been enacted through better promises" (8:6).

In all of these references, we discover that *liturgy* refers to a kind of service or ministry done by someone, with or on behalf of another. We also begin to see that liturgy is not limited to what we do in church. Our "giving worth" to God continues beyond the doors of the church, beyond Sunday morning.

To talk about worship as a liturgy, then, is to understand that what we do in worship is a ministry or service to God and to one another. The liturgy of worship, perhaps more familiarly the "service of worship," is the work of the Christian people praising God in the midst of the world. If we think about liturgy as public service or work, and worship as giving worth to God, we begin to see what we as Christian communities are planning for and doing as we engage in the "public work of worship." Worship is our liturgy, our service; and our liturgy is worship.

THE COMMUNITY AT WORSHIP

In talking about *liturgy* as our "public work of worship," we discover several things. First, Christian worship is directed toward the One who is worthy—the triune God of Christian faith—not at those who come to worship. Second, worship is an activity the Christian community is called to do: Worship is our work in response to the presence and grace of God. Third, as work that the community does, the "ministers" of worship are not only those involved in preparing or leading worship—preachers, readers, musicians, and others—but the whole of the community called out and gathered together by God in Christ Jesus. This is even to say that the primary actors and "ministers" in worship are not the worship leaders but those who gather to worship in Christ's name—the whole of the Christian community. Although the chapters that follow focus on those whose ministries or liturgy are the planning and leading of worship, the starting point for our consideration of people in worship must be the community gathered for and engaged in its work of worship. As I argued in "The Role of the Presider" in Volume I of *Worship Matters* (pp. 123–29), this work is not reserved for the ordained, consecrated, or licensed. It is the common work of the baptized community to praise, worship, and glorify God.

The Danish theologian Søren Kierkegaard provided a helpful, and now familiar, analogy for the work of worship when he described worship as a drama.[4] This analogy in itself was not unusual; the musical style of the evangelical (Lutheran) and Catholic churches of Kierkegaard's day drew more from the opera house than from the prayer meeting. What was unusual was the way in which he assigned the parts of actors, director, and audience. For Kierkegaard, the actors were the gathered community; the congregation enacted its worship of God. Worship leaders functioned as directors or prompters in this drama, assisting the congregation in its work, cuing lines, directing movement, enabling the action to take place. The audience? God, of course.

What Kierkegaard understood of worship in his own Lutheran church in the nineteenth century, the Roman Catholic community claimed for worship in the reforms of the Second Vatican Council in the 1960's: Vital and faithful worship requires the "full, conscious, and active participation"[5] of all the faithful in the work of worship. As United Methodists on the cusp of a new century and millennium, we are aware that planning and implementing vital and faithful worship requires not only a recovery of the dramatic sense of a community enacting worship in the presence of God, but also the education and formation that will enable such full, conscious, and active participation by our congregations in the work of worship. At the least, this requires a recovery of worship that engages and involves the hearts, minds, and bodies of the whole congregation. In doing so, we may recover a sense of worship as a credible and public witness of our sacrifice, service, ministry of praise and thanksgiving to God, rather than one product among others the church offers for the spiritual consumer.

Finally, while we have emphasized the character of worship as the work of the community of faith, we would be typically, but incorrectly, self-(human)centered to think that it is our work alone. At this point we discover the inadequacy of Kierkegaard's analogy. God is not only the audience distantly observing our work of worship; God is also *host to* and an *actor with* us in this work. The discussion of our doctrinal heritage in the *Book of Discipline* reminds us of the distinctive Wesleyan emphasis on the cooperative nature of God's grace and human work: "We see God's grace and human activity working together in the relationship of faith and good works. God's grace calls forth human response and discipline" (*BOD,* ¶60, p. 45).[6] Worship is, at one and the same time, the cooperative work of the Christian community with God in Christ Jesus through the abiding presence and power of the Holy Spirit, even as it is our work in response to God's grace. That is, the work and the theology of United Methodist worship are trinitarian at their core and in their fullness. It is the recognition of the presence of the triune God, the One who is worthy, in our midst that evokes our worship. This is and must be our foundation for planning and implementing vital and faithful worship as United Methodists.

OVERVIEW

The two volumes of *Worship Matters—A United Methodist Guide to Ways to Worship* (Volume I) and *A United Methodist Guide to Worship Work* (Volume II)—have a common starting point: Worship *matters* because it is at the heart of and vital to the work of the local church as it makes, nurtures, and sends disciples in ministry to the world. Although Volume I is more theological in its approach and Volume II is more practical, both draw upon the close relationship between theology and practice. The work of planning worship must build upon informed and critical reflection on Scripture, tradition, and experience. At the same time, our reflection must account for the realities of our practices in particular places and times. In this, the *how* and *why* of United Methodist worship must answer more than the pragmatic question, What works? It also must answer the question, What is this work doing?

In preparing these volumes, we understand reflection and action to be mutual partners, joined hand in hand, for the work of worship. Volume I provides basic perspectives on worship for the emerging missionary context in North America, emphasizing the importance of worship in making, nurturing, and sending disciples. Volume II provides a practical guide for

Worship is an activity the Christian community is called to do: Worship is our work in response to the presence and grace of God.

planning and implementing vital and faithful worship, emphasizing the materials of worship. Both volumes support the work of worship with the basic United Methodist patterns and practices. Both volumes address the importance and materials of United Methodist worship. Worship *matters!*

INTRODUCTION TO VOLUME II

This second volume of *Worship Matters* provides pastors and other worship leaders and planners with practical resources for vital and faithful worship. It focuses on the people, places, and planning of United Methodist worship. Because of this emphasis on people and planning, local churches are permitted, as stipulated on page 2 in this book, to make photocopies of the articles for use with local church worship committees, leaders, and planning teams.

PART ONE: PEOPLE IN WORSHIP

In the preceding pages, we sought to name the congregation as the primary minister of worship. Worship is first and foremost the congregation's work. In Part One, we look beyond these roles to the diverse ministries involved in planning, leading, and supporting the work of worship: planning teams, readers, musicians, acolytes, Communion stewards and servers, ushers, dancers, videographers, video technicians, and visual artists. The role of the presider in worship, with particular attention to the work of elders and deacons, was discussed in Volume I.

PART TWO: CREATING SPACE FOR WORSHIP

As some architects would argue, form follows function. If the shape of United Methodist worship is changing, then we must pay attention to the spaces in which that worship happens. Whether we are involved in building new worship spaces or in redesigning old ones, we must ask about the spaces for Holy Communion, baptism, and preaching, as well as the space for storing and preparing the things necessary for use in worship. The articles in this part of the book explore each of these spaces.

PART THREE: PLANNING AND GUIDING WORSHIP

Part Three is clearly defined as the how-to section, with each article addressing a particular planning question. After attending to perspectives, people, and places of worship, we are ready to talk about how congregations can welcome and include children in worship, how to learn and sing new songs and hymns, how to make music without a choir, how to introduce baptism by pouring and immersion, and how to make the offering a vital part of worship. We also look at particular planning contexts: small-membership congregations, multicultural congregations, worship in an oral context, and worship with people who are deaf, deafened, or hard of hearing.

A congregation's work of worship in each place and time requires thoughtful planning and careful reflection. How we worship must be closely joined with why we worship, who (or what) we worship, and who is worshiping. We hope this volume will nurture vital and faithful worship work in your congregation.

ENDNOTES

1 From *The Book of Discipline of The United Methodist Church—1996,* ¶1112.3. Copyright © 1996 by The United Methodist Publishing House. Used by permission.

2 From "The Order for Consecrations and Ordinations," © 1979 by Board of Discipleship, The United Methodist Church; © 1992 by The United Methodist Publishing House; from *The United Methodist Book of Worship,* p. 690. Used by permission.

3 In *Introduction to Christian Worship,* Revised Edition (Nashville, TN: Abingdon Press, 1990), James F. White provides a helpful review of the various names and definitions for worship, as well as the implications of these for how we worship (pp. 25–37).

4 See *Purity of Heart Is to Will One Thing: Spiritual Preparation for the Office of Confession,* by Søren Kierkegaard, translated by Douglas V. Steere (New York, NY: Harper & Brothers Publishers, 1948), pp. 180–81.

5 From "Constitution on the Sacred Liturgy (Sacrosanctum Concilium)" in *The Documents of Vatican II,* edited by Walter M. Abbott, S.J. (New York, NY: The America Press, 1966), p. 144.

6 From *The Book of Discipline of The United Methodist Church—1996,* ¶ 60, p. 45. Copyright © 1996 by The United Methodist Publishing House. Used by permission.

How we worship must be closely joined with why we worship, who (or what) we worship, and who is worshiping.

Part One

PEOPLE IN WORSHIP

The Work of the Worship Planning Team

DAVID L. BONE

Administrator, The Fellowship of United Methodists in Music and Worship Arts, Nashville, Tennessee

MARY J. SCIFRES

Pastor, Fircrest United Methodist Church, Tacoma, Washington

PLANNING CORPORATE WORSHIP PROVIDES AN IMPORTANT opportunity for pastors, musicians, worship leaders, artists, and others to work together as a team. Both paid staff members and volunteers find in team planning a vehicle in which they can minister together. Lay and ordained people have equally important roles to play in this ministry. Such planning also can be a vehicle through which worship committees can begin to provide an important aspect of their ministry—namely, taking responsibility for the worship life of the congregation.

Unfortunately, the most common worship planning model in churches seems to be one that could easily be termed the "lone-ranger" model. The preaching pastor chooses the Scripture readings, often picking one or more from the Revised Common Lectionary; chooses a sermon topic to correspond with the reading(s) and writes the sermon; chooses hymns to correspond with the sermon topic for the coming Sunday; and writes or chooses liturgical responses, readings, and prayers for the bulletin only minutes before the last printing deadline. The church secretary or pastor types and prints bulletins. The choir director and/or the organist picks up a note from a mailbox with hymn numbers for the coming Sunday. If time permits, the choir rehearses hymns during rehearsal. Anthem and choral responses for Sunday, which were chosen at least a month ago, are rehearsed as well. Rarely do the musical selections correspond to the Scripture readings and sermon topic. A lay liturgist arrives early on Sunday morning to mark Scripture passages and read over the bulletin; and the musicians arrive to warm up and rehearse the prepared anthem and choral responses. The worship commences.

If this is how worship most often comes together in your church, you may want to consider another model for planning worship. Many pastors find the lone-ranger model the most convenient because all decisions are made by one person (the preacher), with the exception of instrumental music and choral anthems. However, many of these same pastors yearn for an opportunity to work with others in developing worship plans, but time demands and seemingly disinterested musicians and worship leaders discourage pastoral initiative toward team planning. Many musicians, likewise, wish for a more integrated approach to their roles and ministries in worship; but again, time demands and seemingly disinterested pastors discourage their initiative toward team planning. Although the lone-ranger model is common and in many ways efficient, it is not the most effective model. As an alternative, we suggest that pastors, musicians, and worship leaders consider a *team-based* approach to planning. There are many benefits to an approach based on teamwork. Consider the following:

- Even a cursory review of the chosen Scripture readings by the team can yield insights to the preaching pastor. Perhaps the musician remembers a different approach to one of the parables of Jesus that he or she encountered at a summer music conference. Maybe a layperson remembers a time when a Bible passage had a personal, special meaning. A wide variety of responses from team members to a selected Scripture passage can help the preaching pastor better understand the complexity of interpreting that Scripture passage to the congregation. This sharing can help the preaching pastor prepare to preach.

- In the lone-ranger model, musicians often feel that they are providing background music or performing anthems simply for the enjoyment of the congregation. In a team-based planning model, musicians are confronted with the awesome role that music can play in worship where God is the audience. If they know the reason why a certain anthem or prelude is appropriate to the day's worship, they have a greater investment in its offering. Thus, they become ministers of music and worship and not simply hired musicians.

- With a longer preparation time, all the musical offerings in the service can be of a higher quality. The staff and lay musicians can offer the music with confidence and clarity of purpose.

- After a worship planning model has been successfully implemented, many pastors and musicians find a great relief in workload because of the increased number of people participating in the planning of worship.

- Worship leaders (preachers, musicians, artists) who work together often can avoid the danger of burnout that comes from idea wells running dry due to lack of new streams of thought.

- Over time, if a wide variety of laypeople are involved in the process of planning worship, more people in the congregation will begin to understand and appreciate worship on a deeper level.

- Team planning often generates a variety of ideas about how to help people worship God. Because of the increased diversity of worship styles presented by a team, worshipers of many different spiritual types find their needs met in one church's worship services.

One of the most crucial aspects of developing a team-based approach to planning worship is establishing communication between pastors and musicians. Whatever the planning approach, pastors need to know the time requirements for planning music. Each choir director can communicate to the pastor the average length of time needed to pick an anthem, order the anthem if necessary, and rehearse it before a Sunday morning worship service. Each organist or pianist can communicate the average time needed to pick a keyboard work, order the music, and rehearse it before worship. Likewise, both organist and choir director need to let the pastor know the amount of time needed to prepare the Sunday morning hymns before Sunday morning.

Pastors may discover that an organist's playing or a choir's singing improves greatly when they are able to rehearse hymns a few weeks in advance rather than a few days, hours, or minutes in advance. Finally, the musicians can communicate with the pastor what their visions are for music ministry as a part of the worship service.[1]

On their part, pastors need to inform musicians of special needs for musical support. Some pastors establish cues that alert the musician that music is needed during an unexpected situation in worship. A pastor can tell the musicians what his or her expectations are regarding worship leadership roles: Listen attentively to the sermon; face the cross during the Doxology; stand as a hymn introduction begins; face the congregation during hymn singing. Additionally, the pastor can communicate with the musicians what her or his visions are for music ministry as a part of the worship service.

These initial communications are essential when the worship planners begin to work together and also when there are personnel changes in the worship planning team. As each of the worship leaders learns about the others' responsibilities, work styles, visions, and gifts, the team will grow and strengthen its ability to plan quality worship services.

Most worship staffs feel at a loss when beginning a team-based approach to worship planning. Thus, in the remainder of the article, we offer a model that many worship planners have found helpful in beginning the process toward team-based planning. Of course, each congregation will need to adapt these ideas to the unique situation, gifts, and interests of the worship service participants and team planners involved.

GATHERING THE TEAM

1. Create a planning process that will work in your congregation. This article can help you design this process, but you and another worship leader are best suited for proposing a process that can succeed in your situation. Your planning process may change over time, but you need an idea of what you are asking others to do before you ask them. Below are some questions to address as you begin the planning process:

- How often will the team meet?
- How many people other than the preaching pastor and the music leaders are needed on the team?
- Will the team do all the planning, or will there be subteams to work on specific services?
- Is it possible to prepare simple job descriptions for each member of the team? What exactly do you expect each person to do in and outside the team meetings?

2. Begin gathering a team. Make a list of possible team members, including the preaching pastor(s), music leader(s), and members of the congregation. Review the talents of individuals in the congregation, looking for artists, visionaries, leaders, organizers, and workers. Try to create a list that reflects a diversity of age, gender, congregational status, and social status. An interested child or youth can often offer insights that would otherwise be lacking. If the Scripture reading for the day is about the ark of the covenant, a child might be the only person to remember that a Sunday school class made a model of the ark only weeks earlier and that this model might be effectively used in the service.

Prioritize the list of names. Balance gifts and talents, as well as time and commitment levels. Members of the worship planning team should expect to meet at least twice a year. Some worship teams find weekly, monthly, or seasonal planning meetings helpful, but even two meetings a year can immensely improve communication and coordination.

Once you have made a list of possible team members in order of priority, begin contacting them, asking them to prayerfully consider

Team planning often generates a variety of ideas about how to help people worship God.

joining the team. Explain the outline of the process you plan to use. It might be best not to contact all the people on the list at once. If one person declines your invitation, you might need to reconsider your list in order to maintain diversity.

3. When you receive a yes, be sure to respond to the team member with appropriate signs of welcome and appreciation. Above all, convene the new team as soon as possible. Avoid letting the excitement of participating in a new venture be lessened through delays in getting started.

PREPARING THE TEAM

1. A team leader should be selected to coordinate the meeting. This duty might rotate among the team members. The leader should be sure that all information about the worship services to be considered has been distributed to the team members. The leader also should take charge of the following logistical arrangements for the meeting:

- Where will the team meet? A retreat setting is appropriate, especially if this is to be a biannual event. Many times, a Saturday spent around a kitchen table can yield a wealth of worship ideas and planning. The process of working, eating, and sharing fellowship is essential to this creative task.

- Determine how often the team will meet and what worship services it will plan. Many teams find that planning for a liturgical season is the most appropriate. Other teams meet monthly or even weekly to look at upcoming services. It is probably best to begin your process with a defined group of services. Plan just the services for Advent and Christmas, or for Lent and Holy Week. After the team begins to function well, the members may want to meet more often and spend more time on each service.

- When will the team meet? The team should meet for a designated period of time. After a few meetings, it will become clear how much time the team needs to plan a given number of worship services. Obviously, the less often the team meets, the more time it needs for each planning meeting.

- What will the team need? Team members will need access to several resources. At the least, these should include: a Bible, a copy of *The United Methodist Hymnal* (or the hymnal used in your services), *The United Methodist Book of Worship*, *The United Methodist Music and Worship Planner* (particularly for use of Scripture readings and hymn lists), and a planning sheet (sample sheets may be found in *The United Methodist Music and Worship Planner,* on pp. 138–39). Musicians may also find it helpful to have access to copies of each of the music collections suggested in *The United Methodist Music and Worship Planner* (pp. 6–7), as well as a single-copy file of the anthem collection of your church.

2. Prior to meeting, the preaching pastor should prepare preliminary Scripture selections and sermon outlines for the worship services the team will consider. Many preachers find that looking at these projected over an extended period of time helps them maintain a logical movement of proclamation themes. For example, during the long period of Ordinary Time (season after Pentecost) in the summer and fall of each year, the Revised Common Lectionary has semicontinuous readings from the Old Testament, the Epistles, and the Gospels. The Scripture readings in Ordinary Time are not designed to support one another but rather to

give the lectionary user a chance to experience a narrative progression from Sunday to Sunday. For someone choosing Scripture readings one Sunday at a time, the advantages of this narrative approach are lost.

The pastor also should prepare a general outline of the worship services the planning team will consider. This outline should focus on the Scripture passages to be read, the sermon themes, and any seasonal emphases (such as Christmas or Lent) or denominational emphases (such as Native American Awareness, Boy/Girl Scouts, or Festival of the Christian Home).

3. Musicians need to have prepared preliminary repertoire lists for the planning meeting. This is especially important for choir directors. Many times, it is easy to get bogged down in trying to select the perfect anthem to go with a given Scripture or Sunday. It is more advantageous to prepare a list of possible works that can be selected from within the planning process. When planning for a liturgical season, it is much easier to select from a list of seasonal works that are already in the church's library or are on the director's wish list. Generally, if the musician creates a list that is twenty-five percent larger than the number of Sundays under consideration, the remaining seventy-five percent will fall neatly into the services being planned.

4. The team leader should disseminate the information from the pastor and musician to the team members. Each team member should review this information prior to the planning meeting. The team leader should contact each member just prior to the meeting to confirm participation and to remind each member to pray for the work of the team.

USING THE TEAM

1. Open the planning meeting with a brief time of worship and prayer. Worship planning in itself can be worship. By worshiping together, team members can open themselves to the working of the Spirit within the planning process. Sharing song, Word, and prayer reminds us of our personal and corporate purpose: to glorify God and to encourage others to share in God's presence. Consider the Orders of Daily Praise and Prayer in *The United Methodist Hymnal* (pp. 876–79) as an order of worship. Do not rush this important step. Allow the group to be open to God's presence. "For where two or three are gathered in my name, I am there among them" (Matthew 18:20).

2. At its initial meeting, the team might begin with a discussion of worship and what it means to each team member. You might ask members to remember and relate a profound worship moment from their own lives. What aspects worked together to create the experience? Was it an experience that seemed planned, or did it develop spontaneously? There is no need to come up with one particular philosophy or purpose of worship; the diversity in team members' opinions can enhance the planning and implementing processes. Over time, the team will develop its own philosophy and theology of worship.[2] It may take some time for team members to work out the differences in these areas and for the team to work together seamlessly. The journey to this agreement will be one of the positive byproducts of the team's work.

3. The preaching pastor should introduce the Scripture readings he or she has selected for each worship service, providing a rationale (if any) for the selections as well as further explanations of the chosen topics and themes. The best worship usually springs forth from the

> **Worship planning in itself can be worship. By worshiping together, team members can open themselves to the working of the Spirit within the planning process.**

Scripture; therefore, it is best to start the discussion with the Scripture readings rather than with specific holy days in the church calendar or special events.

The preaching pastor also should introduce and outline his or her sermon topics or emphases at this time, noting especially any continuing themes or narratives. The team evaluates this general outline and adds items as determined by seasonal needs or special Sundays. Remember to include celebrations of Holy Communion and baptism according to the congregation's practice.

4. The team should begin looking at specific items within each worship service. Hymns can be chosen by the team, keeping in mind thematic and scriptural emphases, musical abilities, sermon topics, congregational hymn preferences, and desire for the introduction of new hymns. The pastor and musician may have prior thoughts about this that can be brought to the meeting.

Look for nontraditional ways to use hymns. Don't settle for the same two or three slots normally reserved for hymns in the congregation's worship services. If a hymn has one stanza that is particularly related to the Scripture reading, use it as a response to the reading. This could be sung by the choir alone, or by the choir and congregation together. If a hymn text is narrative in nature, look to see if the stanzas of the hymn could be logically interspersed with the reading of the Scripture passage on which the hymn is based. Look for ways to use hymn stanzas as congregational calls to worship, calls to prayer, and benedictions. Be creative and use the congregation as another choir.

Introduce and discuss in the planning team special ideas or plans for specific worship services. For example, you may have to incorporate a Palm Sunday cantata or Christmas Eve candlelight service into your plans. Your church may also recognize its own series of special days such as Children's Sunday or Laity Sunday. The Scripture reading for the service might also lead you to plan for a special dramatic reading of the text or a special visual element.

5. Once these ideas have been discussed by the entire team, convene small groups to work on specific worship services. People who are most familiar with a particular aspect of worship should be in the same small group. For example, a small group consisting of the preaching pastor and lay liturgist (or worship committee chairperson) may choose the spoken words (prayers, responsive readings, blessings) to be used in a worship service. The choir director and keyboard player may form a group to select the vocal, choral, and keyboard music. Visual artists on the planning team may want to have time alone to brainstorm about altar decoration or banner creation ideas. If your church is blessed with a drama team or children's performing arts group, those leaders may want some time to discuss where their group's talents might best be used in the coming worship season.

6. After the small groups have had time to develop their specific plans, convene the whole group and begin to focus on specific services. Working on one service at a time, ask a representative from each small group to share her or his group's ideas with the whole planning team. The team leader should ensure that all the ideas are recorded and, when possible, integrated into the worship service being planned.

Now the entire service is ready for review. The team should evaluate the service in terms of how well it is integrated, as well as in terms of its unity and diversity. As the plan for the service is finalized, ask about the placement of specific worship acts. For example, if there is a confession, should it come at the beginning of the service or as a response to the Word? Does the anthem function best as a general act of praise, or does its specific reference to the Scripture reading suggest that it should immediately precede or follow the reading of the Word?

7. Finally, discuss any concerns members of the planning team might have about the service. For example, does the congregation need to be educated about a new liturgy, such as a congregational reaffirmation of baptismal vows? Should the musician lead a few minutes of congregational music rehearsal of a new musical response prior to the service? Create "to-do" lists and discuss what items need to be delegated to other subcommittees or work areas.

8. The team meeting should close as it began, with a brief worship service consisting of at least prayer time and hymn singing. Thank God for the guidance that the team received during the planning. Ask God for continued direction as the plans become reality.

ADJUSTING THE PLAN ALONG THE WAY

For many people, the planning model outlined above may sound ideal but unrealistic. What if the pastor doesn't write sermons more than a week or two in advance? In this case, ask the pastor simply to notify the planning team of chosen Scripture readings or sermon themes as far in advance as possible. If this information is not available, the team can follow the Lectionary and church year to a satisfactory result.

What if the planning team doesn't have time to plan everything together? Be sure that the planned Scriptures and themes are very complete and effectively communicated to the team. The team can then discuss the general outline of the services. Also, smaller teams or individuals might work on other steps prior to the meeting. The choir director and preacher could meet to discuss hymns and anthems and then offer these suggestions at the team meeting. Likewise, the preacher and worship chair could meet to choose liturgy items and prepare copies for review at the team meeting.

How much planning is too much? Sometimes, a team can get so caught up in planning a service that the outcome seems heavy-handed and overdone. A service based on Psalm 23 with one too many references to "sheep" may send the congregation home with only "baa" on their lips. Usually, the simplest ideas are best. Choose the ideas that best express the Word and sermon theme, and pray that God will use them to inspire the worship. In many situations, one good idea is enough to add excitement to a service, to make its theme memorable, and to inspire the worshiper to service in the world.

How much personal investment should we make in a plan? Enough, but not too much. Worship planning and leading is more like leading a choral rehearsal than presenting a planned lecture. In a lecture, the words are prepared in advance, the listener is prepared to listen to whatever the lecturer has to say, and there is little deviation from the prepared text. In a choral rehearsal, the prepared director uses a plan to teach the music to the choir. The good director also listens to the choir and makes small and large adjustments to the plan as the rehearsal proceeds. Maybe the basses are not as proficient on a phrase as the director thought and additional time must be used to give them security. If the director is too attached to a plan and does not revise it, the singers are frustrated. The guidance of

Usually, the simplest ideas are best.

the Spirit is important not only in the planning of worship but also in the leading. This does not mean that last-minute decisions can be made on a regular basis. Musicians should not be expected to perform a hymn at the drop of a hat, just as preachers should not regularly be expected to preach extemporaneously. But with a good working relationship, worship leaders can make adjustments to the worship plan even as the service is unfolding.

CONCLUSION

Worship planning can be a point of unity and team building. The team that works together serves as a model of corporate worship for the congregation. If we expect people to walk in the church doors on Sunday mornings from their many walks of life to have a corporate experience, we need to reassess the lone-ranger approaches with which we have planned worship services. In so doing, we may find that the Holy Spirit has found a new freedom in which to work.

FOR FURTHER READING

The Fellowship of United Methodists in Music and Worship Arts. A membership organization of The United Methodist Church for people who employ any of the arts in worship. The Fellowship publishes a bimonthly journal (*Worship Arts*) and sponsors local, jurisdictional, and national training events. For membership information, contact: The Fellowship, P.O. Box 24787, Nashville, TN 37202-4787. Phone: 800-952-8977. FAX: 615-749-6874. E-mail: FUMMWA@aol.com. Internet: *http://members.aol.com/fummwa/fummwa.htm*

Fellowship Lectionary Guide. This annual publication lists all the lectionary readings for a year, with a short description of each reading. For membership information, contact The Fellowship at the address listed above.

The United Methodist Music and Worship Planner: 1998–1999, by David L. Bone and Mary J. Scifres (Nashville, TN: Abingdon Press, 1998).

Trouble at the Table: Gathering the Tribes for Worship, by Carol Doran and Thomas H. Troeger (Nashville, TN: Abingdon Press, 1992).

ENDNOTES

1 A wonderful exploration of the differences that exist between pastors and musicians can be found in Chapter 2 of *Trouble at the Table: Gathering the Tribes for Worship,* by Carol Doran and Thomas H. Troeger (Nashville, TN: Abingdon Press, 1992).

2 See the articles on the shape and theology of United Methodist worship in Volume I of *Worship Matters,* Part One (pp. 15–69).

The Work of Reading the Word in Public Worship

Come, divine Interpreter,
bring me eyes thy book to read,
ears the mystic words to hear,
words which did from thee proceed,
words that endless bliss impart,
kept in an obedient heart.

(*UMH*, 594)[1]

GRANT S. WHITE

Assistant Professor of Church History and History of Christian Worship, Saint Paul School of Theology, Kansas City, Missouri

THE WORD OF GOD IN SCRIPTURE IS BREAD FOR FAMISHED pilgrims on the long road to Zion. Yet how often does our reading of Scripture in worship obscure or even negate that fact! In this article, I discuss some theological and liturgical questions that touch on why we read Scripture in public worship and how we might read in a way that most fully sets the table of the Word for hungry people today.

WHY READ THE SCRIPTURE IN WORSHIP?

The church sees the Bible as a living book. Hearing the Word is an encounter with God, who continues to speak to the church through the Scriptures. Thus the reading of Scripture is a sacramental event—an occasion for God's self-giving (to use the phrase of James F. White in *Sacraments as God's Self Giving*).[2] God speaks to us today in the Scriptures, both in their reading and in their being broken open in the sermon.

Because Protestants have tended to focus exclusively on the sermon, the public reading of the Scriptures functions as a "lesson"—a didactic event—in most mainline Protestant worship services. I submit that the act of reading is itself an act of *proclamation*—an act that deserves the best that the church has to offer. To say this doesn't mean, however, that the church will define "best" as the world does (as we will see).

WHAT AND HOW MUCH SHOULD WE READ?

Probably the majority of United Methodist congregations use the Revised Common Lectionary. I suspect, however, that United Methodists use this Eucharistic lectionary, with its three readings and psalm, largely with liturgical assumptions deriving from their use of a Sunday service that centers on preaching, not on Word and Eucharist.

What this means in practice is that often not all of the Scripture readings (least of all the psalm) are actually read in the service. Instead, only

Worship Matters: A United Methodist Guide to Worship Work (Volume II) © 1999 Discipleship Resources. Used by permission.

Telling God's Story Through the Lectionary

The common lectionary used by The United Methodist Church and other churches in North America provides a structure of readings over three years, following the outline of the Christian year. (See *UMBOW,* pp. 227-37.) Each Sunday is provided with a reading from the Old Testament, the Epistles, and the Gospels. A psalm is always appointed as a response to the first reading, rather than as a "lesson" in its own right.

On the Sundays from Advent through Epiphany and from Transfiguration through Pentecost—that is, on those Sundays that narrate the birth, life, death, and resurrection of Jesus—the Gospel lesson governs the choice of the other texts. The Old Testament and Gospel lessons on these Sundays are linked thematically or typologically.

On the Sundays between Epiphany and Transfiguration, and the long season of Sundays after Pentecost (often called Ordinary Time), the three lessons are structured to provide a continuous reading through major biblical cycles. In year A, we read from the Gospel of Matthew, the letters to the Romans and Thessalonians, and hear the stories of Abraham and Moses. In year B, we read from Mark, the letters to the Ephesians and James, and hear the stories of Samuel and David. In year C, we read from Luke, the letters to the Galatians, Colossians, and Hebrews, and hear the stories of the prophets, including Amos, Hosea, Isaiah, and Jeremiah. The Gospel of John is read in the course of Lent and Eastertide over the three years.

the Scripture text to be preached on is read. The assumption behind reducing the Lectionary's three readings to one is clear: The only Scripture reading that has meaning in worship is the passage actually addressed in the sermon. This assumption needs rethinking.

At best, the sermon can address only certain issues and themes in the Scripture readings appointed by the Lectionary for the day. But the Service of the Word—the first part of the Sunday service, including the "Concerns and Prayers" (*UMH,* pp. 6–7)—is about more than addressing a particular congregational need or issue through the lens of Scripture. It is equally about proclaiming in all its fullness the story of God's saving love for us. A lectionary allows us to tell that story through the systematic reading of Scripture keyed to the celebrations of the liturgical year.

Reading all the appointed Scripture readings in the Lectionary helps the congregation to experience the larger context of the story of salvation, in which the specific word of the sermon finds its place. Reading only one reading deprives the congregation of that larger context, a situation that can lead to serious distortions of our understanding and practice of the good news. For example, if a congregation never hears the readings from the Old Testament (Hebrew Bible), it would be missing a vital element of God's story: God's gracious covenant with Israel and God's faithful relationship with Israel, of whom Jesus Christ is a member.

Worse yet, omitting the Old Testament readings might even lead this congregation to imagine that the story of God's loving relationship with Israel has nothing to say to Christians, or that the Christian church has replaced the Jews in God's sight—Christians have actually made both of these assumptions at one time or another. As our baptismal liturgy reminds us, United Methodists profess the Christian faith as found in the Scriptures of *both* the Old and New Testaments (*UMH,* pp. 35, 40, 46, and 50). The Christian church is not a church exclusively of the New Testament, but of the Old and New Testaments together.

WHO SHOULD READ THE SCRIPTURE IN WORSHIP?

The short answer is: Anyone who wants to read! The church does not operate on the basis of the canons of theatrical or oratorical competence. The church's criteria have to do with faithfulness and love. Thus it would be profoundly contrary to the gospel to limit the office of reader to people whom we think can read with good voice, intonation, and feeling. I know that saying this runs directly counter to the popular idea of worship as an "art," with all the notions of performance, quality, and perfection that come with it.

The reader gives voice—a distinct, human, audible voice—to the word of God in Scripture. Limiting the enfleshment of that word to a select number of voices runs counter to a Christian view of the human person. If we say that only those who can "speak well" can read Scripture in worship, we are tacitly suggesting that those voices are somehow more worthy for the clothing of God's word in Scripture. Yet we proclaim that all people are made in the image of God, and that God's saving love embraces all people. If we truly believe this, we will not place limits on who can read Scripture in worship.

At the same time, I am not arguing for an off-the-cuff approach to reading! It is important to hold an occasional training session for readers, in which they learn about the mechanics of reading. The following topics might fall under "mechanics":

- What is the location in the worship service from where the Scriptures are read? Which versions of the Scriptures ought to be read?
- What is the proper way to introduce and conclude the reading of Scripture?
- Where should the reader stand during the singing of the psalm after the first reading?

In addition, it would also be good to gather the readers together occasionally (perhaps over a meal) to reflect on the ministry of reading and its impact on the congregation and its ministry.

HOW DO I READ THE SCRIPTURE IN WORSHIP?

The short answer, again: Read to the best of your ability. The mechanics of fulfilling this basic requirement will differ from person to person. Obviously, the point of reading is to make the Scripture audible to the congregation. Beyond that, it is difficult to say. Instead of talking about matters of voice, tone, and projection, let's turn to the work of reading in the context of the Sunday liturgy. This work involves how one introduces the readings, the general pace of reading, and the use of silence.

In The United Methodist Church (and in many other denominations), a certain chaos reigns when it comes to how the reading of Scripture is introduced in worship. Although the *Book of Worship* suggests ways to introduce the readings (pp. 22–23), these seem to be observed more in the breach than in actual practice.

The way a reading is introduced frames the congregation's expectations of it. In other words, the introduction directs the hearers to hear or listen to the reading in a specific way. For example, if the reader begins with, "Today's lesson is taken from the eleventh chapter of the Book of Isaiah, verses one through ten," the congregation will approach that reading as a *lesson*, something to be heard. They will hear the passage in a variety of ways, depending on how they see their role as "student."

On the other hand, if the reader introduces the day's Scripture passage with, "Today's reading is from the Book of Isaiah. Listen for the word of God," a completely different expectation is established. The congregation is directed to *listen*, to be *attentive*, to *wait* for the word of God in the Scripture reading. This introduction also places the proper emphasis on the act of hearing rather than on the act of following along in a text (whether in a Bible or in a printed insert). After all, the Scriptures were intended to be read and heard in the context of public assemblies for worship.

Should your congregation use a more extended literary or theological introduction to each reading? I suggest that you avoid them. While by and large our congregations suffer from acute biblical illiteracy, extended introductions to the public reading of Scripture will not solve this problem. This is so primarily because such introductions tend to create new problems for the hearer, providing ready-made theological interpretations of the readings. This is particularly dangerous with regard to the first reading, when almost invariably (especially during Advent, Lent, and Easter) a typological approach to the Old Testament often appears in introductions of this kind. Books of introductions are now available keyed to the Roman Lectionary and striving to introduce each reading in ways free from anti-Jewish theological biases.

The reader gives voice—a distinct, human, audible voice—to the word of God in Scripture.

Yet I cannot help but feel that the best place for theological introductions, if they are to be used at all, is in the bulletin; this allows congregation members to read them at their leisure. If your congregation has members who cannot read, why not institute a brief time (five or ten minutes) prior to the worship service during which a worship leader can place the day's readings in their literary and canonical contexts? Of course, one of the best ways to bring about congregational biblical literacy is to have ongoing lectionary discussion groups. Church school curriculum resources, such as *The Whole People of God* and *The Inviting Word,* also provide week-by-week companions to the Lectionary, thus enabling the work of worship to move into and overlap with the classroom.

The pace of reading Scripture should be unhurried and with as much attention as possible to the sense lines of the text. The point of doing so is to allow the congregation to hear the text. This may sound like an obvious point; yet, often in United Methodist congregations, the reading appears to be viewed as one of the "preliminaries" to be gotten through on the way to the sermon. As I have argued throughout this article, that is an inadequate approach. The reading of Scripture is an event of proclamation in its own right. It requires and deserves an adequate amount of time to accomplish effective proclamation. Just as a congregation would not want the pastor to rush through the sermon, so a congregation should not want the Scripture readings to be hurried through either.

To facilitate this kind of reading, you may wish to purchase a suitably bound lectionary book from which to read. Or, each week someone in the congregation might type up the week's readings into a large-print, sense-line format. Ideally, it's better to read from a book (whether lectionary book or Bible) than from a single sheet of paper. The book is itself a sign of the word of God in Scripture. It is an important part of the liturgical space, just as much as the altar-table, the font, and the pulpit.

Silence is a necessary counterpart to speech. Just as the depth and joy of feasts cannot really be appreciated without the experience of fasting or abstinence, so too the words of the Scripture readings need to be balanced with an expectant silence that nourishes our reflection on what has been read. We need the silence to be able to hear the thundering echoes of what God is saying in and through the reading.

How long a silence is long enough? There are no hard and fast rules. For a congregation not used to silence, even fifteen seconds can seem like fifteen minutes! Yet, as a congregation's experience with silence after the reading grows, you may discover that people want more silent time, not less. To begin, try fifteen seconds of silence and gradually work up to thirty. As with so many aspects of liturgical change, it is absolutely vital that the congregation understand why there is silence. For the first six to eight weeks, make a brief announcement before the service begins about some of the dimensions of the practice of silence.

Another important place for silence is after the Scripture reading has been introduced but before the reading of the text itself begins. This silence allows people to focus their attention on the coming word, and underlines the importance of the acts of reading and hearing. Such silence might also follow a Prayer for Illumination prior to all of the readings. (For examples and resources for a Prayer for Illumination, see *UMH,* pp. 6 and 602; *UMBOW,* p. 22.) The congregation also might sing the first stanza of "Come, Divine Interpreter" (*UMH,* 594), sung to the tune "Ratisbon" (*UMH,* 85, 173), or "Blessed Jesus, at Thy Word" (*UMH,* 596).

CONCLUSION

I conclude with a grab bag of questions having to do with reading Scripture in public worship:

- Should United Methodists stand for the Gospel reading?
- Who should read the Gospel?
- Should a special ceremony be used for the reading of the Gospel?
- What is the status of the psalm as a reading?

United Methodists have the option of standing for the Gospel reading; they are not required to do so. To some, standing for the Gospel reading elevates the Gospel above the rest of the canon of Scripture; therefore, they reason that this practice should not be followed. To others, standing for the Gospel reading shows reverence for Christ, who is proclaimed in the Gospel. I suggest that those who are able stand for each of the readings in worship.

In some denominations, it is the prerogative of the deacon, presbyter, or bishop to read the Gospel. The United Methodist Church has no such official practice. Often, one will see the pastor read the Gospel, while laypeople read the other two readings. Given the emergence of the ordained permanent deacon, it may be worthwhile to assign the Gospel reading to the deacon.[3] This practice would be consonant with ecumenical practice, and symbolizes the relationship between proclamation of the Gospel and service in the world in Christ's name.

United Methodists generally have not practiced a special ceremony at the reading of the Gospel, such as the use of special responses, a Gospel procession into the midst of the congregation, or incense. However, some United Methodist congregations may well want to consider using some or all of these ceremonial practices on special occasions such as Easter, Christmas, Epiphany, and Pentecost. The ceremony could contribute to a joyous incarnation of the good news proclaimed on each of those feast days.

Finally, the psalm: Put briefly, the psalm is not a reading. The psalm appointed for each week in the lectionary cycle is appointed as a response to the first reading (from the Old Testament most of the year, from Acts during Eastertide). It is intended to be sung. Since 1905, American Methodists have experienced the psalms as responsive readings. The 1989 *Hymnal* confuses the issue somewhat by including settings and antiphons for the psalms it includes, and by printing the psalms in alternating light and bold type for congregational reading. Thus the *Hymnal* makes possible both the old Methodist use and the much older practice of singing the psalms. On a purely practical level, a sung psalm breaks the pattern (even tedium, on occasion) of spoken speech, and can make possible a more attentive hearing of the readings.[4]

In a time of increasing biblical illiteracy, people are hungry for a word of hope that tells them, as our African-American brothers and sisters remind us, "There is a way out of no way." By careful attention to the proclamation of Scripture in its fullness week by week, we provide a response, if not a remedy, to such illiteracy and hunger. By faithful proclamation of the Word in worship, we begin to fulfill the prayer that we may "hear…, read, mark, learn, and inwardly digest" the Scriptures, so "that we may embrace and ever hold fast the blessed hope of everlasting life" (*UMH*, 602).[5] This, finally, is why we read Scripture in public worship and why we need to give attention to how we read.

> The reading
> of Scripture
> is an event of
> proclamation in
> its own right.

FOR FURTHER READING

A Guide to Church Ushering, Revised Edition, by Homer J. Elford (Nashville, TN: Abingdon Press, 1983).

Training for Hospitality: The Ministry of Ushers and Greeters (video-cassette), by Delores Dufner, O.S.B. (Collegeville, MN: The Liturgical Press). To order this videocassette, call: 800-858-5450.

ENDNOTES

1 From "Come, Divine Interpreter," by Charles Wesley, in *The United Methodist Hymnal* (Nashville, TN: The United Methodist Publishing House, 1989), 594.

2 See *Sacraments as God's Self Giving: Sacramental Practice and Faith,* by James F. White (Nashville, TN: Abingdon Press, 1983), pp. 13–22.

3 See "The Role of Deacons and Assisting Ministers," on pages 130–36 in Volume I of *Worship Matters.*

4 See "The Work of Singing the Psalms," on pages 29–37 in this volume, for a discussion of how to sing the psalms in worship.

5 From "Concerning the Scriptures" in *The United Methodist Hymnal,* 602. Copyright © 1989 The United Methodist Publishing House. Used by permission.

The Work of Singing the Psalms[1]

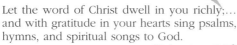

Let the word of Christ dwell in you richly;…
and with gratitude in your hearts sing psalms,
hymns, and spiritual songs to God.

(Colossians 3:16)

DWIGHT W. VOGEL

*Professor of Theology
and Ministry,
Garrett-Evangelical
Theological Seminary,
Evanston, Illinois*

SINGING THE PSALMS WAS PART OF THE EXPERIENCE OF THE early church. It was natural for them to do so. Jesus and his disciples sang psalms in Temple worship, at synagogue gatherings, and at observances of holy days such as Passover. In the accounts of the Last Supper, the statement "when they had sung the hymn, they went out to the Mount of Olives" (Matthew 26:30) probably refers to the psalms sung at the conclusion of the Passover meal. Singing the psalms was significant not only for the early church but also for John and Charles Wesley. In their time, the only congregational songs permitted in the Church of England were metrical settings of the psalms.

The metrical forms of a few psalms are still sung; for example, Psalm 90, "O God, Our Help in Ages Past" (*UMH*, 117), and Psalm 23, "The King of Love My Shepherd Is" (*UMH,* 138). Yet, the experience of most United Methodist congregations with singing psalms and canticles— including "Canticle of Mary (Magnificat)" (*UMH*, 199) and "Canticle of Zechariah (Benedictus)" (*UMH*, 208)—has been limited. There remains good reason for the tradition of singing the psalms and canticles, for it enables worshipers to participate in praying the psalm or canticle at a deeper level.

How did the early church, in a time before musical notation and printing, provide a way for the psalms to be sung? To compose a melody for every line of every psalm would have been an overwhelming task for the early church. More important, that much material would not have been easily accessible for congregations in the years before printing made hymnals a possibility.

What the church did was to adopt a pattern of singing that goes back to a time before there was "written" music. We still find that pattern in the way a small child sings: (1) much of it is on one note; (2) there is lots of repetition; and (3) there is just enough movement to keep it interesting. These are the same characteristics as what we know as *psalm tones*. Psalm tones are among the earliest and easiest forms of musical expression.

Today, as in the past, psalm tones are "music of the people," rather than being restricted to those with musical training. (Psalm tones are not to be confused with the Gregorian chant, a highly developed form that

Worship Matters: A United Methodist Guide to Worship Work (Volume II) © 1999 Discipleship Resources. Used by permission.

grew out of them.) Part of your ministry in introducing the singing of the psalms is to enable people to experience singing the psalms as something that grew out of folk culture. It is music that belongs to them and not to professional musicians.

THE BASIC PATTERN OF A PSALM TONE

What is a psalm tone like? What makes it so easy for people to learn? Knowing the basic pattern of a psalm tone will help you in teaching others about it. Psalm tones are based on a simple pattern:[*]

Notice the following about this pattern:

1. Each psalm tone has two parts that are divided by a bar line. Each part of the psalm tone has four notes.
2. Each part of the psalm tone begins with a note called the "reciting note," to which one word or a number of words may be sung.
3. In each part of the psalm tone, the reciting note is followed by two notes that are called "passing notes." Passing notes appear like eighth notes, but that has nothing to do with how quickly they are sung. It merely sets them apart from the other notes in the pattern.
4. Together with the last note (written as a half note), they lead to the half-way point, called a "half cadence." The last three notes in the second part can be called the "ending."
5. Each psalm tone, then, is a pattern of only eight notes, which are easily learned and remembered. They also arc sung easily without accompaniment.

To make it easier for your congregation to appropriate the singing of psalms and canticles in worship, I have included a few psalm tones in this article. (*The United Methodist Hymnal* contains five of these psalm tones, on page 737.)

LEARNING TO SING PSALMS AND CANTICLES

When introducing the singing of psalms and canticles to a congregation, remember that psalm tones grew out of the experience of a culture in which the congregation did not have hymnals. One does not have to read music in order to sing psalm tones because this kind of music is best learned by hearing it.

However, it is important for both the cantor (a kind of "liturgical song leader," who is going to lead the congregation in singing the psalm) and the accompanist to know the rules for singing the psalms. The rules are few in number and easy to understand. The rules also appear in abbreviated form in the Keyboard Edition of *The United Methodist Hymnal* (pp. 737 A–C).

A dot known as a "point" (a red dot in the *Hymnal*) indicates the word or syllable where the singers move from the reciting note to the black notes at the half cadence or ending. All the words in the phrase that precede the point are sung to the reciting note. These words are not sung in strict rhythm, but rather in the natural pattern we would use when speaking them. Punctuation in the text sung to the reciting note should be observed with a slight pause.

The following rules guide what happens after the reciting note is sung:[*]

1. When there are three or four syllables from the point to the half cadence or ending, they are sung in this way, with the additional syllables sung to the last note:

2. When the point is over the consonants joining two syllables, the text may be sung in this way:

3. When the point is over the second word of a phrase composed of three one-syllable words, the text is sung in this way:

4. When a final word of three syllables falls on the half note, the middle syllable may be elided, or all three syllables may be sung to the half note. A three-syllable word pointed over the consonants may be sung to the two black notes by eliding the middle syllable. For example:

5. Occasionally, one line will be marked with two points. The guidelines given above should be followed. For example:

6. The last syllable sung to a reciting note should receive a slight retard. When there is only one syllable for the reciting note, as in the example under rule three above, the syllable should be held somewhat longer than would otherwise be the case.

Psalm tones grew out of the experience of a culture in which the congregation did not have hymnals.

PUTTING THE RULES TO USE

Although there are only six rules, they may make singing the psalms and canticles sound more complicated than it actually is. We discover that when we put the rules to use. First, let's look at Psalm 134 as we find it in the *Hymnal* (850–851):***

Psalm 134

RESPONSE *(Evening Prayer & General)*

Ps. 141:2
Arlo D. Duba

My prayers rise like in - cense, my hands like the eve - ning sac - ri - fice.

R

1   Come, bless the Lord, all you servants of the Lord,
    who stand by night in the house of the Lord!
2   Lift up your hands in the holy place,
    and bless the Lord!
3   **May the Lord who made heaven and earth**
    bless you from Zion.   R

Since the response is in D minor, it will be easy for us to use Psalm Tone Two, which is in the same key:**

1. Note that the first three lines have the point over the syllable that is the third from the end, so that each syllable will have one note.
2. In the fourth line ("and bless the Lord!"), there is only one syllable before the pointed syllable, so we will want to hold it. The same thing is true of the last line of the psalm.
3. Verse 3a has the point over the *v* in "heaven," so we sing both syllables of that word to the first passing note.

The way the text is pointed in the *Hymnal* makes it easy to sing without musical notation. Look at the text from the *Hymnal* reprinted above. Try singing it using only the points to remind you what to do.

SELECTING AN APPROPRIATE PSALM TONE

Each psalm tone communicates its own feeling. Certain psalm tones are more appropriate than others for a given psalm or canticle, although any psalm or canticle can be sung to any psalm tone.[2] You will notice also that the feeling of the psalm tone changes when it is sung quietly and reflectively rather than in a strong, vibrant manner. The nature of the text and the context (how it is being used in prayer and worship) will help you decide which way is most appropriate. The accompanist and cantor will set the mood for the singing of the psalm at the outset.

Let us look at each of the psalm tones, noting their characteristics.[3]

Psalm Tone One**

This psalm tone, which is one of the easiest to sing, is a good one for you to use in introducing psalm tones to your congregation. It is written in the major mode. When sung vibrantly, it gives a feeling of strength and certainty. When sung reflectively, it communicates a sense of quiet security.

Psalm Tone Two**

This psalm tone is written in a minor mode. Sung reflectively, it can express longing, pain, or anguish. There can be a sense of strength and stability if you choose to sing the tone vibrantly. (Important Note: In early printings of the *Hymnal*, the last note of this psalm tone—a *D*—is misprinted as a *C*.)

Each psalm tone communicates its own feeling. Certain psalm tones are more appropriate than others for a given psalm or canticle.

Psalm Tone Three

This is a very adaptable psalm tone. The same melody line may be used with both major and minor accompaniment. The minor form appears in the Keyboard Edition of the *Hymnal* (p. 737 A):

Psalm Tone Three in Minor[**]

This tone is a good example of the fact that the minor mode can communicate strength and firmness. It can express praise, thanksgiving, and affirmation, even when sung reflectively.

Psalm Tone Three in Major[**]

Interestingly, the key signature and one chord change are the only changes in this form of tone three. It shares all of the characteristics noted above, but also may be used when a major tone is needed.

Psalm Tone Four[**]

Sung reflectively, this psalm tone can express a deep sense of supplication and a longing for deliverance. However, it changes character when sung vibrantly, giving evidence of strong affirmation and assurance.

Psalm Tone Five[**]

If you are looking for a psalm tone with a limited vocal range that is easy to sing, this may be the answer! Like Psalm Tone Four, it changes character when you change the way in which it is sung. A word of warning: This psalm tone is easily confused with Psalm Tone Four because the first three notes are identical!

Having looked briefly at the psalm tones provided by the *Hymnal*, remember it is wiser to begin by introducing only one of the psalm tones (probably Psalm Tone One) until people are familiar with it, and then gradually introducing them to the others.

TEACHING THE CONGREGATION TO SING PSALMS AND CANTICLES

At first, the cantor may sing the verses to the psalm tone while the congregation joins in singing the response. Some pastors and church musicians prefer to sing the words of the response to the psalm tone being used rather than to the melody for the response provided in the *Hymnal*. The responses are pointed for those who wish to use them. (When used in this way, the melody line for the response as printed in the *Hymnal* is ignored.)

If you choose to have the congregation sing the response to the music provided in the *Hymnal*, note that the key in which the psalm tone is to be sung will have to be adapted to the key of the response. A list of recommended psalm tones and the appropriate key for each response appears in *The United Methodist Hymnal Music Supplement,* on pages 371–73. Transpositions of the psalm tones into the keys needed appear on pages 367–70.

Important Note: In the *Hymnal*, the pointing of the text of the psalms follows the meaning of the biblical passage and is not related to either verse divisions, or to divisions between light- and bold-faced type. The assignment of the light- and bold-faced type for use by two voices or for liturgist and congregation was done for speaking, not for singing.

When introducing the singing of the psalms, only the cantor and accompanist need to be familiar with the rules that appear above. The choir also may help introduce the singing of the psalms, with the cantor singing through the entire psalm tone the first time, the choir "answering" the second time, and so forth, alternating with each other.

Sometimes the psalm (for example, Psalm 82) can be sung antiphonally (in an alternating manner) between two voices, using the light- and bold-faced type as a guide. In many psalms, however, it is better to use one of the approaches listed below, ignoring the light- and bold-faced type divisions.

After hearing a psalm tone several times, the congregation may join the choir in answering the cantor. The only rule the congregation needs

> Begin by introducing only one of the psalm tones...until people are familiar with it.

to know is that the (red) point indicates when the singers move to the next notes. It is helpful for the cantor to indicate to the congregation when they are to sing.

There are many variations on this approach that may be used in time. The left and right sides of the congregation (or choir and congregation, or men and women) may sing antiphonally. In singing antiphonally, one voice can sing from the reciting tone through the half cadence to the ending, with the other voice answering in the same way. Clusters of meaning are thus preserved. In some psalms (for example, Psalms 47 and 150), it is effective to have one voice sing from the reciting tone to the half cadence, with the other voice answering from the second reciting note to the ending.

You may want to invite the congregation to sing the entire psalm in unison. This is particularly effective with shorter psalms (for example, Psalm 100). In order to establish the tonal pattern in either antiphonal or unison singing of the psalm, it is advisable for the cantor to sing the psalm tone through when the congregation hears it for the first time. Thus, in Psalm 100, the cantor would sing the first two lines, with the congregation singing the remainder of the psalm, either in unison or antiphonally.

Take care not to introduce the congregation to a wide variety of ways of singing the Psalter (*UMH*, 735–862) at the same time they are learning the psalm tones. Select the way that is most appropriate for your congregation and use it consistently, especially at first.

PREPARING TO SING A PSALM IN WORSHIP

If you are going to be leading the psalm, you will be more effective if you have spent some time preparing for it. Even when you are familiar with the process, reviewing the psalm text will help you lead the congregation more effectively.

- Decide who is going to sing what parts of the psalm or canticle.
- Review the musical response. Is it a hymn fragment that the congregation already knows well? (For example, Response 1 of Psalm 31 [*UMH*, 764] uses a part of "A Mighty Fortress Is Our God.") If so, having the accompanist play through it once will be sufficient. If the response is unfamiliar, or if the congregation doesn't have hymnals available, you may want to say: "After we have heard the response played, I will sing it, and then invite you to join me in singing. We will sing it together whenever an *R* appears in the text."
- If you are going to sing the entire psalm text, with the congregation singing the response, you may want to circle the *R* wherever it appears so that you will remember to invite the congregation to join you in singing at those points. Extending your arm with your palm toward the congregation is an effective signal of invitation.
- If you are going to sing the psalm tone through the first time and then have the choir or congregation sing the rest of the psalm text with you, note where the first two points in the text occur, and place a bracket in the left margin around those lines to indicate what you will be singing alone.
- If you are going to sing the psalm tone antiphonally with the choir, the congregation, or another singer, go through the text and mark with a bracket in the left margin the parts you will be singing. Remember that in doing this you will usually have to ignore the bold-faced type divisions.

SINGING PSALMS AND CANTICLES IN WORSHIP

The traditional place in the worship service for singing the Psalter, and the basis on which psalms are chosen in the Lectionary, is as a response to the first Scripture reading. This position unites the psalm with Scripture, providing a musical bridge between the first two readings. Most of the psalms appointed in the Revised Common Lectionary appear in the *Hymnal.* Some of those used only every six or nine years have been omitted and must be replaced with psalms of similar content. However, this is the most complete liturgical Psalter that American Methodists have had since the one recommended by John Wesley, and it makes the Psalter as designated by the Lectionary available for consistent congregational use.

Psalms also may be sung as acts of praise. Psalms 8, 24, 47, 95:1-7, 100, and 150 are examples of psalms that may be used in this way. Psalms also may be used as prayers of confession (for example, Psalms 51:1-7, 90, and 130). Sections of psalms may be appropriate responses to the reading and/ or proclamation of the Word (for example, Psalms 46:1-7 and 116:12-19).

The responses may be effectively used as "introits" sung by the choir or the entire congregation, coupled with verses selected to serve as the "Scripture sentences" that begin a service (for example, the responses provided for Psalm 67 and verses 1-4, for Psalm 92 and verses 1-4, for Psalm 34 and verses 1-3).

CONCLUSION

Singing psalms and canticles can be an important way of involving the congregation in acts of worship, as well as uniting them with the practice of the church through the ages. It is said that those who sing "pray twice." Singing the psalms is a way of recovering praying the psalms in worship. That connection with the spiritual experience of Jesus and the early church can deepen our own pilgrimage of faith together.

FOR FURTHER READING

Handbook for Cantors, Second Edition, by Diana Kodner (Chicago, IL: Liturgy Training Publications, 1997).

United Methodist Hymnal: Music Supplement, edited by Gary Alan Smith (Nashville, TN: Abingdon Press, 1991), Appendices B & C.

Worship Resources of the United Methodist Hymnal: Introduction to the General Services, Psalter, and Other Acts of Worship, edited by Hoyt Hickman (Nashville, TN: Abingdon Press, 1989), Chapter 7.

ENDNOTES

1 This article is adapted from *Your Ministry of Singing the Psalms,* by Dwight W. Vogel. Copyright © The Order of Saint Luke. Used by permission.

2 For an example of a canticle, see "Canticle of Simeon" in *The United Methodist Hymnal,* 225. All the canticles included in *The United Methodist Hymnal* have been pointed and appear in Appendix C (pp. 374–89) of *The United Methodist Hymnal Music Supplement.*

3 The melody line for these psalm tones are found in *The United Methodist Hymnal* (p. 737). The accompaniment for each of the tones are in the Keyboard Edition of *The United Methodist Hymnal* (pp. 737 B and C).

* Psalm tones adapted from *The United Methodist Hymnal,* pp. 737, 769, 818, 821, 854, 862. Copyright © 1989 by The United Methodist Publishing House. Used by permission.

** Psalm tones reprinted from *Lutheran Book of Worship,* copyright © 1978, by permission of Augsburg Fortress.

*** Words adapted from *The United Methodist Hymnal,* pp. 850–51. Copyright © 1989 by The United Methodist Publishing House. Music © 1980 by Arlo D. Duba. Used by permission.

Singing psalms and canticles can be an important way of involving the congregation in acts of worship, as well as uniting them with the practice of the church through the ages.

MICHAEL J. O'DONNELL, O.S.L.

United Methodist Pastor, Townsend, Tennessee

The Work of Acolytes

A COLYTES ARE AN IMPORTANT PART OF THE WORSHIP SERVICE because they help the pastor and other leaders make the service go smoothly. My years as an acolyte—starting when I was eight and ending when I graduated from high school—were a significant part of my development as a Christian. Therefore, I see the role of the person in the congregation who oversees the work of the acolytes as important to the nurturing of young people in the faith.

Acolytes have been a part of the church in one form or another for nearly two thousand years. They have ministered to the church by carrying in the light for the service and assisting the pastor with Holy Communion and baptism. Today, it is customary to have children serving as acolytes; however, in many churches adults serve well in this capacity. While not excluding adults and youth, this article focuses on children serving as acolytes.

Acolytes may be asked to do many tasks during the service, depending on what the pastor wants and on the customs of the congregation. The way a church is built also will affect how the acolytes go about their work. This article introduces the work of the acolyte in worship and provides suggestions to acolytes and their leaders for integrating the role of the acolyte meaningfully in the congregation's worship experience.

DUTIES OF AN ACOLYTE

The understanding is growing in the church that children and youth need to be involved in worship. Asking children and youth to serve as acolytes is a wonderful way to involve them. As a pastor, I am always delighted with the work of acolytes. Together we show that we are all ministers in the church. Because it is crucial to always involve a willing participant in this ministry, it is better to create a job for an enthusiastic acolyte than to tell the acolyte that he or she is not needed.

Acolytes perform a variety of tasks, each of which is important. Many acolytes have a favorite job, but it is important for them to share responsibilities. An acolyte who has not done a particular job before or has not done it in a long time should take time to practice, which will make him or her feel more comfortable on Sunday morning.

This section discusses duties that a congregation may ask acolytes to perform. Among the many possible tasks an acolyte may perform, the following are particularly important.

Worship Matters: A United Methodist Guide to Worship Work (Volume II) © 1999 Discipleship Resources. Used by permission.

CANDLELIGHTER

Jesus said: "I am the light of the world" (John 8:12). The presence of the light reminds us of Jesus' coming into our world and into our lives. The light is carried into the worship service as a symbol of Jesus' coming into the presence of the worshiping community. Many congregations use two candles on the altar to point out that Jesus was both a human being and God. At the end of the service, the light is carried out into the world to show that Jesus Christ is for all people everywhere.

It is important to tell the acolyte at what point in the service to bring the light into the sanctuary. It may be before the music starts. Or, if the congregation uses a processional, the acolyte may lead the choir and the pastor.

The acolytes carry a candlelighter with a lit flame to the candles on the altar. The candlelighter has a long stem with a wick (taper) at the top on one side, and a bell-shaped part on the other side of the top. On the stem is a lever to push the wick up, which regulates the length of the wick and, therefore, the size of the flame.

The acolyte should carry the candlelighter with the handle at his or her waist and the stem pointed forward and up. The wick should be pointing up and just far enough out to get a strong flame. The acolyte should watch the flame while walking slowly (not dragging). If the flame starts to go out, the acolyte can push the wick up with the lever. The acolyte may cup one hand over the flame to protect the flame from a sudden breeze—perhaps from a fan, from a window, or from a breeze caused by walking too fast.

Sometimes the flame goes out even when the acolyte has done everything to prevent it. In such a case, another acolyte may assist in relighting the taper. If there is only one acolyte, it would be a good idea to have some matches hidden near the altar.

Where a single acolyte is lighting two candles, he or she should first light the candle on the right (that is, on the right side when facing the front of the sanctuary) and then the candle on the left. When two acolytes are working, the candles should be lit at the same time.

Where the acolyte has to light a candelabra in addition to the candles on the altar, the altar candles should be lit first, in the manner outlined above. Afterward, the acolyte should light the candelabra, starting with the candle closest to the cross, and moving outward from there. Lighting the candelabra in this order symbolizes the light of Christ radiating from the cross.

If a candle will not light, the acolyte may try to straighten the candle wick with a finger (if he or she can reach it). If unsuccessful, the pastor or another adult may help. If the candle still won't light, the acolyte should leave it and take a seat.

When all the candles are lit, the acolyte pulls down the lever in the stem until the wick is extinguished. (The flame should not be blown out.) The acolyte takes a seat and quietly places the candlelighter by his or her side or under the seat, making sure it is far enough out of the way so that it will not be kicked accidentally. The candlelighter should not be leaned up against the wall because it might fall over in the middle of the service.

At the end of worship, the acolyte extinguishes the candles in the order opposite from the way they were lit. The acolyte first lights the wick on the candlelighter from the candle on the left side of the altar-table. Then he or she turns the candlelighter over and gently lowers the bell over the candle, taking care not to smash the candle wick. The candle will go out when the air supply is cut off.

Asking children and youth to serve as acolytes is a wonderful way to involve them.

The acolyte leaves the worship service at the pastor's direction, carrying out the lighted candlelighter. This symbolizes the light of Jesus Christ going out into the world where believers are to serve. Once the acolyte has left the worship area, he or she extinguishes the candlelighter and stores it appropriately.

PROCESSIONAL CROSS BEARER (CRUCIFER)

Many congregations use a processional cross every week or on special occasions. This cross is carried in at the beginning of the service and carried out at the end. It reminds Christians of Jesus' death on the cross and his triumph over death. The person who carries this processional cross is often referred to as a "crucifer" (cross bearer). Usually, the acolyte carrying the processional cross follows the acolytes carrying the candlelighters. The crucifer carries the cross high and straight, not like a flag that is carried at an angle.

In many congregations, the crucifer stands at the top of the steps facing the congregation as other worship leaders go to their places. At the end of the opening hymn, the crucifer puts the cross in its stand and then takes a seat.

If the cross is carried out at the end of the service, the crucifer retrieves the cross when the final hymn begins. He or she stands at the top of the steps, then follows the acolytes who are carrying the candlelighters.

OFFERING ASSISTANT

Acolytes may be asked to help take up the offering. Traditions regarding the offering vary from congregation to congregation. In many congregations, the offering assistant goes to the altar, retrieves the offering plates, and hands them to the ushers. After the ushers have taken the plates through the entire congregation, they line up at the back of the church. When the musician begins the Doxology, the ushers come forward. The offering assistant takes the plates from the ushers and hands them to the pastor or takes them to the altar. If the plates are taken to the altar, the assistant may also be asked to hold them for the duration of the Doxology. The plates should be held at about eye level. Holding the plates up high symbolizes that the congregation is making an offering to God. If a prayer follows the Doxology, the assistant holds the plates until the prayer is finished and then sets them down where directed.

If the congregation does not have the custom of singing a doxology, the assistant should be instructed about how to handle the offering plates. In some churches, the plates are not brought back to the altar. In such cases, the prayer is usually said before or while the ushers receive the plates.

BANNER AND FLAG BEARER

Banners are used to signify important times, seasons, or events. Banners should be carried with the front facing the congregation as the banner bearer enters the sanctuary. The bottom of the pole is put at the bearer's waist and is held up, slightly forward, so that the banner hangs free. The banner will either be placed in a stand or hung on the wall.

Some congregations also use flags during the procession/recession. The best way to carry a flag is to put the bottom of the pole at the waist and angle the pole out (slanting) so that the flag can be seen. As the bearer comes in with a banner or flag, he or she should go directly to the place where the banner or flag resides during the service and should put it in its holder. At the end of the service, the order of the process is simply reversed. In some congregations, the banners are not removed at the end of the service, especially if they have been hung on the wall.

BIBLE BEARER

In many congregations, acolytes carry the Bible into the service during the procession. The Bible is held just below face level, but without obstructing the acolyte's view. Upon reaching the chancel, the acolyte places the Bible on the pulpit, lectern, or wherever directed. He or she then opens the Bible at the middle.

In some congregations, the pastor may stand in the aisle for the reading of the Gospel. When this tradition is followed, the acolyte takes the Bible from the lectern or pulpit and carries it to where the pastor directs.

COMMUNION SERVER

Acolytes may be asked to help with the preparation and serving of Communion.[1] One task may be to receive the bread and cup brought forward during the offering. Upon receiving the elements, the server hands them to the pastor.

Communion servers may also give the bread or cup to members of the congregation as they come forward to receive, but in many congregations this responsibility is reserved for the pastor and other worship leaders. However, if asked to serve Communion, the acolyte should be taught the appropriate words to say while serving (for example, "The body of Christ, given for you" and "The blood of Christ, given for you"). If the congregation uses individual Communion cups, the acolyte may be asked to collect the cups as each group of worshipers leaves. It is important for the pastor and Communion servers to rehearse the process before the worship service.

Communion servers may also be given the responsibility of assessing the supplies of bread or wine (juice) during the service, making sure fresh supplies are always available.

BAPTISM ASSISTANT

Acolytes are sometimes asked to assist with the sacrament of baptism. The acolyte may serve by holding the water pitcher, a towel, the baptismal certificate(s), or the pastor's book. Watching the pastor for clues, the acolyte can provide valuable assistance during the service by helping the pastor keep organized the several items he or she consults as the service progresses. It is important for the baptism assistant and the pastor to coordinate duties and set expectations prior to the service.

When I am baptizing someone, I have the acolyte hold the water pitcher with the handle toward me. At the appropriate time, I take the pitcher and pour the water into the font. After the baptism, I dry my hands on a towel that the acolyte has draped over one arm. The acolyte then hands me the baptismal certificate(s). In some cases, depending on the size of the pitcher and the size of the acolyte's hands, one acolyte may be able to hold more than one item. In other cases, it may be better to use more than one acolyte.

If every acolyte knows her or his place and role, the service will go smoothly.

CHECKING EQUIPMENT

Before the worship service begins, acolytes should make sure that they have all the equipment needed during the service and that these are in working order. The candlelighters should have enough wick, and matches should be available. Candle wicks should be free of wax and pointing upright. If the acolyte carries a banner, cross, or flag during the service, he or she should be ready in plenty of time. After the service, the acolytes should properly store the equipment (including robes).[2]

ENTERING AND LEAVING WORSHIP

Entering and leaving the sanctuary should be done in an orderly and dignified fashion. This may become difficult, however, when several acolytes are serving in various ways. If every acolyte knows her or his place and role, the service will go smoothly. The following processional order is suggested when several acolytes are performing several tasks:
1. Candlelighters
2. Cross Bearer (Crucifer)
3. Flag Bearer
4. Banner Bearer
5. Choir
6. Lay Worship Leaders
7. Pastor

This is only a suggested order. Often the candlelighters follow the crucifer, with the other acolytes following the choir.

SPECIAL EVENTS AND SERVICES

During the year, special services in addition to the normal Sunday service may be held. Within a regular Sunday service, some special event may need the careful attention of an acolyte.

ADVENT

During the season of Advent, many congregations have an Advent wreath in the sanctuary to remind worshipers of the coming of Jesus into history and to prepare them for his coming into their lives. The Advent wreath has five candles—usually four purple candles (or three purple and one pink) and one white candle in the middle.

The custom in many congregations is to have a family or members of the congregation light the candles. However, if an acolyte has the duty of lighting the candles, he or she will need to know the order for this ceremony. On the First Sunday of Advent, the acolyte lights one purple candle. On the second Sunday, the first candle is relit and a second purple candle is lit. On the third Sunday, a third purple candle is lit after the first two candles have been relit. (If there is a pink candle for the third Sunday, it is lit after the two purple candles have been relit. The pink candle symbolizes the heightening of joy as Christmas approaches.) On the fourth Sunday, all four purple candles (or three purple and one pink) are lit, so that all the candles in the outer ring of the wreath are lit.

On Christmas Eve or Christmas Day, all five candles are lit. The white candle in the center (the Christ candle) is lit last. All the candles should continue to be lit throughout the Christmas season.

ASH WEDNESDAY

As a way to signal the beginning of the season of Lent on Ash Wednesday, many congregations celebrate Holy Communion and also place ashes on people's foreheads as a sign of penitence. This service may afford the acolyte a special role; therefore, acolytes and their leaders should ask the pastor what task the acolyte may fulfill during the service.

HOLY (MAUNDY) THURSDAY

Pastors often use Holy Thursday as an occasion to celebrate Holy Communion in a way that is not the usual practice. For example, a table might be set up for worshipers to sit at (rather than coming to the altar rail or being served in the pew). Acolytes may be asked to act as Table servers, helping people to be seated, making sure that the Table is in order, and ensuring that all the supplies are at hand as needed. Acolytes and their leaders should consult with the pastor ahead of time about possible roles and tasks during this service.

EASTER SUNDAY

Many churches light a paschal candle on Easter Sunday. This is a tall candle that usually stands by itself on a floor stand. When Jesus died on the cross, the world was cast into darkness. On Easter Sunday, when the church celebrates Jesus' resurrection from the dead, the paschal candle is used to symbolize Jesus as the light of the world. The paschal candle is the first candle lit on Easter Sunday; all the other candles are lit using its light.

WHAT ACOLYTES WEAR

Acolytes may wear a variety of clothes. In some congregations, acolytes wear their regular Sunday clothes. This may be a pair of pants and a shirt for boys, a nice dress or skirt and top for girls. Other congregations use children's choir robes for the acolytes. In still other congregations, acolytes wear one of several different kinds of robes (vestments). The two most common types of vestments are the *alb* and the *cassock and cotta*. Both kinds of robes go back a long way in history.

The alb is a long white robe that is fairly loose-fitting and is usually tied around the waist with a rope called a *cincture*. The alb reminds us of the kind of clothes Jesus wore. Church leaders also have worn the alb throughout the centuries.

The cassock is a tight-fitting dark robe. It usually extends from shoulder to ankle, but sometimes it extends only from the waist to the ankles. It is fastened with buttons, a zipper, or velcro. A cotta, which is worn over the cassock, is a short white vestment that fits over the shoulders and extends to just below the waist. Like the alb, this garment was normal attire many years ago.

HOW ACOLYTES BEHAVE

People look up to acolytes with respect; they are glad to have them as leaders in worship and want them to do well. Members of the congregation notice how acolytes behave during the worship service. How

A proper approach to worship can be summed up as "joyful reverence."

acolytes act helps set the mood for everybody else in the service. If the acolytes approach the experience with a sense of joy and reverence, people notice that. If they pay attention to what is going on when someone else is praying, reading, or speaking or singing, the members of the congregation will follow suit. On the other hand, people also notice when acolytes are chewing gum or talking; therefore, proper training is important.

Perhaps a proper approach to worship can be summed up as "joyful reverence." When acolytes feel joyful reverence, they take their responsibilities seriously, remembering that it is God they are serving in worship.

QUESTIONS ACOLYTES ASK

Those interested in serving as acolytes often have many questions related to the nature of this ministry. Below are some common questions that leaders with responsibility for acolytes can anticipate. Possible ways to respond are also included.

1. WHY DO ACOLYTES WEAR ROBES?

People have been wearing special clothing (vestments) to lead worship for many centuries. Also, wearing clothes that look alike makes us more equal. It eliminates any differences between rich and poor, designer and second-hand clothing. All people are equal in God's eyes, and wearing a robe like everybody else's symbolizes that equality.

2. I'VE HEARD DIFFERENT WORDS USED TO DESCRIBE PARTS OF THE CHURCH BUILDING. WHICH TERMS ARE CORRECT?

Confusion often arises because people use different words to name the same thing. The architecture of every church building is different. Have the acolytes meet with the pastor for a walk through the church building. Ask the pastor to point out the various parts of the building. Acolytes will see, in one form or another, the following parts:

The *nave* is the area where the congregation sits. Some people refer to this area as the *sanctuary*. Traditionally, the sanctuary is the area that contains the *altar-table*. The altar-table (or *altar* or *table*) may be either against the wall or free-standing. During Holy Communion, the pastor stands at the altar. In Old Testament times, altars were used for sacrifices. The New Testament contains the account of the table Jesus used when he celebrated the Last Supper with his disciples.

An *altar* or *Communion rail* surrounds the chancel area. In many congregations, people kneel at the rail for prayer, for healing, or to receive Communion. The *chancel* is the area behind the altar rail, which includes the altar and the area where the choir sits. The choir area also may be known simply as *the choir* or *choir stalls*.

The Scriptures are read and the Word proclaimed from the *pulpit* and/or *lectern*. Usually the pulpit and lectern are at opposite sides of the chancel. If they are different sizes, the pulpit will be larger than the lectern. The lectern usually holds a Bible, from which passages are read during the service. (The word *lectern* comes from another word that means "to read.") Most of the worship service is led from the lectern. The pastor preaches from the pulpit and also may read Scripture from it. Many churches have a only a pulpit, from which the entire service is led.

3. WHY DOES THE PASTOR WEAR A COLORED SCARF?

The colored scarf, called a "stole," symbolizes the yoke of Christ. Pastors are "yoked," or connected, to Christ in their service to the congregation and to the world. Only ordained (or consecrated) ministers may wear stoles, although the choir may have a modified form of a stole.

4. WHAT IS THE RIGHT AGE TO SERVE AS AN ACOLYTE?

The first acolytes were adults; so, being an acolyte is not just for children or youth. I was an acolyte from the time I was eight years old until I graduated from high school.

HELPS FOR LEADERS

Each congregation should have an adult to serve as acolyte coordinator or acolyte parent. This person is responsible for making assignments, notifying the acolytes weekly of their duties, and overseeing the work of the acolytes each week.

Children are an important part of the life of the worshiping community; therefore, they should be given the opportunity to feel involved in worship, no matter the age. Serving as an acolyte is one way of being involved. Local custom usually dictates when a child is old enough to begin serving as an acolyte. Generally, children who are in the third grade are old enough to grasp the importance of worship and can perform the various tasks easily. Both boys and girls are equally able to serve. The coordinator should be careful not to differentiate assignments by gender—the church is no place to reinforce sexual stereotypes.

If a child has a physical or mental disability, the child should not be excluded automatically from serving as an acolyte. For example, if a child uses a wheelchair, he or she could carry a banner in the procession. The banner could be attached to the chair, or the acolyte could hold it while someone pushes the wheelchair. The banner would then be placed in a location that is wheelchair accessible, such as in front of the altar rail.

Care must be taken to allow all acolytes to be involved in duties that reflect their abilities. Some children are physically stronger than others, and some are taller. Every job is important. No job has a higher honor than another.

I remember struggling to reach very tall candles when I was the "littlest acolyte." The acolyte coordinator should exercise sensitivity and not ask a child to try to reach candles that are obviously too high, or to carry something that is too heavy. Each acolyte should be allowed to do what he or she can do. It should be kept in mind that children at this age grow quickly. What was difficult or impossible last year may not be this year.

Each acolyte will have favorite duties. (Mine were serving as crucifer and Communion server.) It is wise to rotate assignments, if enough acolytes are available. A schedule with job assignments should be posted at least a month in advance. This eliminates most arguments about who does what. One good reason to rotate assignments is so that each acolyte will become comfortable in all roles.

If enough acolytes are available, one or two may be kept in reserve in case an acolyte who is scheduled to work does not show up. Establish a policy for acolytes who consistently arrive at the last minute. Ideally, the acolytes should be in place five or ten minutes before the service starts. If

When acolytes feel joyful reverence, they take their responsibilities seriously, remembering that it is God they are serving in worship.

one of the acolyte is not there, call on one of the reserves. If the scheduled acolyte arrives late, he or she misses the turn for that Sunday. The exception is if the acolyte notified the coordinator in advance about a delay.

The acolyte coordinator should contact the acolyte or acolyte's parent during the week preceding the day the child is to serve. This can be done either by postcard or telephone. If the congregation depends on just one or two children to serve as acolytes, prior confirmation will probably not be necessary. In any event, the coordinator will want to make a special effort to thank acolytes and parents at various times throughout the year.

As has become clear from this article, acolytes perform many different duties in a worship service. Generally speaking, the more the children are involved each week, the more the congregation will be inspired. With more involvement, children also gain a greater sense of their importance to God and to the church. If several children want or need to be involved, the coordinator may create extra duties that acolytes do not usually perform in your congregation (for example, serving as baptism assistants or Communion servers).

The acolyte coordinator should make sure that robes are clean and pressed and that all equipment is in working order (for example, the wicks in the candlelighters). He or she should always be ready with matches or a lighter.

Each congregation will need to adapt the practices described above to its particular needs and customs. The degree of formality that acolytes practice in their work also will be dictated by local custom.

CONCLUSION

The duties of the acolyte are an important part of the worship service of God. Tasks and how they are approached vary from church to church. Remember that whatever you do as an acolyte you are doing for God.

FOR FURTHER READING

Children Worship! by MaryJane Pierce Norton (Nashville, TN: Discipleship Resources, 1998).

The New Handbook of the Christian Year, Second Edition, by Hoyt L. Hickman, Don E. Saliers, Laurence Hull Stookey, and James F. White (Nashville, TN: Abingdon Press, 1992).

Worshiping With United Methodists: A Guide for Pastors and Church Leaders, by Hoyt L. Hickman (Nashville, TN: Abingdon Press, 1996).

Your Ministry of Being an Acolyte, by Michael J. O'Donnell (Nashville, TN: Discipleship Resources, 1997).

ENDNOTES

1 For more information about the work of Communion servers, see "The Work of Communion Stewards, Servers, and Altar Guilds," on pages 54–60 in this volume.

2 For helpful guidance about creating and maintaining a sacristy, see "Creating Space for the Sacristy," on pages 111–16 in this volume.

The Work of Music Leaders

M. ANNE BURNETTE HOOK

*Music Resources Director,
The General Board of Discipleship,
Nashville, Tennessee*

Wanted: First United Methodist Church of Fantasy Land is looking for a full-time director of music/organist. A large suburban congregation with a small-church feel, we are seeking a professional musician and minister to do the following: oversee an extensive graded-choir program in choral and instrumental music; accompany all church services (including the contemporary praise service on Saturday nights); supervise and train volunteer musician leaders; provide creative leadership for the worship planning teams for each service (including monthly special services throughout the year); recruit new members into the music ministry; administer an active after-school music and drama school; and be shepherd for all one thousand members who are currently a part of this vital ministry. We desire someone who is proficient in all types of music, ranging from Gregorian chant to praise choruses, and who loves the Lord. A Ph.D. in conducting and organ and an M.Div. (or equivalent) are preferred. It would be nice if your spouse is also a professional musician who would accompany without pay the choirs you direct....

SOUND IMPOSSIBLE? CONGREGATIONS TODAY ARE SEEKING church musicians who can do a number of things, ranging from the traditional choral conducting to the relatively recent job of "praise-team" leader. As with many professional ministry positions, the job description is often daunting and apparently impossible to do well.

What is the real work of the music leader? Is it to be all things musical to all people in the congregation? Or is it to be a spiritual leader in the congregation who focuses intentionally on the music life of the congregation as a part of the larger ministry context?

This article explores the specific jobs of the music leader of the congregation. It names specific tasks that must be done by the music leader and those that should be delegated to gifted helpers. It helps church musicians understand more fully their unique roles in the congregation and, it is hoped, how to do them more effectively.

THE MANY ROLES OF THE MUSIC LEADER

It may be true in every organization and institution—but it is especially true in the church—that musicians who work there must wear many hats to fulfill the task of music leadership. The job description may be limited to directing the choir, planning worship, and attending occasional worship committee meetings. However, the work of the church music leader—whether part- or full-time, paid or volunteer—is usually much larger than the job description.

A church musician should be prepared to undertake four major roles to be an effective leader of a congregation: congregational song leader, worship planner and leader, music educator, and spiritual leader. Although other roles also may be identified, these four make up the major work of the church musician.

CONGREGATIONAL SONG LEADER

This role is an important and often overlooked task of the music leader. Although much of the work of a church musician is with other musicians in the church—choir members and accompanists—a major task of the music leader is to lead the song of the most important singing ensemble of the church: the congregation. "Song leader" in this case is much more than just a worship designation or task; it is the work of equipping and enhancing the song of the congregation.

Every musician would love to work in a congregation where the congregation sings as robustly (but perhaps not as slowly) as the gathered assembly at an annual conference worship service sings "O for a Thousand Tongues to Sing." It is the job of the church musician to equip the congregation to do just that.

Much of what will enable the congregation to become a singing congregation has to do with careful worship planning. Planning worship with a singing congregation in mind is one of the first steps in enhancing a congregation's singing. I discuss that role further in the next section.

After careful planning, effective song leadership in worship will greatly strengthen the congregation's ability to sing with vitality and meaning. Congregations tend to rely on one of four possible song leaders for worship—the choir or a small ensemble such as a praise team, the accompanist (organ or piano), a song leader, or another worship leader, such a pastor who can also sing. Any of the above leadership styles may be effective in congregational worship, and it is important that worship planning teams decide which will be most effective given the style and form of worship in their particular settings. In my opinion, for most United Methodist congregations with a middle-of-the-road worship style and form (somewhere between "high-liturgy" and "camp-meeting" styles of worship), a visible, upfront song leader is the best means to more lively, involved, and spirited congregational singing.

An important role of the song leader is to introduce the hymn or song with a brief statement that helps connect the song to the rest of the service. Some worshipers do not pay close attention to the texts of the songs or to the way the texts relate to the Scripture readings or the sermon. A *brief* statement that relates the song to the service may help the congregation sing with more meaning and intent. It also may help to indicate the worship form of the song. If the song is a prayer, for example, the song leader may invite the congregation to pray the words as they sing.

After introducing the song, the song leader should sing the song strongly enough to lead but not overpower the congregation. It is important that the song leader sing the melody and not a harmony or descant part. This assures the congregation that they are singing the right music. (The exception to using the melody guideline is when singing a Taizé song. After the assembly is familiar enough with the song, it is appropriate for the song leader to sing the harmony if he or she chooses.) A microphone may be used if necessary; however, the microphone is a tool for amplification and not a nightclub singer's prop!

The song leader should use his or her hands only to indicate when the congregation is to sing and not to direct worshipers as if they were a choir. A congregation that does not know the song will look at the printed music instead of the song leader; a congregation that knows the song well does not need gesturing. Instead of elaborate arm movements, the song leader can effect a change in tempo by announcing it or by speeding up the accompaniment. If the song is new to the congregation, the song leader should decide before worship how to teach the song to the congregation. Most congregations will not sing if they do not know the song.[1]

The choir can also be used to lead and support the congregational singing. The song leader should help choir members understand that their role is more than providing music for the service; they are first and foremost leaders of the congregation. For this reason, it is important for the choir to sing the hymns and songs with correct singing technique and energy and to be active participants in worship at all times, not just when they are singing the choral anthem.

The choir should never be allowed to usurp the congregation's singing. I was worshiping at an assembly where the choir in residence did a lot of performing outside of worship. During worship, we sang "When I Survey the Wondrous Cross" (*UMH*, 298) as a congregational hymn. On the last stanza, the organist suddenly modulated to a much higher key and the choir began singing a very familiar and popular choral setting in place of the congregational setting of this hymn. The rhythm was different, the key was higher than most worshipers could sing, and the transition was abrupt. The ending was very exciting musically, but the congregation dropped out. They did not know the music and could not sing the song. The choir took the congregation's song from them.

The choir's task of facilitating the congregation's song does not allow for such musical showcases. The same rule applies to the song leader: His or her task is to *lead* the congregation's singing, not to sing *for* the congregation. When a solo voice is required, as in a psalm setting (or in a call and response song such as "Come Out the Wilderness" [*UMH*, 416]), the song leader is not replacing the congregation but assisting its song.

Finally, the song leader should look for opportunities outside of worship to sing with the assembly or any gathering within it, teaching them about the great hymns of faith as well as some of the new hymns and songs of faith. Sunday school classes, meetings of small groups, even church or administrative council meetings can be opportunities for hymn singing.

WORSHIP PLANNER AND LEADER

The music leader functions not only as a song leader but also as a worship planner. Working cooperatively with other worship leaders such as the pastor, the music leader plans music in worship in such as way that the people can experience God's presence in powerful ways through singing as well as hearing the music in worship.

Several strategies will help increase the effectiveness of music in worship. First, it is crucial that the music leader know the musical character of the assembly. That means he or she should find out which hymns the congregation collectively knows and loves and should regularly choose those hymns for worship. Additionally, the music leader can do a congregational "favorite-hymn" survey or ask members to mark their favorites in a "community hymnal" kept in an accessible place.

> **It is crucial that the music leader know the musical character of the assembly.**

Second, the worship leader should devise creative ways to increase the singing in worship. If the congregation is not singing the psalm responses because the responses are unfamiliar, the worship leader should select appropriate familiar hymn phrases or refrains to use as responses. For example, the first stanza or the refrain from "How Great Thou Art" (*UMH,* 77) can be used as a musical response to a psalm in praise of the God of creation (Psalm 8, for example). This will touch many people for whom this is a favorite hymn. Instead of a spoken Prayer for Illumination or prayer before the sermon, a familiar hymn or praise chorus can be sung during a specific season, such as "Spirit of the Living God" (*UMH,* 393) during Pentecost. Also, the Scripture or prayers of the people can be framed with an appropriate hymn or song, such as "Praise to the Lord, the Almighty" (*UMH,* 139). The worship leader also can invite the congregation to sing a closing song of dismissal, such as "Shalom to You" (*UMH,* 666).

Communion Sundays offer several opportunities for creative worship planning with music and the congregation in mind. A good idea is to teach the congregation one of the musical settings of the Great Thanksgiving (*UMH,* pp. 17–25). If the congregation has never sung these before, many worshipers find the call and response form of "Musical Setting B" (pp. 18–20) or the echo of the familiar hymn "Holy, Holy, Holy! Lord God Almighty" in "Musical Setting A" (pp. 17–18) accessible and easy to learn.

Instead of choral or instrumental music during the serving of Holy Communion, the worship leader may prepare a list of familiar hymns, or a series of new and old Communion hymns, for the congregation to sing as people are being served. The numbers of the hymns can be listed in the order of worship. It is important to move smoothly from one hymn to the next. These hymns should be changed rarely, especially if the congregation celebrates Communion only once a month; this helps the congregation become familiar with both the hymns and the order in which they are sung.

Introducing different types of congregational music for use in worship increases the opportunities for the congregation to sing as a community. (This practice will be most successful if you use a lot of hymns they know and love.) Moderation is the key; therefore, it is unwise to sing, on a given Sunday, every prayer that the congregation is accustomed to speaking. Instead, only one or two of the prayers should be sung.

The worship leader should think carefully about songs that may get used on only one Sunday (such as a psalm response), and those songs that are used for longer periods of time (such as over the course of a liturgical season, or on Communion Sunday during a whole year). The congregation should have enough time to learn a response well enough to be able to sing it from the heart, but not so long that it becomes routine and mindless.

Finally, as the worship leader plans music for the choir, he or she should intentionally select music that includes the congregation whenever possible. Festive hymn settings provide exciting choral experiences; they also allow the congregation to participate in the music-making. Several music companies, such as G.I.A. Publications, Inc., publish a lot of choral literature with congregational responses. Again, while this form should not be used every week, it should be used often enough so that the congregation feels comfortable participating.

It is important for the worship leader to remember that his or her goal in planning worship is to help people both experience and worship

God. Creative, innovative worship planning is irrelevant if it impresses people but does not lead them into God's presence. This is as true for the magnificent cathedral choir singing classical choral literature as it is for the energetic praise band encouraging everyone to "put their hands together for Jesus."

MUSIC EDUCATOR

There was a day in our culture when learning how to read music and play an instrument was considered integral to the well-educated person. Today, school systems that are drained by declining tax revenues and rising costs are often forced to eliminate the arts from their curriculum. Because of this reality, the role of music educator for the church is vital. However, the purpose of such music education is not to create musicians, as valuable as such a goal would be. The task of the church is to make disciples of Jesus Christ. The task of the church musician as music educator is to teach musical skills as well as how these skills can be used to share the gospel, increase people's experience with God, and increase their ability to share their faith through and with music.

The role of music educator in the church often begins in the choir room, where the director teaches the vocal and other musical skills for effective music-making: how to have strong vocal production and clear diction so that the message in the words can be heard and understood by the assembly; how to blend and sing as an ensemble so that the congregation can focus on the message and not be distracted by a less-than-beautiful sound; how to read the notes on the page and interpret those notes so that people can experience the love and grace of God through the music that is presented.

While making music is possible without all or most of these skills, it is much more difficult. It is possible to teach an anthem by rote if choir members cannot read music, but it is more time consuming than relying on their ability to read the notes. In the long run it is more effective to teach music skills than to teach the music every time. This is especially true in children's choirs, where we are charged with training the church musicians of today as well as of tomorrow and are often tempted by the short-term ease and success of rote learning. If we are going to have musicians in the church in the future, it is up to the church musician to train them today.

The role of music educator is not limited to the choir. The congregation can be taught about the great hymns and music of faith. They can learn about various styles of music through hearing a variety of music in worship, through reading educational write-ups in a worship order or newsletter, or during gathering time for learning (Sunday school, Wednesday-night fellowship dinners, and so forth). Every congregation can learn to sing better, especially if they are taught by a congregational song leader and choir who sing correctly and enthusiastically. Good singing, like worship, can be "caught" as well as taught by the music leadership of the church.

SPIRITUAL LEADER

While the task of spiritual leader may require little or no musical training, it may be the most important role of the church musician. If the task of the church is to make disciples of Jesus Christ, then every

Creative, innovative worship planning is irrelevant if it impresses people but does not lead them into God's presence.

aspect of the church must be engaged in that task, including—and perhaps especially—the music ministry.

Music is one of the most effective tools for conveying spiritual truths. John and Charles Wesley knew the power of music as they wrote hymns for the purpose of teaching doctrine to the people they were leading. Ask any worshiper to quote from a sermon he or she heard last week, and you will probably get a blank stare. Ask this same worshiper to recite a line from his or her favorite hymn, and he or she can sing for days. Music both shapes the faith of those who sing and hear it and offers a vehicle for sharing that faith.

The congregations that music leaders serve, and especially the choirs they lead, need them to be spiritual leaders for them. They need the music leader to fulfill the other roles mentioned above; but if the music leader is not a spiritual leader, he or she might as well be leading a civic chorus or teaching music in the school system.

To be a spiritual leader as a musician does not require seminary training or advanced theological degrees. It does require that one be a Christian on the journey, willing to lead and to walk with others on their journey. If you are currently a music leader in a congregation but are not actively engaged in a personal spiritual life, ask your pastor or another trusted Christian friend how you might begin. Here are some additional ideas to get you started:

• Set aside time daily for prayer and study.
• Join an accountability group to support you in your spiritual disciplines.
• Make your relationship with God through Christ a priority, not just an exercise you go through in order to be a more effective worship planner.
• As you begin to grow in your faith, provide opportunities for spiritual growth in the groups you work with.
• Talk with them about why you chose a particular anthem or how it relates to the Scripture reading(s) for the Sunday.
• Invite them to share stories of what an anthem text means to them.
• Lead the choir in regular worship together as a community.
• Foster a nurturing, caring community in the group by following up when people are absent, praying for them regularly, encouraging them to pray for each other, leading them in acts of compassion and mercy outside the choir room.

The music leader's role as spiritual leader is perhaps her or his most important role to the people with whom she or he works.[2]

WHAT A MUSIC LEADER IS NOT

A church musician cannot be all things musical to all people in the congregation. As effective as one might be, there will always be people in the congregation with whom one will disagree and from whom one can learn. There are also gifted people who will need to do much of the work in the music program instead of the music leader.

There are many tasks, both musical and nonmusical, involved in the music ministry of a congregation. Some of these things the music leader must and should do him or herself, such as picking out music for the choir and planning the rehearsals he or she is to lead, or picking out and learning the music he or she will play in worship.

There are other tasks the music leader can do well, such as direct a children's choir. In some settings, the music leader may be the only one who can do that task; in that circumstance, the music leader has to decide if his or her job description and time allow doing this job. Or, if there are gifted individuals who also can do this task, the music leader's skills may be better used equipping these people to lead the children's choir.

In addition, there are other tasks that many people could do, such as making costumes for a musical or keeping the music library in order. Often these tasks require little or no musical training—only a willingness to learn and to serve. In these circumstances, it is often more appropriate for the music leader to delegate that task to someone else. Even if it seems to take more time to help someone else do the job than to do it oneself, it is better stewardship and leadership to offer the chance to serve to someone else.

Delegating responsibilities is not an excuse to avoid the servant tasks to which Christ calls all of us. It would be poor leadership on the part of the music leader to take a youth choir on a mission trip and then to refuse to help repair a front porch, claiming that God has called him or her to music ministry and that, therefore, the work of serving others should be left to those who are "gifted" to do so. Indeed, God has given each of us gifts and expects us to live on the basis of our giftedness, but God also expects us to be obedient to the call to servant ministry as shown to us by Jesus Christ.

Finally, the music leader is called not only to the ministry of leading music. He or she will assume many roles—child, spouse, parent, friend, worker, musician, disciple. At times, one of these roles may take precedence over the others. The music leader will never be a balanced spiritual leader in the congregation if he or she allows the role of music leader to exclude all the other roles. To be sure, God has called the person to be a music leader, but God has called him or her to be much more than that.

> To be a spiritual leader...does require that one be a Christian on the journey, willing to lead and to walk with others on their journey.

CONCLUSION

It is true that the music leader has many roles. But there is one God who calls us into ministry; one God who provides us with gifts for leadership; one Spirit who equips and inspires us to lead others into ministry. The music leader who leads out of a sense of giftedness and in obedience to God's direction will be blessed by God and be a blessing to others.

FOR FURTHER READING

Grace Notes: Spirituality and the Choir, by M. Anne Burnette Hook (Nashville, TN: Discipleship Resources, 1998).

The Church Music Handbook for Pastors and Musicians, by N. Lee Orr (Nashville, TN: Abingdon Press, 1991).

The Church Musician, Revised Edition, by Paul Westermeyer (Minneapolis, MN: Augsburg Fortress Press, 1997).

ENDNOTES

1 See "How to Sing a New Song," on pages 126–33 in this volume, for suggestions about how to teach the congregation a new song.

2 See *Grace Notes: Spirituality and the Choir,* by M. Anne Burnette Hook (Nashville, TN: Discipleship Resources, 1998) for a more extensive exploration of the role of spiritual leader and its possibilities in a music ministry.

6

HOYT L. HICKMAN

*Worship Consultant,
Nashville, Tennessee*

The Work of Communion Stewards, Servers, and Altar Guilds

WE WORSHIP GOD NOT ONLY WITH OUR VOICES BUT ALSO with our whole bodies, our entire being. God comes to us not only through hearing but also through *all* our senses. In this article, we explore some of the ways in which lay members of the worship planning and leadership team can enable this to happen. We discuss the ministries of Communion stewards, servers, and altar guilds.

Material things such as bread, wine, water, furnishings, textiles, and flowers play a major role in Christian worship. They are things we can see, touch, taste, and smell. God has used them through the centuries as means of grace. The sacrament of the Lord's Supper is a prime example of how God uses material things and works through every one of our senses. This should not surprise us. The material world is God's creation, and God has called it good. In Jesus Christ God's "Word became flesh and lived among us" (John 1:14).

Every congregation needs someone to prepare and maintain the material things used in the celebration of the Lord's Supper. Just as "Jesus sent Peter and John, saying, 'Go and prepare the Passover meal for us that we may eat it'" (Luke 22:8), so congregations choose individuals to prepare the holy meal that Jesus instituted. Just as the title *steward* is given to an officer of a ship who is in charge of dining provisions and arrangements, or to any of the staff who serve food and drink, so in The United Methodist Church the title *Communion steward* is given to those who prepare the bread and wine (grape juice) and set the Lord's Table. In some congregations, one person performs this ministry. In others, especially larger congregations or those with more frequent Communion, several people or a committee may be needed.

Often the ministry of Communion stewards is part of the larger ministry of an *altar guild*, whose responsibilities extend beyond the Lord's Supper to other matters of chancel and sanctuary care. In addition, laypeople often assist the pastor or other ordained presider in serving or distributing Communion to the people. Sometimes such people also are called "Communion stewards" or "Eucharistic ministers," but here we shall call them "Communion servers" or "servers."

Worship Matters: A United Methodist Guide to Worship Work (Volume II) © 1999 Discipleship Resources. Used by permission.

These people are part of the larger worship team and need to work closely with the pastor and with one another. They need to learn from the pastor when and how the Lord's Supper is to be celebrated and exactly what is expected of them. They in turn make important contributions to congregational worship and deserve respect and recognition for their ministries.

THE ENVIRONMENT OF THE LORD'S SUPPER

Because the Lord's Supper is a meal, it is held at a table. This table has been called the Lord's Table, the Communion Table, or the altar-table.[1] It is here that the pastor presides in the Lord's name at the Lord's Supper, and it is from here that the people are served. This is the focal point of the Communion steward's ministry.

The Lord's Table is located in an area, sometimes called the chancel, that is the focal point of the congregation's attention. In this area are also the other basic furnishings used in the conduct of worship—the pulpit, baptismal font, and perhaps a lectern. There also may be a rail with kneeling pads in front of it, where people may kneel to receive Communion.

The arrangement of the chancel area and the placement of the Lord's Table in it vary widely from one congregation to another, depending on the theories, fashions, or practical considerations that governed the original design or later renovations. The Lord's Table may be free-standing, designed to look like a table, and emphasizing that the Lord's Supper is a holy meal. Or it may be an altar-table set against the wall, designed to look like an altar and suggesting that we are making a sacrifice. The arrangement of the furnishings in a congregation and the local traditions that have developed over the years will greatly affect how the Lord's Table is to be set for the Lord's Supper.

The Lord's Table may be covered with a parament (altar cloth) and may be set with appointments such as cross and candles. Paraments may include matching scarves or bookmarks that hang in front of the pulpit and lectern. The parament colors may be changed to signify the day or season of the Christian year. An altar guild or other designated individuals may care for these paraments and furnishings. They also may have responsibilities for banners and other hangings and furnishings throughout the sanctuary. The handbook for those with this responsibility is *United Methodist Altars*. (See "For Further Reading," on page 60.)

As Communion stewards gain understanding, they may come to favor changes in how the Lord's Table in their sanctuary is designed, placed, or appointed. Current understandings of the Lord's Supper strongly support that the table be free-standing; thirty-nine or forty inches high; and free of crosses, candles, or flowers so that the presiding minister can stand behind it facing the people. Any changes, however, should be made carefully by a process that gains the understanding and ownership of the congregation. The book *Church Architecture: Building and Renovating for Christian Worship* will prove extremely valuable in planning any changes. (See "For Further Reading," on page 60.)[2]

PREPARING THE LORD'S SUPPER

For festive meals we commonly cover the dining table with a tablecloth, so for the Lord's Supper we customarily place on the Lord's Table a fine white cloth, traditionally of linen. Congregations that use

Every congregation needs someone to prepare and maintain the material things used in the celebration of the Lord's Supper.

a colored seasonal parament on the Lord's Table may place the white Communion cloth on top of it. The paraments used when the Lord's Supper is celebrated should be of the color appropriate to the day or season; they are white only when the day or season calls for white. If the parament and the Communion cloth are unattractive when used together on the Lord's Table, the Communion cloth may be used alone.

Just as a dinner table is set with plates, glasses, and silverware, so the Lord's Table is set with Communion ware—a plate (paten) or basket for the bread, a large chalice or small individual cups for the wine, and often a pitcher or trays. Cloths similar in material to the Communion tablecloth (but smaller) may be used for covering the Communion ware or for wiping the lip of the chalice.

Preparations for the Lord's Supper will be much easier if the Communion ware and cloths have been properly cleaned and stored since they were used last. It is important that the whole cycle of preparation, cleanup, and maintenance be entrusted to one or more stewards who will see this as Christian stewardship to be done with the fidelity and reverence appropriate to the character of this holy meal.[3]

United Methodist churches today are increasingly returning to the New Testament and early Christian practice of using an uncut, common loaf of real bread. As Paul tells us in 1 Corinthians 10:17, this signifies that we Christians are "one body." It is especially meaningful when the bread is homebaked. Either leavened or unleavened bread is suitable for United Methodists. The bread should not be crumbly, especially if it is to be dipped in the cup. It is vital to ensure that there is enough bread for everyone. The number of people who can be served from a loaf of bread depends not only on the size of the loaf but also on how large the pieces are that are broken off and given to the people. Pastors and Communion stewards can judge from experience how large a loaf—or in a very large congregation, how many loaves—is needed.

Scripture refers to the contents of the cup as the "fruit of the vine" (Matthew 26:29). The juice of the grape is always to be used. Neither any other kind of juice nor any artificial beverage, even if it is grape-flavored, is acceptable. Christians traditionally have used wine; therefore, the word *wine* is frequently used for the contents of the Communion cup. Since the late-nineteenth century, The United Methodist Church and its predecessors have used unfermented grape juice. For United Methodists, the decision to use grape juice and not wine expresses pastoral concern for individuals recovering from alcoholism and makes possible the participation of children and youth. It also reinforces the church's witness of abstinence. It is especially meaningful when the grape juice is homemade.

Use of a single large cup, called a *chalice*, on the Lord's Table is, like the common loaf of bread, a powerful symbol of unity. Many older congregations have one or two historic chalices that can be brought out and used for the Lord's Supper. Chalices are traditionally made of (or plated with) silver or gold, but ceramic or other materials are often used today. Metal chalices that are actually used should be gold-lined, as other metals taint both grape juice and wine. It is not hard in any large city to find someone who can line or reline a chalice with gold.

Although the historic and ecumenical Christian practice has been for the people to drink from one or more common cups, following the practice of Jesus and his disciples, hygienic considerations have led most United Methodists to abandon this practice. If the people drink from a common cup, the rim of the cup should be wiped with a clean, white cloth after each person drinks from it. These cloths should be reserved for use at the Lord's Supper and should be carefully maintained along with the other Communion cloths.

Another way of using the common cup is for people to dip their piece of the bread into it. This practice, called *intinction*, has become increasingly common among United Methodists. When intinction is used, some pastors prefer to have a spoon handy for removing particles of bread that may fall into the chalice. Special spoons with a perforated bowl are made for this purpose, but any fine spoon may be used.

Small individual cups may be used. They may be filled from a siphon-operated cup filler that is available from Cokesbury and other church supply houses. These cups are customarily placed in round metal (or occasionally, wooden) stacking trays for serving and are filled with grape juice before the worship service. If these trays have a lid, there is no need for a white cloth covering. The pastor removes the lid when taking the bread and cup before giving thanks.

Again, it is vital to make sure there is enough grape juice for everyone. If individual cups are used, enough of them should be filled to cover the maximum expected attendance. If one or more chalices are used, Communion stewards can judge from experience how much grape juice is needed.

If a chalice is filled in advance, it should be covered with a white cloth, or with a white cloth-covered square of stiff cardboard or other lightweight material, until the pastor takes the bread and cup before giving thanks—at which time the pastor removes the covering.

An alternative is to not fill the chalice(s) in advance but to pour the grape juice into a fine flagon, cruet, or pitcher—one that will not taint the contents and is reserved for use at the Lord's Supper. This is then either placed on the Lord's Table in advance or brought to the Lord's Table immediately before the pastor takes the bread and cup—at which time the pastor pours the grape juice into the chalice(s).

SERVING THE LORD'S SUPPER

Many United Methodist congregations have discovered that properly trained laypeople perform a valuable ministry assisting the pastor in serving Communion to the people. The serving of one person by another—passing on the grace we have received from Christ—is crucial to the symbolism of the Lord's Supper. It is our historic custom to serve each person individually, with appropriate words. This should be done in a warm, personal, reverent manner. While *presiding* at the Lord's Supper is the function of the pastor or other ordained elder, *serving* Communion under the pastor's direction is a powerful demonstration of the priesthood of the whole body of believers. This lay ministry is encouraged by both *The Book of Discipline of the United Methodist Church—1996* (¶1115.9) and *The United Methodist Book of Worship* (pp. 28–29, 51–53).

There are other practical reasons for this ministry. Many congregations, especially large ones, experience a problem with the time required for the pastor to serve both the bread and the cup to everyone. A pastor trying to do this in a reasonable period of time can easily lapse into a rushed and less personal manner. After the service, if there are large numbers of people who are sick or who are limited in their ability to leave home, it may take too long for the pastor to get to all of them with Communion. Some congregations have additional ordained clergy who can assist, but most congregations do not.

The serving of one person by another— passing on the grace we have received from Christ—is crucial to the symbolism of the Lord's Supper.

The ministry of serving the Lord's Supper can be done in several ways, depending in part on how Communion is served. However it is done, it is important that servers be carefully selected and trained by the pastor and work closely under the pastor's direction. It is a sacred ministry to be carried out with dedication and reverence.

In some congregations, the people receive Communion while seated. The ushers or other designated servers bring the bread and cup to each row. The people in each row pass the bread and cup(s), serving one another. The whole congregation has the opportunity to minister as well as be ministered to, but they lose the more active response of standing up and going forward.

A few congregations form a large circle and pass the bread and cup around the circle to one another. The people have made the active response of standing up and going to a place in the circle. Everyone has the opportunity to minister as well as be ministered to. It is a powerful symbol of unity. But it is feasible only if those present are not too numerous and want to commune in this manner.

Most United Methodists come forward to receive Communion. Traditionally, this has been done kneeling at a rail, but increasingly it is done standing at Communion stations. In either case, the use of laypeople as well as the pastor(s) has both symbolic and practical value.

When people receive the Supper while kneeling, one or more pairs of servers move back and forth behind the rail, serving the people as they come. Each person receives the bread first, then the cup. In large congregations with long rails, two or more pairs of servers may take responsibility for designated sectors of the rail. If individual cups are used, empty cups may be placed in racks attached to the rail for that purpose.

When people receive the Supper while standing, they go to a Communion station consisting of two servers: one with the bread, the other with the cup. The sanctuary may have one station in the center at the front, or it may have any number of strategically located stations, depending on the size of the congregation. Individuals come to the nearest station and are served standing. If a kneeling rail is available, people have the option of kneeling afterward at the rail for as long as they wish before returning to their seats. If individual cups are used, empty cups may be left at designated places, or a cup collector may be added to each Communion station.

Whether Communion is received while kneeling or standing, it works best if the pastor or a more-experienced server serves the bread. That person makes any necessary split-second decisions about such matters as who needs assistance in receiving. This in turn alerts the server following with the cup to any special needs.

As soon as feasible after the service, lay servers may assist the pastor in distributing the consecrated Communion elements to people who are sick or who are limited in their ability to leave home, and to others who are prevented from attending. This extends the congregation's worship to include those who are unwillingly absent.[4] Some pastors choose to bring a layperson representing the congregation with them when they make Communion calls. Some pastors need the assistance of lay servers because they have so many parishioners they need to visit that it is not feasible for them to do it soon after the service. A Service of Word and Table V (*UMBOW*, pp. 51–53) is an excellent resource for this ministry. Note that the Great Thanksgiving is omitted if a layperson is distributing the consecrated elements, but that thanks should be given after the bread and cup are received (pp. 52–53).

AFTER THE LORD'S SUPPER

After the congregation has been served, the Lord's Table is put in order. The pastor and any who may be assisting reverently return the bread and cup(s) to their places on the Lord's Table. They may wish to replace whatever lids or coverings had been in place at the beginning of the service. This is a visual sign that the Lord's Supper is over.

What is then done with the remaining bread and grape juice should express our stewardship of God's gifts and our respect for the holy purpose they have served. Here are some possibilities suggested in *The United Methodist Book of Worship*:

1. They may be set aside for distribution to the sick and others wishing to commune but unable to attend. [This was discussed above.]
2. They may be reverently consumed by the pastor and others while the table is being set in order or following the service.
3. They may be returned to the earth; that is, the bread may be buried or scattered on the ground, and the wine [grape juice] may be reverently poured out upon the ground—a biblical gesture of worship (2 Samuel 23:16) and an ecological symbol.[5]

We don't know who did the clearing and cleaning up after the first Lord's Supper, but someone must have done it. Clearing and cleaning up after Holy Communion is an important part of a Communion steward's ministry. It is a sacred ministry just as surely as is preparing and serving the Lord's Supper.

The Communion steward should wait until the people have left before clearing the Table, but should take care not to show disrespect for the Lord's Table by leaving it uncleared for hours, or even until the next day. One certainly would not want people coming into the sanctuary later and seeing the Lord's Table uncleared.

Any stains should be removed and the cloths laundered after each use, so that they are always spotless. The cloths should never be sent to a commercial laundry or laundered in a load with other items. Wax drippings can be removed in this way: First, scrape the drippings with a blunt instrument; then, place a blotter or paper towel under the cloth and press over the spot with a warm iron until the wax is absorbed. Wine (grape juice) stains can usually be removed by placing the cloth over a bowl and pouring boiling water through the stain until it fades from view. The sooner stains are treated, the easier they are to remove. More stubborn stains may require a bleach solution.

The cloths should be ironed while they are still quite damp, first on the underside and then on the side that will show. The cloths should not be folded, as they should be uncreased. Smaller cloths can be stored flat in clean drawers. After the tablecloth is perfectly dry, it should be rolled on a heavy tube and wrapped in tissue paper for storage.

If a cloth is on the Lord's Table during the week, it may be covered with a protective cloth or even a plastic sheet when the sanctuary is not open for public or private worship; but the covering should be removed for services.

The bread plate(s), cup(s), and other Communion ware should be carefully washed and stored. Special equipment for efficiently washing individual cups is available from Cokesbury and other church supply houses. Any glasses that are chipped or cracked must be discarded. Washing a gold-lined chalice or bread plate should be done gently so as not to rub off any of the thin gold lining. Each item should have a storage place and should be labeled to prevent unnecessary handling.

> What is then done with the remaining bread and grape juice should express our stewardship of God's gifts and our respect for the holy purpose they have served.

Silver Communion ware requires special care. The following process is proper: Wash it in hot, soapy water and rinse it in clear, hot water. Dry it immediately with a soft cloth or paper towels. Polish silver two or three times a year with a fine grade of silver polish. Never allow polish to dry on the surface. Maintain the shine between polishings by rubbing with a soft cloth or treated polishing gloves. Store in clean cotton flannel bags to prevent tarnishing.

CONCLUSION

The faithful stewardship of the Communion stewards, servers, and altar guilds brings to mind the saying, "God is in the details." Stewards and servers are essential to this holy meal, in which the congregation has been renewed as the body of Christ and given a foretaste of the heavenly banquet. Altar guilds greatly enhance all worship in the sanctuaries where they minister. They have every reason to give thanks for the sacred ministry entrusted to them.

FOR FURTHER READING

Church Architecture: Building and Renovating for Christian Worship, Second Edition, by James F. White and Susan J. White (Akron, OH: O.S.L. Publications, 1998).

Eucharist: Christ's Feast With the Church, by Laurence Hull Stookey (Nashville, TN: Abingdon Press, 1993).

United Methodist Altars: A Guide for the Congregation, Revised Edition, by Hoyt L. Hickman (Nashville, TN: Abingdon Press, 1996).

Worshiping With United Methodists: A Guide for Pastors and Church Leaders, by Hoyt L. Hickman (Nashville, TN: Abingdon Press, 1996). See especially Chapter 7, "Thanksgiving and Communion."

ENDNOTES

1 See "Creating Space for Worship," on pages 155–59 in Volume I of *Worship Matters.*

2 See also "Creating Space for Holy Communion," on pages 85–92 in this volume.

3 See "Creating Space for the Sacristy," on pages 111–16 in this volume, for more information about how to prepare and maintain a sacristy.

4 See "The Distribution of Communion by the Laity to Those Who Cannot Attend Worship," on pages 147–54 in Volume I of *Worship Matters.*

5 From "An Order of Sunday Worship Using the Basic Pattern," copyright © 1985, 1989, 1992 by The United Methodist Publishing House; from *The United Methodist Book of Worship,* p. 30. Used by permission.

The Work of Ushers

KENNETH M. JOHNSON

Retired United Methodist Pastor, Lake Junaluska, North Carolina

W ORSHIP THAT MATTERS TAKES PLACE IN A CONGREGATION that cares. Such a gathering resembles a symphony orchestra. While the presider is the "conductor" or host extending hospitality to the gathered congregation, the "first chairs" in the orchestra belong to the ushers and greeters! The difference between the "conductor" and "first chairs" is in location, not function. Both extend ministries of hospitality. Strategically located at doors and in heavy traffic areas, ushers extend the warmth of the church with caring eyes, with gestures of inclusion, and with body language that communicates real love. Finding seats, distributing bulletins, directing traffic, and receiving the offering are secondary to their care for the individual.

When everybody in the gathered community is "in tune" with the ministry of hospitality, people are able to experience worship of incomparable beauty and effectiveness. Christ is truly glorified, and one leaves the sanctuary alive and refreshed, with a desire to return. Such an ideal, however, calls for a different orientation for ushers and greeters, requiring them to shift their focus from functions to relationships, and to a priority of "being" over "doing."

How do we move toward this ideal of hospitality? What practical steps can ushers take to make their work more effective? In this article, we look at one way to respond to questions such as these.

DOORKEEPERS AND PEOPLE MANAGERS

Hospitality begins before one enters the sanctuary—in the parking lot. If parking is a problem, having an usher or "parking attendant" point to an empty space is very helpful. I know of several United Methodist congregations that reserve accessible parking spaces not only for people with disabilities but also for church visitors. This says a lot about that church's priorities! The term *visitor* is usually applied to the newcomer. A more appropriate term is *guest*, which communicates greater warmth and care.

When hospitality reigns, doors are opened individually to worshipers. This is especially appreciated in inclement weather. Whenever doors are opened in a hotel or at some other place of business, guests invariably experience a warm feeling of appreciation. When a door is opened for someone in or out of a church building, the response "Thank you!" invariably follows.

Ushers should pay special attention to the elderly and to those with disabilities. Nowadays most churches are barrier-free, but the location of the barrier-free entry is not always obvious. Meeting the newcomer at his or her level and then walking with him or her up a ramp, or toward an opened door or an elevator, are greatly appreciated.

When newcomers inquire about the location of the nursery or a telephone or restroom, the magic words for ushers and greeters are, "Let me show you," followed by leading the newcomer within sight of the telephone or restroom door. It is important for the newcomer to be introduced to the nursery staff. When nursery attendants introduce themselves and repeat the names of newcomers, they add immeasurably to the warmth of their greeting.

Ushers greet visitors at the door of the sanctuary. While their role has changed across the centuries, one consistent function for the usher has been the opening and closing of church doors. We would never think of inviting a guest to our home and then limiting our hospitality to the inside only! We tend to forget that strangers approach a church building with some apprehension, not knowing if they will be received warmly or coolly. A door that is opened for them dispels their anxiety. Such loving care by the usher or greeter eliminates any feelings of being conspicuous, uncertain, or fearful. If this care is extended to all worshipers, the usher or greeter does not have to know if they are members or not.

Rather than ask, "Where would you like to sit?" the usher should mention the available seating options and then take the worshiper to the seat of preference. Handing a bulletin to a person so that he or she receives it right-side up is also helpful! Of course, such hospitality should be extended to all, not just to visitors.

Some ushers should always remain on duty during a service. On some occasions people become ill and need assistance. Parents with small children may have to take them to the restroom in an unknown location of the building. Emergency calls to doctors, nurses, or others may come during the service. The usher should move to assist these people as unobtrusively as possible, opening doors and providing information.

No greater opportunity for hospitality is found than at the close of a service. Most churches ignore this opportunity. Recently when I visited a colleague in his home for the first time, we were in a third-floor room when I realized I was supposed to meet my wife at that time. Even though another friend was also visiting, my host excused himself and walked with me to the first-floor entrance and opened the door, saying, "Come to see us again!" Can ushers not model that kind of hospitality in the church? Should hospitality in a church be less than hospitality in a home? Such an act requires no more than an additional ten minutes at the close of a service, but it creates a warm and friendly feeling of inestimable value, making the guest want to return!

Ushers in most congregations are probably unaware that in the early church the symbol of their office was a golden key, presented to them at their installation. Thus, the key became a perpetual reminder of hospitality at the threshold.

In most churches, people tend to drift away at the close of a service without being shown any sign of appreciation for their coming. Therefore, those same doors that were opened by the usher or greeter for the worshiper to enter should be reopened for him or her to leave. Having a greeter or usher on the walkway or in the parking area who smiles, nods, and says, "Thank you for being with us!" makes for a memorable experience. For the usher or greeter to regard his or her work as complete after the offering is to miss a real opportunity for service afterward: creating a friendly and lasting impression.

Hospitality is also conveyed nonverbally. Once while recuperating from an illness, I was able to slip into a neighboring church service while my wife and other family members attended our church. I got out of my car in the large parking lot, walked down a long walkway—passing several people coming from the earlier service—into the doorway leading down a hallway to the sanctuary. To my shock and amazement, at no place in or out of the sanctuary did anyone smile at or greet me. I got the impression that worship for these people is a self-centered experience. Either they didn't know about or they had forgotten their ambassadorial mission to the world! I felt more like an alien in that congregation than a fellow Christian.

Newcomers to a church service often arrive early and show by cautious movements that they are unfamiliar with the surroundings. If uncertain, the usher or greeter may say, "Hello, my name is _____," whereupon the worshiper will usually introduce him or herself. If the usher is uncertain about the worshiper's name, the usher may simply say, "I don't believe I know you. I am _____," whereupon the newcomer will usually introduce him or herself. The usher should make sure that he or she understands the name of a guest, asking for a spelling if in doubt. This may seem awkward to the usher or greeter, but it is flattering to the guest. Then, as an aid to memory, one can jot the name on a slip of paper afterward, to be reviewed before the person leaves the sanctuary. Thanking a guest by name afterward is "icing on the cake"!

Ushers move toward the ideal of hospitality in the church when they understand their ministry as one of people care rather than people management.

TRAINING AND PRACTICE

Pastors and usher leaders cannot assume that people know about ushering and greeting; nor should they assume that good ushering is learned overnight. Being an embodiment of the gospel is an awesome task! Thus, a time for training and orientation is necessary if new recruits are to understand their work as ministers of hospitality.

A practical thing such as opening a church door by pushing it outward is clumsy for many people because they are accustomed to opening a door toward them. The tendency for the usher is to follow the door outward with his or her back turned toward the worshiper; this makes greeting the worshiper awkward. A rule of thumb for the usher: Never turn your back on anyone. This requires the usher, then, to push or follow the door with one hand while greeting the worshiper with the other. Such a procedure sounds simple enough, but it often is not done gracefully without practice.

Church ushers are always volunteers, so scheduling takes place in an atmosphere of shared leadership. If an ushering board or committee does not exist, one should be established by working through the worship committee and pastor. An ushering committee can develop and coordinate a rotation plan that also will ensure the cultivation of new leadership. It can also coordinate ongoing training for new ushers. One other reality is that ushers are taken for granted by many congregations. The choir is often recognized, but ushers are seldom thanked. Having

Ushers move toward the ideal of hospitality in the church when they understand their ministry as one of people care rather than people management.

an occasional dinner or recognition service in their honor will show the church's appreciation for the work ushers do.

Here is a three-step plan to help ushers in a church of any size or makeup to move toward excellence in hospitality:

1. Meet people warmly at the threshold with caring eyes and doors that are opened. Remember the Scripture: "Do not neglect to show hospitality to strangers, for by doing that some have entertained angels without knowing it" (Hebrews 13:2). By viewing their work from the perspective of a stranger, ushers and greeters are able to disperse themselves to strategic areas of greeting, such as doorways. It also avoids the temptation for ushers and greeters to bunch up and engage one another in small talk!

2. Practice the habit of people care until doors are opened naturally and inconspicuously. Remind yourself that the historic role of usher and greeter, explicitly expressed in the Bible, is that of doorkeeper (Psalm 84:10). The challenge is to give caring attention to the worshiper and not inordinate attention to oneself.

3. Use every opportunity for hospitality from the time worshipers arrive at the church building until they leave. Every church has the potential for receiving compliments like that of the ancient church in Corinth, which was cited for the magnificence of its people's hospitality (1 Clement 1:2).

In the parable of the Last Judgment (Matthew 25:31-46), those whom Jesus recommended for inheriting the Kingdom were not self-conscious in their service for the Lord. Such is the ideal for hospitality in the local church. The modern usher may be initially self-conscious in his or her service, but through practice it becomes spontaneous and natural. Based on this parable, the usher can actually chart his or her progress in achieving a higher level of hospitality.

CONCLUSION

Worship that matters takes place in a congregation where ushers and greeters are so trained and dedicated in their work that caring ministry is spontaneously and even unconsciously expressed to all who worship, fulfilling the biblical mandate: "Be hospitable to one another" (1 Peter 4:9).

FOR FURTHER READING

Reading Scripture in Public: A Guide for Preachers and Lay Readers, by Thomas Edward McComiskey (Grand Rapids, MI: Baker Book House, 1991).

The Word in Season: Essays by Members of the Joint Liturgical Group on the Use of the Bible in Liturgy, edited by Donald Gray (Norwich, England: Canterbury Press, 1988).

The Work of Liturgical Dancers

ROSALIE BENT BRANIGAN

Director of Dance Ministry, Central United Methodist Church, Albuquerque, New Mexico

Dance is a word used to describe one of the most basic ways humans express feelings and faith through body movement. Dance is said to be our oldest art form. Every culture throughout history has used dance to express religious faith and to celebrate important events in life—birth, death, healing, natural phenomena. Sacred dance includes individual forms (private meditation) and liturgical forms (within a communal liturgical framework). Liturgical dance has as its purpose the deepening and focusing of the worship event; it is not merely ornamental or decorative. This article discusses the place and uses of liturgical dance in worship and ministry.

LITURGICAL DANCE IN SCRIPTURE AND CHURCH HISTORY

There are many biblical and historical references to dance: Psalms 149 and 150 instruct us to praise God with dance; the apocryphal Acts of John has a description of the disciples at the Last Supper circling around Jesus as he calls them to dance; Romans 12:1 and 1 Corinthians 6:19-20 bless the body as a worthy instrument. The word *rejoice* in Aramaic (the language Jesus spoke) is said by some to mean "to jump or dance." The original meaning of *choir* referred to a group of dancers. *Stanza* meant that the dancers stood still while the soloist danced; the *chorus* was when the group danced.

Dance was common in early Jewish and Christian worship; but as Western civilization progressed, dance took on a life of its own—as did each of the arts, developing sacred, social, and profane aspects. In religious teachings there was a constant conflict between the spiritual (the soul and spirit) and the earthy (the body and the physical) through the Middle Ages, and especially in the Protestant Reformation, when many of the arts were ejected from Christian worship. Music eventually returned, but dance in liturgy remained in only a few countries. The Puritans and Victorians continued the renunciation of the body. It has been only in the last fifty years, as many Christian groups recovered their liturgical heritage, that dance has begun to regain a place in worship.

INTRODUCING LITURGICAL DANCE IN THE CONGREGATION

Dance is a powerful art form in which people of all ages can participate and to which all ages can and do respond. Nevertheless, introducing dance in a local congregation must be carefully planned. Fall, when new groups often begin, is a good time to start liturgical dance choirs. These groups can be organized in the same way as singing choirs: open to anyone in the age group—adult, youth, or children—and meeting on a weekly basis during the school year.

Auditions should not be required, and training or experience should never be a criterion for membership. Dancers do not need to be thin or young to make a contribution. All God's children, including those with disabilities or special needs, should be welcome in all liturgical dance groups. Being in a wheelchair does not prevent someone from dancing.

All of us are dancers. Some of us may have studied more, but all of us have the ability to express ourselves with movement. Some dancers who do the most authentic work have never had a formal dance class, and some of the best-trained dancers are so concerned with technique that they forget that they are a part of worship. Most worshipers would rather watch someone with faith share through their dance than someone with simply superb technical ability.

Try to start with adults. It is always possible to involve children and youth later, but if an art form is introduced by these younger age groups, it may be branded as not worthy of adult attention. Often the arts are used as interest groups to get youth and children to be active in the church. This is fine, but only after the art form has been established as having validity for all ages.

How often dance occurs in a year is a matter for the worship committee or team, the pastor, the director of music, and the dance choir to decide together. Don't be greedy; it is better to leave the congregation wanting more dance, not less. Dancing once in each liturgical season or once a month plus special services and events is enough to keep the dancers interested.

Congregations may not totally accept dance initially; therefore, the leaders should be ready to patiently field questions and comments and not cancel the program based on a few negative remarks. Before sharing dance in worship, it helps to introduce dance to the congregation in informal settings, such as Sunday school classes and church dinners. At these events, talk about the history of dance, the importance of dance to you, and the symbols to look for in choreography. Teach a simple dance to be done with a prayer or Scripture. Have the people sing a familiar hymn while it is danced. When they have had an actual experience with movement in a religious setting, they will have more empathy when dance occurs in worship.

Volunteer to discuss dance with any group that will listen, and be able to defend dance historically, theologically, and scripturally. Be sure the pastor has materials and knowledge to do the same. The pastor's active support from the pulpit and in the bulletin or newsletter can help immeasurably in preparing the congregation.

Never forget that God, not the congregation, is the focus of our worship and that we as artists must be instruments used to bring the people to a deeper level of understanding and feeling. Dance in worship must never be thought of as performance, but always as ministry.

When dance is used for the Scripture, call to prayer, response to the Word, call to worship or benediction, it will be perceived as an integral part of the liturgy. The Lectionary can be invaluable in planning how dance will relate to worship. The Lectionary Scripture readings do not have to be read; they can be sung, prayed, or danced, with their scriptural reference noted in the order of worship. Using the Scripture themes, other hymns, anthems, and texts may be choreographed that will enhance the service.

Plan at least one liturgical season at a time, starting the planning two or three months before the season begins. Choreography cannot be created and learned in as short a lead time as other components of the service. Ask: Who will accompany? Who will order and pay for music? When will joint rehearsals occur? All such matters must be worked out, with nothing left to chance.

When choosing material to be danced in worship, either to a musical setting or to spoken word, consider that the congregation may not be ready for complex or abstract choreography set to music without a text. Liturgical dances that have the most impact are usually very simple and straightforward. Less is more! Too often, because we are afraid of stillness, we make dances too busy or too complicated. Start with conservative material, careful costuming, and restrained choreography. Proceed slowly and prayerfully.

In many congregations, those in the chancel area can be seen only from the waist up by people sitting past the third row. Thus, time spent on footwork is wasted, but expressive arms and faces can convey a great deal. Dancers should know their space and sightlines and should ask themselves, *Can I be seen when kneeling? Does the pulpit block the chancel?* Using different levels and areas in choreography makes the dance more interesting, but not if the dancers periodically disappear from view. Be creative in using space. Strange architectural quirks can be turned into exciting opportunities.

CHOREOGRAPHING THE CONGREGATION'S DANCE

Choreographing or "composing" a dance can be challenging. There are few sources of written choreography and no consistent method of writing it. Even teaching someone how to choreograph is an inexact science.

Dance does not have to be pretty or sweet. In fact, in worship it should never be either. Our lives run the gamut from extreme love and joy to rejection, despair, and death. All of these experiences are present in the worshiping community on any given Sunday. While we may express beauty or happiness, we do not have the right to trivialize any emotion. Observing how real people move when experiencing intense feelings can bring to choreography an authenticity to which people of all ages will respond. Dance during Lent, for instance, allows us to deal with not only Christ's pain and death but also with ours.

If the choreography is not being based on Scripture, look for material that is theologically sound and that is good musically, with a strong melodic line and a text that "moves." "Holy, holy, holy!" is much harder to choreograph than "Were you there when they crucified my Lord?" or "I lift up my eyes to the hills." Look for active verbs and images that lend themselves to "pictures."

Spoken words, either read by a liturgist or spoken by the dancer, can be very effective. The psalms are wonderful when done this way and can bring the Psalter to life. The beauty of the spoken word is that the dancer is not restricted by the rhythm or music.

All of us are dancers.... All of us have the ability to express ourselves with movement.

One method of choreographing is to create "pictures" or "poses" on key words and then to find ways to move from picture to picture. Another is to find all the nouns or verbs (or emotions or symbols) that can become a shape or describe a movement and to let the dancers explore them individually. Encourage them to use open, asymmetrical shapes on different levels and to be strong and forceful rather than timid. Allow room for individuals to express themselves in unique ways. When dancers are given encouragement and confidence, incredible and sincere expressions of faith become glorious dances.

Collect photographs—dance pictures, newspaper and magazine photos of people expressing raw emotions—that will inspire you or will save many words if you are trying to get an idea across.

The earliest dances in worship were folk dances—dances of the people. Using material from such dances, particularly with ethnic hymns or anthems, is quite appropriate. Use what you know and what is comfortable for you. Deaf signing also can be incorporated into choreography.

Modern dance allows more freedom of technique and expression than classical ballet. Dance can border on mime, be static, or use large movements and require more dance technique; the text, music, and occasion will dictate the style. When the movement is sincere and honest, there is no right or wrong way to do it. Sincere movement that expresses faith and conviction is always more important than style or technical ability. The objective is *communication,* so the choreography must be appropriate to that end.

Dancers risk a great deal when participating in worship. Directors must never forget or belittle dancers' courage. They must enable and build confidence, creating safe situations where miracles can occur as feelings and faith are laid bare for the congregation to see.

Much of a dancer's confidence and liturgical dance's acceptance is dependent on what is worn. Due to the long religious history of making the body something to be negated, some congregation members may have real problems in dealing with their own bodies—let alone having to look at the dancer's—for few of us are truly self-confident.

Designing a costume that is modest enough to make the congregation comfortable and that allows the dancer to move is not easy. Form-fitting costumes and sheer fabrics suitable for the secular stage are too revealing for most congregations. One design for both men and women starts with a long-sleeved leotard and stirrup tights. The women wear an ankle-length skirt, and the men wear knit pants. Over this is worn a sleeveless tunic made of double-knit fabric with a gold cross embroidered on the chest; the tunic is open on the sides except from the armhole to the waist. The women's tunic is ankle length; the men's tunic comes down to cover the hips. Each costume is all one color— the women in bright, vibrant tones (pastels look washed out), and the men in darker colors. Remember that it is better to err on the side of being too conservative.

Costumes for children and youth should also be carefully designed. Youth may wear the same costumes as the adults. Or, the girls may wear loose-fitting, solid T-shirts, ankle-length skirts, and stirrup tights; the boys may wear T-shirts and loose-fitting pants. Children's skirts may be shorter and be worn with a leotard and tights; however, as soon as little girls' bodies start to develop, some sort of a loose-fitting top will become necessary.

UNDERSTANDING THE SKILLS, PRINCIPLES, AND GUIDELINES OF LITURGICAL DANCE

Children remember ten percent of what they are told, sixty percent of what they see, and ninety percent of what they do. Television and computers have made us a people dependent on visual stimulation. These facts help to justify the inclusion of the arts in worship and religious education. If our faith, heritage, and value systems are to be perpetuated, they must be internalized in ways that will succeed in an experiential world. The arts answer this need, illuminating and illustrating our faith stories, Scriptures, and moral teaching as the child participates in the production of dances, dramas, or visual arts.

The arts give children, youth, and adults experiences that become ends in themselves. They learn to praise, pray to, and worship God through the arts. While having these experiences, they also are learning the following:

- cooperation and interdependence
- self-reliance and self-esteem
- coordination and dexterity
- creativity and discipline
- memory and physical skills
- fitness and healthy fun
- rhythm and sequence
- spatial and human relations
- patience and dependability
- confidence to work alone
- confidence to work in front of others to witness and to celebrate

Many Christian educators believe that an important objective of religious training is to teach children and youth how to worship. By having ongoing groups, rehearsals can become classes where children are prepared to become part of the worshiping community; where Scripture is studied while technique is taught; and where a graded body of increasingly significant material is used for the dances that are created.

When working with children and youth, remember these principles:
- Children and youth should never be exploited by being presented as "cute," or by being used merely to entertain the adults.
- Dance movement for children and youth should never be sexy.
- We must be constantly vigilant in preventing the perpetuation of racial and sexual stereotypes.
- People of all ages respond to quality.

Once children or youth understand a text or story, let them do their own choreography (with veto power and supervision by an adult). What they create, they will remember and will be less likely to desecrate.

Sometimes parents, coming from a recital or performance mentality, believe that technique is all that is necessary to have a successful dance choir. The need for a strong spiritual emphasis and understanding never enters their minds. So, time must be spent stressing that technique must be a tool and not an end in itself, and that the instrument—our body—must bend, stretch, and move to the best of its ability but must never be a slave to the demands of technique.

Liturgical dance requires the dancer to bare his or her soul in worship. There are no words to hide behind, rarely a character to portray, no literal use of facial expression or gesture—only the abstract essence of a basic idea, text, or piece of music. The body does not lie; therefore, raw, real

When the movement is sincere and honest, there is no right or wrong way to do it.

emotions, shapes, and feelings must be wrung from the depths of the soul in each dance in worship for the dance to be the powerful conduit to God that it is capable of being. Unless this occurs, dance in worship becomes, at best, a technical exercise or, at worst, a mechanical performance.

So how do we get people to join our dance choirs and be willing to get up in worship and dance? Consider the following guidelines:

1. Love and believe in the ministry of liturgical dance and be willing to defend its validity.

2. Love the dancers unconditionally and believe that they are always more important than the dance.

3. Believe that every person has worth and beauty and has a soul that longs for a means of expressing feelings that are too deep for words.

4. Realize that inside each dancer there is a collection of memories and experiences, both positive and negative, that if remembered and tapped can inform the body and add depth and conviction to the dance; but tapping these memories can be painful, though cathartic.

5. Know that helping another person find a way to delve into her or his soul, risking exposure of her or his inmost feelings, is an enormous responsibility that is not to be taken lightly. We must be ready to help bring about healing.

6. Remember that discipline and criticism are not bad if they are done in love and are constructive in nature.

7. Never forget that after a dancer has given his or her dance as a gift to God, we must never in any way belittle it; for once given, it cannot be changed.

8. Have enough enthusiasm and energy for everyone, and use it to carry the dancers through the rough spots, by cajoling, crying, laughing, loving, caring, feeding—whatever it takes.

CONCLUSION

If you believe that you are in ministry and that what you do is for God, if you think and pray before you speak or choreograph or dance, and if you love what you do and the people with whom and for whom you dance, your ministry will be blessed and be a blessing.

FOR FURTHER READING

Introducing Dance in Christian Worship, by Ronald Gagne, Thomas A. Kane, and Robert VerEecke (Laurel, MD: The Pastoral Press, 1984).

The Spirit Moves: A Handbook of Dance and Prayer, by Carla De Sola (Collegeville, MN: The Liturgical Press, 1986).

Organizations you can contact include:

Sacred Dance Guild. Contact: Carla Kramer, Membership Director, Sacred Dance Guild, 2558 Delaware Street, Wickliffe, OH 44092. Phone: 440-585-1676. E-mail: Rkram@aol.com. Internet: *www.us.net/sdg*

The Fellowship of United Methodists in Music and Worship Arts, P.O. Box 24787, Nashville, TN 37202-4787. Phone: 800-952-8977. FAX: 615-749-6874. E-mail: FUMMWA@aol.com. Internet: *http://members.aol.com/fummwa/fummwa.htm*

The Work of Media Ministers

THOMAS E. BOOMERSHINE

*Professor of New Testament,
United Theological Seminary,
Dayton, Ohio*

LEN WILSON

*Minister of Media,
Ginghamsburg Church,
Tipp City, Ohio*

THE DEVELOPMENT OF ELECTRONIC COMMUNICATIONS technology and its growing use in worship is only the latest stage in the integration of technology in worship. In earlier periods, architects, stone masons, stained-glass designers, scribes, printers, organists, pianists, icon painters, artists, typists, and mimeograph-machine operators mastered technologies that have become an integral part of the community's worship. The integration of these technologies in worship has been essential to the vitality of worship in each new cultural setting. As the technologies have been gradually integrated, they have become a seamless part of the overall fabric of worship.

In the first period of the use of electronic media in worship, its role has been to broadcast the worship service to a radio or television audience. In worship services that are being audiotaped or videotaped for broadcast or cablecast, the work of the audio technicians, videographers, and directors is to provide a high quality audio and/or video experience for the radio, tape, or television congregation in as unobtrusive a manner as possible. The role of the media minister in these contexts is to provide high-quality documentation and reproduction of the worship service for electronic distribution.

In an increasing number of worship services, the work of the media ministers is to be an integral part of the worship design and leadership team for the development and delivery of audio, video, computer graphics, and music as structural elements of the worship service. In these contexts, the media ministers' work may include the co-creation of virtually every part of the service: the sermon, the recital of the Scriptures, the prayers, announcements, hymns and anthems, call to worship, testimonies/personal stories, and mission connections. The call to worship, for example, through a graphic image of some kind often functions as the crucial metaphorical representation of the theme of the worship service. The media ministers' role, then, is to manage the system so that the images and sounds flow smoothly throughout the worship service.

THE ROLES OF MEDIA MINISTERS

The particular roles of media ministers, which are becoming increasingly diverse, include at least the following:

Worship Matters: A United Methodist Guide to Worship Work (Volume II) © 1999 Discipleship Resources. Used by permission.

DIRECTOR

The work of the director is to coordinate the production of the audiotaping and videotaping of the worship service and/or the delivery of the sound and image elements of the service. The director, who is the leader of the production crew, works with all crew members—including the sound and lighting directors, the speaker, and the floor director—to coordinate all aspects of the media presentation during the service.

By communicating with the team through an intercom headset system, the director integrates the various elements of worship into a cohesive package. Other responsibilities include meeting with the speaker for a sermon rehearsal to gain a firm understanding of the in- and out-cues for sermon graphics, Scripture readings, video clips, and so forth. The director also supervises the development of preproduced segments by storyboarding, scripting, coordinating shots, and editing the final segment.

TECHNICAL DIRECTOR

The technical director operates the mixing device, through which the various sources of video are mixed for projection. This is the last step before an image hits the screen. The technical director takes commands from the director about when to choose a particular source, keeps tabs on the quality of video coming from cameras, and assists both the camera operators and the director if something is not working correctly.

The primary requirement for this position is a cool head. The technical director must be able to operate the video mixer without hesitation, in order to execute commands correctly and on time. Other functions include ensuring that the cameras are set up and white-balanced prior to the technical rehearsal. The technical director assists the director during technical rehearsal, which gives the technical director a better feel for what will be expected during the service itself.

ENGINEER

The work of the audio, video, and computer engineers is to ensure that the equipment is working properly and to handle the technical aspects of the delivery of the audio, video, and computer materials to the director.

SOUND DIRECTOR

The sound director operates all elements of the sound related to worship. This includes setting up sound for musicians, establishing appropriate levels and equalization, wiring speakers and microphones, operating various auxiliary sound sources (including CD, cassette, mini-disc, and DAT), and mixing these various elements through the soundboard during worship. The sound engineer also preproduces sound that will coordinate with video and graphic images.

VIDEOGRAPHER

The work of a videographer is to videotape preproduced segments for the worship service and to record/project the live video-feed of the service in a way that enhances the worship experience and deepens meaning. Video in worship is more than the documentation of an event on a screen.

The video creates an emotionally charged atmosphere and a visual subtext that enhances meaning. It takes viewers outside of the worship context to places that are being addressed in the service, and it enhances the experience for the people present in the worshiping community.

GRAPHIC ARTIST

The work of the graphic artist is to create and deliver graphics and images that become the visual representation of elements of the worship service: the words of the hymns and/or prayers, outlines of the sermon, and graphic images for virtually any element of the service.

The graphic artist does not so much *represent* elements of the service as *create* them in new ways—saying things with images that cannot be said with words. For example, behind a song about the community of faith being radically inclusive, there might be a series of images of people from a variety of races and cultures. The images also can be interpretive. For example, a recital of Jesus' parable of the rich fool with his plan to build bigger barns (Luke 12:13-21) might be accompanied by images of bigger and bigger suburban homes.

LIGHTING DIRECTOR

The lighting director operates the lighting board during worship. During rehearsal this person programs the board for various light configurations. He or she then implements that program during the worship service.

THE WORK OF MEDIA MINISTERS

The work of media ministers is determined by the cultural character of the worship service. In a traditional service, the work of the media ministry team is to record the worship service for transmission; this work is primarily technical. In a contemporary worship service, the work of the media ministry team is to participate in a creative group that designs the service, and then produces and delivers electronic sounds and images as an integral part of the service.

In contrast to the more individual work of worship in print culture, teamwork is essential in electronic media ministry. Because of the wide range of technical skills and capabilities that are needed, the spiritual and pragmatic work of team building is the only way to develop effective media ministry. Two teams of ministers are involved in planning and executing a worship service for an electronic culture; they are the worship design team and the media ministry team.

THE WORSHIP DESIGN TEAM

Only by being included in the planning process for worship can electronic media be an integral part of the worship experience. Otherwise, the role of media in worship will not move beyond the instrumental delivery of technological functions. Worship for an electronic culture involves a reconceptualization of the theory and design of worship. For example, the decision about what images will best help to interpret the Scripture of the week is an essential element in the planning of the sermon, the Scripture reading, the congregational hymns, and the prayers. The worship design team includes the preacher, the minister of music, the media minister, and others responsible for planning worship.

> **Only by being included in the planning process for worship can electronic media be an integral part of the worship experience.**

THE MEDIA MINISTRY TEAM

Once the overall design for the worship has been decided, the work of the media ministry team is to generate appropriate sound and images and to get these into the system in time for the service. This may involve shooting and editing new video, scanning photographs, selecting and editing music into a multimedia montage, generating computer graphics, recording new sound (speech or music), and editing. These elements, once produced, generally also need to be tested and rehearsed for timing and for practicing the various moves. If the role of the media ministry team includes taping the worship service for audiotape or videotape distribution, the team also needs to practice its ways of working together in order to produce a quality production.

The members of the media ministry team need to have a thorough mastery of the equipment they will use. The easiest way to do this has been to hire professional technicians. However, the experience of many congregations is that it is preferable to empower members of the congregation with those technical skills. Giving people the opportunity to develop the technical and creative aspects of doing media in worship for an electronic culture uses and develops gifts that would otherwise be lost in the church. In this way, the congregation is involved in the use of the technology, and members have opportunities to learn new skills.

Also, it has become clear that congregations who let it be known that they want to develop these ministries often find that there are people who are technically skilled who are looking for a place to use their skills in the service of something other than the business world. Many people who work in the communications and computer industry want to use their knowledge and skill for the church but have never had the models or means to do so.

Another part of the work of media ministers is making and distributing audiotapes and videotapes of the worship service to people who are unable to leave home, people who are hospitalized, people who are in prison, and people who are elderly. The delivery of the tape is best done in person and is itself an occasion for a short visit. On days when Holy Communion is served, it is both efficient and symbolically proper to deliver the Communion elements and the tape together. Also, the gift of an audiotape and especially a videotape of the service is an ideal way of introducing people who have just moved into the community to the church. The tape can be delivered or, even better, parts can be shown as an occasion for conversation.

Thus, the work of media ministers follows a rhythm of preparation prior to worship, the worship service itself, and post-service distribution. All of these elements are occasions for prayer and study. It is clear that the more the media ministers understand and spiritually participate in the worship, the more integral the images and sounds are to the worship. There will always be those technicians who will simply observe the worship. But everyone wins when the technicians are spiritually involved in the worship.

To a significant degree, the role of the media minister is to develop a vision for the church's ministry in an electronic culture and to provide electronic media literacy training. Essential aspects of this ministry are to
- build teams;
- keep up with what is happening in electronic culture and technology;
- attend to the spiritual lives of the members of the media ministry team.

CONCLUSION

Just as ministers in the past needed mastery of literary communication systems, so media ministers now need to be masters of electronic communication systems. Their task is to continue the work of worship in a new cultural context.

FOR FURTHER READING

The Spectacle of Worship in a Wired World: Electronic Culture and the Gathered People of God, by Tex Sample (Nashville, TN: Abingdon Press, 1998).

The Wired Church: Making Media Ministry (book and CD-ROM), by Len Wilson (Nashville, TN: Abingdon Press, 1999).

> The more the media ministers understand and spiritually participate in the worship, the more integral the images and sounds are to the worship.

16

ASHLEY M. CALHOUN

Pastor, Beulah United Methodist Church and Hendron's Chapel United Methodist Church, Knoxville, Tennessee

The Work of Visual Artists in Worship

WHAT IS VISUAL ABOUT WORSHIP? PERHAPS THE QUESTION should be: What is *not* visual about worship? Of course, the spiritual aspects of worship—the sounds of music and spoken word, the aromas, and mystery of God's presence—are not visual. But is not the impact of the nonvisual dimensions of worship and the proclamation of the Word strengthened or weakened by the visual in worship? Does not the worship environment—the architecture, furnishings, color, equipment—play a significant role in the total experience of worship?

AN IMAGINATIVE WALKING TOUR OF YOUR WORSHIP SPACE

Step for a few moments into the shoes of a first-time visitor to your church. This is often difficult because we quickly adjust visually to our worship environment and lose the freshness of the first impression.

Begin your tour either physically or mentally at a time when no one else is present. What do you notice first? What grabs your attention? Is there order or disarray? Is your line of sight directed to the altar and/or the cross or to another symbol of God's presence, power, and grace? Do the architectural elements evoke harmony or confusion? How does light affect the space? color? texture? What emotional responses might one experience simply by entering this space? Awe, wonder, peace, excitement, joy, warmth? Or perhaps confusion, disappointment, apathy, even repulsion? Any or all of these responses are possible in churches today.

More pointedly, as you tour the sanctuary or other worship space, say on a Monday morning, do you find hymnals askew, bulletins from the past few Sundays on the floor or sticking out of pew racks, an empty vase or a stack of literature on the altar? Are the paraments appropriate to the season? Are banners changed with the season, or are they left up indiscriminately? Is it obvious that thought and care go into maintaining this place where the community gathers to worship God and find fellowship with the family of God? Is the space welcoming? Would you want to come back to worship here?

Now stand back and imaginatively observe what happens visually as your worship hour approaches. What happens as people begin to arrive in the worship space? Is everything in order and prepared, inviting worship? Does it encourage fellowship or quiet meditation? informality or formality?

Worship Matters: A United Methodist Guide to Worship Work (Volume II) © 1999 Discipleship Resources. Used by permission.

Is it clear to the newcomer what is expected? Are there greeters or ushers to welcome guests? Is there anyone to give direction or assistance? Are directions clear as to the location and hour of worship? Is there any indication outside the worship space that calls attention to what one might expect in the service, such as a special observance or theme for the day?

What does this have to do with visuals in worship? I believe that all of the above is as much a visual representation of who we are as a worshiping community as what happens in the service itself. It sends a message—whether clear or blurred, positive or negative—that can strengthen or weaken the experience of worship and the proclamation of the gospel, especially for newcomers and the unchurched.

What kind of a message is sent by the leaders of worship? Is there order or chaos, or something in between? If the worship is informal, are technicians still setting up microphones as the music begins, or is everything ready? Is there an air of expectancy, anticipation that something wonderful is about to happen? As the musicians, acolytes, liturgists, preacher, and other worship leaders enter, what is conveyed by their demeanor and dress? Are robes and vestments appropriate for the occasion? Would less-formal attire be more fitting to the service? (Clothing does have a visual impact.) Do the worship leaders appear prepared, confident, expectant?

The movements and gestures of the participants and leaders in worship communicate what we believe about worship and about who we worship. Processions, lighting of the candles, the collection and receiving of offerings, the consecration of the elements of Communion, posture in prayer, administration of baptism, standing and sitting, dismissal and recession—all these reflect our theology of worship and convey visual messages that may or may not be consistent with that theology or with the gospel. There is great beauty, grace, and power both in formal ritual and in orderly informality. We can also overritualize or so informalize our worship that it loses its vitality. How we conduct worship is visual, and it can either help or hinder the good news we gather to proclaim.

> **How we conduct worship is visual, and it can either help or hinder the good news we gather to proclaim.**

BIBLICAL PRECEDENTS FOR USING VISUALS IN WORSHIP

Probably the earliest use of a visual in worship that we have in Scripture is the Passover experience of the Hebrew people. The blood of the lambs on the doorposts and unleavened bread became ritualized, forever symbolizing God's deliverance of the people out of the bondage in Egypt.

Later followed the elaborate system of sacrifices and rituals that God ordained to engender discipline and obedience within a rebellious and willful people. One only has to read the detailed directions in Exodus and Leviticus to see how important the visual representations in the Tabernacle were for the relationship between God and the people of Israel. God called upon the skills of the best artisans to create the magnificent symbols of God's presence and power: the mercy seat, the altar, candelabra, the ark of the covenant, the elaborate vestments of the priests, the curtain separating the Holy of Holies, and even the tent posts. Everything was to be of the finest materials, created by the skilled artists, all to the glory of God. The elaborate instructions were carried over into the construction of a succession of temples and restorations of the Temple down to the construction of Herod's Temple that was standing in Jesus' day and was destroyed in 70 C.E. (Common Era).

There is precedent for the elaborate and for the simple use of visuals as means of instructing people about who God is and who we are in relation to God. After the destruction of the Temple and suspension of the sacrificial system, worship moved to the local synagogues and was less elaborate ritually as well as visually. In the early Christian era, worship was also very simple.

In his teaching, Jesus created simple yet powerful word pictures in his parables. Who can erase the image of the father racing out to embrace his wayward son, or the older brother's disapproval? Or the lost lamb enfolded in the arms of the Good Shepherd? What more powerful image is there than Jesus reaching out, gently lifting a child, and setting the child in the midst of a circle of adults to teach what it means to enter God's kingdom? Jesus took everyday objects and ordinary people and gave them extraordinary significance.

He did the same in his actions toward people. He was himself a living object lesson as he spoke to the woman of Samaria and showed her who she was and who she could become; and in so doing, Jesus brought her to perceive who he was. Jesus' actions revealed his identity as he went home and ate dinner with Zacchaeus; as he stood before the Sanhedrin in silence and before Pilate as Pilate washed his hands; as he hung on the cross crying out to God, pleading forgiveness for those who had nailed him there; and as he appeared to the disciples cowering in an upper room that first Easter night and showed them the nail prints in his hands and the spear wound in his side.

WHY VISUALS IN THE CHURCH?

As Jesus used the simple objects and images to teach in his day, so we may use the same gospel and other common things to teach and inspire an increasingly visually oriented, contemporary audience. We do so because of the material, incarnational nature of our faith. The church, as did Jesus, uses in its worship things of the earth—clay, oil, water, wine, bread. The psalmist invites us to "taste and see." John the evangelist proclaims, "Behold, the Lamb of God." Jesus invites us to take and eat. The Revelation of John recounts a vision of the New Jerusalem. The visual arts often speak more clearly and universally than words.

Even today we see everywhere the earliest Christian visuals: the cross and the fish. In the simplest forms, lines, and arcs, we find the earliest creeds symbolized. The cross says without words, "Christ is risen! Christ is risen, indeed!" The fish proclaims, "Jesus Christ, Son of God, Savior!" The myriad of Christian symbols that developed quickly and have been used ever since are a universal language that image the doctrines and experiences of the Christian faith. They express our faith and strengthen the proclamation of the gospel. The visual arts often speak more clearly and universally than words.

PARTNERSHIP AND THE WORK OF THE VISUAL ARTIST

If the visual artists, worship leaders, and proclaimers of the Word form a partnership and work as a team, much can be accomplished to more effectively proclaim the good news and affect the lives of those who come asking, searching, and knocking at the doors of our churches.

The work of the visual artist is to preach a silent sermon, with or without words. The form of that sermon has endless possibilities. It may be in the medium of fabric: banners, paraments, tapestries and hangings, needlepoint, weaving, quilting—with elaborate detail and stitching, or simply basted and glued. The medium may be photography (for example, still slides); or it may be film or video. Florists might arrange floral displays that suit the season and use plants and flowers that are native to the region, that come out of gardens, or that are mentioned in Scripture. Graphic artists might design posters, bulletin covers, or displays that tie into the Scripture readings of the day or to themes of the church year. Sculptors might produce works that stand alone or can be used in worship settings. Dance and drama are very much a part of the visual experience of worship, as are the musicians, liturgists, and preachers. The silent and the verbal proclaimers of the gospel should form a close and effective partnership in the gospel in order to strengthen that proclamation in worship.

RESOURCES FOR VISUALIZING WORSHIP

A rich store of resources and opportunities for the effective use of visuals in worship exists today. (See "For Further Reading," on pages 81–82.) The richest resources are Scripture (especially as presented in the Revised Common Lectionary), the themes of the church year, and the endless creativity and depth of the souls of the visual artists.

THE REVISED COMMON LECTIONARY

There are numerous visual images in each of the Scripture readings in the Lectionary. Some are obvious; others emerge through reflection and study. Psalm 23, a very familiar example, is rich in imagery that can be reproduced in material objects: shepherd, sheep, water, path, rod, staff, table, oil, cup. Other images (such as green pasture, still waters, the shadow of death, or the presence of God) might be reproduced graphically or photographically on bulletin covers, slides, or video to create visual backdrops for the reading of the passage.

A display might be created in a narthex (or other area adjacent to the worship space) or in the chancel or on a platform transformed into a setting for the psalm. One or more of the objects might be used in the children's sermon, be held in the preacher's hand, or be placed on the pulpit during the proclamation. The psalm might also be pantomimed as it is read or interpreted in movement.

THE CHURCH YEAR

The seasons of the church year are a visual cornucopia. Christ is the dominant figure in all that happens throughout the seasons. The Christian calendar developed around the events of Christ's life, death, resurrection, and ascension; his teachings; his relationship within the Trinity; and the manifestation of the Holy Spirit as his continuing and empowering presence in and for the church. From Advent through Christ the King Sunday, we have countless opportunities to present Christ and all he represents through visual imagery. It is this story, in part, that the Revised Common Lectionary helps us proclaim.

The church year encourages change as well as creativity. In the majority of our sanctuaries, much of the visual artwork—stained-glass

The work of the visual artist is to preach a silent sermon, with or without words.

windows, wall crosses, organ pipes, sometimes the pulpit and chancel furniture—is fixed. They cannot be changed unless a major renovation is undertaken. Some visual art is fixed, not physically but by tradition. Many of our churches have a portrait of Christ that has hung in the same spot for who knows how long. No one dares move it. Other portraits are rarely seen in our churches.

Yet there are hundreds of portraits depicting the life of Christ from infancy to ascension. The choices include ancient, classical, and modern periods, as well as a myriad of cultures. This art can be pulled off the Internet and reproduced on paper, slides, or video, which can be used in many effective ways in worship and display. What an opportunity to fill and expand the minds, hearts, and spirits of our congregations!

Although many congregations have not been introduced to the riches of the church year, many are incorporating Advent wreaths, banners, and blue paraments for the Advent season. Others have begun learning about the wonderful variety of symbols related to Christ in chrismons. Many congregations observe Lent and Easter in some fashion but often ignore Holy Week—except perhaps for Palm/Passion Sunday and a Maundy Thursday Communion service. The Palm/Passion, Maundy Thursday, and Good Friday observances are of equal importance to Easter if the full story is to be experienced and understood.

These events and special days in the church year represent incredible opportunities for visual artists to express the heart of the gospel message. Involving the worshipers in a re-enactment of the events leading up to and including the Last Supper, stripping the chancel and altar, and observing a moment of darkness before leaving in darkness leaves an indelible visual image and emotional experience. Draping the cross in black on Good Friday and then in white on Easter Sunday also adds a visual and spiritual dimension to long-observed Easter traditions that are very visual in nature.

Once Easter Sunday has passed, many churches ignore the rest of the church year. The Great Fifty Days between Easter and Pentecost celebrate the appearances of the risen Christ and his preparation of the disciples for his ascension and the in-filling and empowering work of the Holy Spirit. Simply leaving the cross draped in white can be a powerful visual. Re-creating the sounds and sights of Pentecost can lift up the central importance of the event. Try pulling out all the stops again. Acts 2 can be read as a choral or dialog reading. The sounds of the "rush of a violent wind" (Acts 2:2) can be reproduced on an organ or synthesizer. Tongues of fire can be simulated with seven processional banners in flame colors with bells or wind chimes attached and carried in as the Scripture is read. Members of the congregation who speak foreign languages can be asked to simultaneously repeat the Lord's Prayer or other Scripture verses in those languages at the appropriate time in the story. Dancers may interpret the movement of the disciples praising God. An actor (or the preacher) could deliver Peter's sermon with all the fervor of the first Pentecost.

Trinity Sunday and the Sundays after Pentecost can be used to teach about the doctrines and mission of the church through various symbols, photographic displays, short video presentations, bulletin art, and skits. The possibilities are endless, limited only by our reluctance to take risks and to use the creative gifts God has given to each of us. Not everyone is an artist with pen, brush, needle, or camera; but each of us is given something with which to create an expression of our faith in form or action.

THE CREATIVITY OF VISUAL ARTISTS

Part of the calling of visual artists as well as of pastors and educators in the church is to help people identify and use their natural talents and their spiritual gifts for the work of ministry. While clergy and the lay leadership share in this responsibility, the pastor of the congregation, for all practical purposes, sets the tone. The possibilities are endless if the pastor is open to allowing creative expression of faith through the arts; sees the value and understands the sacredness of the gifts of creativity; and, especially, is willing to discover and use his or her own gifts. To be in touch with our creativity is to be in touch with the Creator. How we use that creativity depends on the maturity of that relationship.

It is wonderful to witness what happens in the lives of individuals, small groups, and congregations when people are given the freedom to use their creativity. In my experience, those involved in projects to create something for worship have gotten in touch with the "holy," and have grown in their self-understanding and esteem, as well as in their relationship with God and the church.

Such experiences of God and such spiritual growth might happen to and through a child whose picture is chosen to be reproduced on the bulletin cover; teenagers who are asked to interpret a song in pantomime; a man asked to help construct a butterfly; a woman asked to construct a banner, frontal, paraments, or stole; people asked to needlepoint on kneelers; a graphic artist asked to design a logo; or a photographer asked to interpret a passage of Scripture in images. In being asked, the gift and the person are affirmed as sacred, important, needed, and wanted. We often lose some of our most creative people from the church because they and their gifts are ignored or unwanted.

CONCLUSION

"In the beginning when God created..." (Genesis 1:1). God is, and always will be, creating. Creativity is a divine principle and a part of the character of God inherent in the divine image in which God has created each of us a human being. God continues to create through us.

It is our sacred privilege and responsibility to put into form what God has placed in our hearts and minds and spirits to glorify God. That is the work of the visual artist in worship.

FOR FURTHER READING

And Also With You—Year A: Worship Resources Based on the Revised Common Lectionary, by Timothy J. Crouch, Mark R. Babb, Nancy B. Crouch (Akron, OH: O.S.L. Publications, 1995).

And Also With You—Year B: Worship Resources Based on the Revised Common Lectionary, by Timothy J. Crouch, Mark R. Babb, Nancy B. Crouch (Akron, OH: O.S.L. Publications, 1993).

And Also With You—Year C: Worship Resources Based on the Revised Common Lectionary, by Timothy J. Crouch, Mark R. Babb, Nancy B. Crouch (Akron, OH: O.S.L. Publications, 1994).

Banners for Worship, by Carol Jean Harms (St. Louis, MO: Concordia Publishing House, 1990).

Christian Symbols Handbook: Commentary and Patterns for Traditional and Contemporary Symbols, by Dean L. Moe (Minneapolis, MN: Augsburg Fortress Publications, 1990).

Events and special days in the church year represent incredible opportunities for visual artists to express the heart of the gospel message.

Church Art (Canton, OH: Communications Resources, Inc). For CD-ROM, call 800-992-2144. Internet: *http://www.ChurchArtOnline.com*

Clip Art for the Liturgical Year, by Clemens Schmidt (Collegeville, MN: The Liturgical Press, 1996).

Creative Ways to Offer Praise: 100 Ideas for Sunday Worship, by Lisa Flinn and Barbara Younger (Nashville, TN: Abingdon Press, 1992).

Symbols for All Seasons: Environmental Planning for Cycles A,B,C, by Catherine H. Krier (San Jose, CA: Resource Publications, 1988).

The New Handbook of the Christian Year, by Hoyt L. Hickman, Don E. Saliers, Laurence Hull Stookey, and James F. White (Nashville, TN: Abingdon Press, 1992).

To Crown the Year: Decorating the Church Through the Seasons, by Peter Mazar (Chicago, IL: Liturgy Training Publications, 1995).

Additional resources may be found at denominational web sites on the Internet, including:

www.gbod.org/worship/resources/planning.html

Part Two

CREATING SPACE FOR WORSHIP

Creating Space for Holy Communion

SUSAN J. WHITE

Lunger Professor of Worship and Spirituality, Brite Divinity School, Texas Christian University, Fort Worth, Texas

"FORM FOLLOWS FUNCTION" IS MORE THAN SIMPLY A clever, alliterative slogan. It has come to encapsulate the whole spirit of the modern age and has grounded the design of everything from can openers to automobiles. Originally, of course, this little formula was applied to architecture to describe what was understood to be the proper relationship between the structure of a building and the use to which that building is put. This interrelationship between form and function is particularly significant when it comes to thinking about the design and furnishing of the places where Christians worship.

Historically, the practice and theology of various kinds of liturgical activity—all the way from reading Scripture to burying the dead—have indeed been a dominant factor in determining the shape of church architecture. One way to study changes in worship over time is to trace the changing shape of church interiors.

Ironically, if "form follows function" is the architectural ideal, "function follows form" is just as often true in reality. Many buildings, designed at cross purposes with the use to which they are put, seriously "de-form" and inhibit the human action that takes place within their walls. This process also has been a part of the history of building and furnishing for Christian worship. With all this in mind, we can see why it is incumbent upon each Christian congregation periodically to ask, "Does the form of our church building adequately reflect its liturgical function?" or perhaps, "Does our building enable or inhibit the worship we envision taking place within it?"

A discussion of such questions is especially important during times of significant liturgical change, when we are introducing new forms of worship and attempting to assimilate and live out the theological vision that undergirds them. Although this process seems straightforward on the surface, it has profound implications. If undertaken seriously, it may well provoke a radical reevaluation of many of our most basic assumptions, and a renewal of our self-understanding as a worshiping community.

This article is intended to be a part of that kind of process, with special attention to the architectural needs of the Lord's Supper. By considering the location and design of the altar-table and the space around it, congregational access (including visual and auditory "access"), and

Worship Matters: A United Methodist Guide to Worship Work (Volume II) © 1999 Discipleship Resources. Used by permission.

the relationship of the Table to the other principal spaces and furnishings in the church building, we will ask how the church building can be designed to enable or inhibit the kind of vital, participatory celebration of the Eucharist envisioned by *The United Methodist Hymnal* and the *The United Methodist Book of Worship*. In this way we will try to answer the question, How can we create a space for Holy Communion in such a way that it helps us deepen our understanding of the meaning of this sacrament in our Christian lives, as well as see its connections with the wider mission of the church?

A SERVICE OF WORD AND ACTION

It would be easy to think from a cursory look at the services of Word and Table in the *Hymnal* (pp. 6–31) that the primary changes that have been made recently in United Methodist Eucharistic worship are changes in the words that are spoken. Of course, many of the words are indeed new; but a closer look at the services reveals that the whole rite is structured as much around significant *actions* as around significant *words*. And it is this centrality of action that makes the first set of demands on the shape of the space within which the Lord's Supper is celebrated. The bringing forward, taking, and blessing of the bread and wine; the breaking of the bread and the giving of bread and cup; the act of receiving Communion: For the full meaning of the new Communion services to be realized, all of these actions must be allowed to communicate clearly to those assembled, in just the same way that the words of the service must communicate clearly. If this is to happen, however, we may need to reconsider certain things we have taken for granted about the kind of space within which the actions are undertaken and the furnishings that fill that space.

In many buildings designed in the past two hundred years, the space around the altar-table is exceedingly cramped. Perhaps the table is very close to (or even directly against) the rear wall of the chancel, hemmed in at the sides by choir stalls and at the back by ornamental chairs for worship leaders. Or perhaps the table is placed in the main body of the church, but the Communion rails—historically, one of the few distinctive features of Methodist Communion space—are placed so close to the front of the table that movement between the table and rail is severely restricted. In addition to these "environmental" considerations, the size and shape of the table itself can also inhibit meaningful action: A very large table can dwarf ordinary human gestures, and a very small table can inhibit a pastor's natural kinesthetic expressiveness.

But, of course, it is not only the action of the pastor that is important to the celebration of the Lord's Supper as envisioned by the services of Word and Table. The full meaning of the Supper is embodied in the actions of all participants; all those who are together members of the Eucharistic community on a given occasion are properly called the celebrants of the rite of Holy Communion. The new services make it clear that neither the words nor the actions of the Lord's Supper are unidirectional: Both the pastor's call to prayer and the congregation's response, both the invitation to the Table and the coming to the Table, both the giving and the receiving of the elements are essential.

For this reason, the "pathways" that allow the members of the congregation to see, to hear, and to approach the action at the Table, as well as the space that allows them to gather around it, need to be considered carefully. If the full participation of anyone present is restricted, then the whole celebration is to some degree deformed. This, of course, includes the participation of children, the elderly, and those with disabilities, for whom special architectural provision may need to be made.

TABLE MOTIFS IN THE NEW SERVICES OF WORD AND TABLE

As we look more carefully at the basic actions of the services of Word and Table, we soon recognize that the altar-table has not one but several different (although mutually complementary) functions. Admittedly, it is a real challenge to design the altar-table and its surroundings to reflect and reinforce these multiple functions, but it can be done with care and imagination. The first task, however, is to get some sense of what these functions are.

THE TABLE AS WORK-SURFACE

The action that begins the Thanksgiving and Communion section in the services of Word and Table is described in the very first rubric: "The pastor takes the bread and cup, and the bread and wine are prepared for the meal" (*UMH,* p. 9).[1] Many of the architectural needs of the Lord's Supper are related to the simple fact that for the Supper to take place, certain quite practical things need to be done. Real work is accomplished at the altar-table; and if aspects of the form or location of the table inhibit that work, a sense of awkwardness will penetrate the whole rite and can overshadow even the most gracious words of invitation.

When we begin to consider the function of the altar-table as a work-surface, two specific design issues immediately present themselves. The first is the height of the altar-table. It is safe to say that most tables currently in use in United Methodist churches are simply too low to be effective work-surfaces. While no particular height is dictated, a pastor ought at least to be able to place the palms of the hands flat on the top of the table while standing upright—as one can when standing at a kitchen counter. This is important for the comfort of the pastor, although this is not the primary factor. It is also important because, as many elements of the preparation of the Supper are accompanied by significant words, the ability of the pastor to work without being hunched over allows a cleaner "flow" between word and action and a greater sense that the words are being spoken to the congregation rather than to the top of the table.

A second issue that arises when the altar-table is looked at as a work-surface is the size of the tabletop. At any given time, a large number of objects may be on the table: offering plates, candlesticks, bread (and the plate it is on), one or more chalices, a flagon containing the wine—or perhaps, if it is the custom of the church, trays for individual cups and smaller plates for the distribution of the bread. These items do not remain stationary, but are handled, moved in various ways, and then put aside when not in use.

If the altar-table is too small, it is difficult to avoid a cluttered and cramped appearance, and it is likely that extraneous noise will be created as pieces of altar-ware are bumped against each other. More important, insufficient space on the table is very likely to cause the pastor to restrict his or her gestures in order to avoid an accident. But if the action of the

It is incumbent upon each Christian congregation periodically to ask, "Does the form of our church building adequately reflect its liturgical function?"

Supper is to speak as loudly as the words, then the symbolic gestures of the pastor need to be generous and expansive (as well as clear and direct), communicating to all present both the dignity of the occasion and the generosity of God. One way of guaranteeing this is to ensure that the tabletop is large enough for the objects that are necessary to the celebration and that nothing that is not used in the celebration of the Supper itself is placed on the table.

But an altar-table can also be too large. Many church architects have made the mistake of determining the size of the table according to the scale of the building, and as a result many existing altar-tables are of considerable size. The work-surface function of the altar-table reminds us that the Lord's Supper is, at least in part, a human action and that the ideal scale is a human scale.

Like a tabletop that is very small, one that is very large also sets the stage for a number of liturgical problems. The pastor is meant to remain fairly stationary behind the altar-table, so that the visual focus will rest securely on the significant actions of the Supper. This means, ideally, that every item used should be within easy reach. If the table is so large that the pastor has to walk from one end to the other to retrieve items needed for the service, visual attention on the main action will be disturbed.

THE TABLE AS MEAL-TABLE

In many different ways, the United Methodist services of Word and Table highlight that the fellowship we share around the Communion table is meal fellowship. This means that the Table is also, in a real sense, a meal-table. The Communion bread and cup are described in the *Book of Worship* as being "given to the people as Jesus gave them to the disciples" (p. 29).[2] This link between Jesus' meal-sharing and ours has already had implications for the type and amount of bread and wine provided for Communion. But it also makes demands on the design of the table around which we gather for Communion.

Some people are inclined to say that if the altar-table looks too much like an ordinary household supper table, its religious significance will be diminished. But Methodist theology has always emphasized that it is precisely in and through such ordinary things that God makes redeeming love visible and tangible. In the Great Thanksgiving we pray that through the power of the Spirit the food and drink will become transparent to that love, and that the Table will become a true place of reconciliation and peace. To suggest, either in its design or in the material out of which it is made, that the Table is something other than a table is to minimize this profound sacramental reality.

The understanding of the Lord's Supper as a meal to which Christ invites those who have gathered in his name has wider architectural implications, since it suggests that those who partake are probably meant to be less sedentary than some have been in the past. To get to our feet and come forward at the invitation is to make a statement about our readiness to respond to Christ's initiative, to join the Host of the meal at the table that has been prepared for us.

In some congregations in which people do come forward, the tradition is to kneel at the Communion rail to receive the elements of bread and wine; in others, standing is the custom. In either case, unless there is sufficient space around the table for a fair number of people to gather, the serving of Communion can be a long process—which fuels the popular impression that "Communion Sunday" is a tedious and drawn-out affair. (This sentiment does little to encourage frequent celebration of the Supper.)

Certain simple architectural changes can make an enormous difference here. If, for example, the space around the altar-table is designed so that people can surround it on three sides (or even on all four sides), either with or without a Communion rail, then Communion can be distributed cleanly and efficiently to a considerable number of people.

THE TABLE AS ALTAR

For many Protestants, the idea that the Communion table might be referred to in any sense as an "altar of sacrifice" is disturbing. The Reformers' rejection of the medieval idea that each Mass was a recapitulation of the propitiatory sacrifice of Christ has cast a long shadow; even to speak of our own sacrifice of praise and thanksgiving in the context of the Lord's Supper (*UMBOW*, p. 38) still makes some Protestants quite nervous. But the services of Word and Table in the *Hymnal* and in the *Book of Worship* have relied on the Eucharistic theology of the early church and of John Wesley; and both the early church and Wesley saw the altar-table as the place where the redemptive effects of Christ's sacrifice and our human self-offering to God are effectively mingled for the sake of the world's redemption.[3]

This means that thinking about the altar-table and its surroundings should be done with a deep sense of the seriousness of the matter. Here, at this table, we recall the shedding of innocent blood on our behalf and declare our own willingness to sacrifice self-interest—even to the point of death—on behalf of others. This is not the place for sentimental or frivolous decoration; weak design; or cheap, dishonest materials. Everything associated with the altar-table should be exactly what it is. If there is a frontal on the altar-table, let it be made of natural, not synthetic, fibers. If there are candlesticks on the altar-table, let them be simple and direct, not fussy, in their design. Let the space around the altar-table be free of unnecessary clutter and the sightlines to and from the table be clear. The image of the table as altar reminds us that what takes place there is, indeed, serious business. The table and the space around it can and should communicate that seriousness to all who gather around it.

THE TABLE AND THE ENCOUNTER WITH CHRIST

In the services of Word and Table, it is clear that the Table is, perhaps above all other things, the place of encounter between the community of believers and the living Christ. From the meal on the road to Emmaus onward, Christians have been clear that Jesus is present in a particularly profound way to those who break bread together in his name and in memory of his life, death, and resurrection. And of course, when we are in communion with Christ at the Lord's Table, we are also in communion with all those who are one in Christ through baptism, and who receive him in faith. This is the "holy mystery" for which we give thanks in the prayer after Communion, and this is the experience that empowers and enlivens our proclamation of the gospel in the world.

A variety of things in the design of the setting for the Lord's Supper can either encourage or diminish the lively sense of the Supper as a direct encounter with the Christ who calls us. When, for example, the altar-table is located deep in the chancel, and the whole chancel area is

The fellowship we share around the Communion table is meal fellowship. This means that the Table is also, in a real sense, a meal-table.

separated from the congregation by a number of steps, the action at the table seems remote and inaccessible, and people can easily have a sense that they are not active participants but merely passive observers. Clutter on or around the altar-table can distract the attention from the Supper, and any triviality in the design and construction of the table and the objects used for the Supper can diminish the dignity and significance of the encounter that is taking place. And of course, when anything about the design of the building isolates people from one another and deforms the sense of Christian community, then our own prayer that we might be "one with Christ, one with each other, and one in ministry to all the world" (*UMBOW*, p. 38)[4] is mocked.

MOVING AROUND THE TABLE IN THE NEW SERVICES OF WORD AND TABLE

We have already spoken of the importance of the pastor's ability to move while behind the altar-table, and to be generous and expansive in gesture. But there are other kinds of movement associated with presiding at the Lord's Table that must be taken into account as we think about the design of space for Holy Communion.

Once the invitation to the Table is made, the pastor needs to deliver the elements to those assisting in the distribution of Communion. The assistants, of course, need to be able to move into the altar-table space by a direct route and to gather around the table without jostling one another. This is another reason why a generous amount of space needs to be provided around the table.

If Communion is received while kneeling or standing at Communion rails, then the space between the table and rails needs to be large enough for two people to pass easily as they dispense the bread and wine. In a building without a Communion rail, the area between the table and the first row of pews must be large enough to accommodate one or more "stations" from which Communion is distributed.

But, of course, it is not only pastor and assistants who move during the Lord's Supper. Members of the congregation are in motion at certain times as well. In many communities, it is the custom for the congregation to stand during the Great Thanksgiving, as a way of signaling their active and joyful participation in the prayer at the altar-table. In this case, it is important to ensure that the distance between the pews is wide enough to allow a person to stand comfortably, without the edge of the seat pressing against the back of the legs. If people are to move forward to receive Communion, the aisles must also be wide enough to permit the circulation of people to and from the altar-table without serious "bottlenecks."

Design questions also arise when thinking about the movement of special categories of people. How will members of the choir and other musicians receive Communion? What provision will be made for people in wheelchairs, people with other mobility difficulties, or people with visual impairments? Can they receive in a natural and comfortable way so that they do not feel singled out for special attention? Generous hospitality is the essential quality of any celebration of the Lord's Supper, reflecting Christ's own hospitality toward us. If these kinds of issues are not handled with care, a feeling of insensitivity may well permeate the whole celebration, contradicting even our warmest words and gestures of welcome.

IMAGERY AROUND THE TABLE

The Christian altar-table is never set in "splendid isolation," but is related both to the worship-space as a whole and to all of the other liturgical furnishings within it. Font, pulpit, and Table together form a symbolic constellation that expresses the essence of the gospel message.

There is, however, an argument for giving visual priority to the altar-table. As we have seen, in its four essential functions—work-surface, meal-table, altar, and place of encounter with the living Christ—the Christian altar-table expresses the complexity of our relationship with Christ and signifies the continuous nourishment of our Christian life and the church's mission. For this reason, if there is any element of church furnishing that deserves to be the visual focus of the worship space, it is the altar-table. Certainly, if anything blocks the congregation's visual or auditory access to the Table, it should be removed. Some people further argue that because of the permanent symbolic significance of font, pulpit, and Table, these furnishings should not be moved about, but should be (and should appear to be) permanently secured in place. They should also be of a design and material that gives a sense of stability and solidity.

Historically, various iconographic motifs have been related to the Lord's Supper and its architectural setting. But the new services of Word and Table make it abundantly clear that the principal symbol of the Lord's Supper is the altar-table itself. The table is the chief sign of Christ's welcome, around which the community gathers; and special care must be taken to avoid anything that detracts from the table's own symbolic significance.

Many altar-tables in current use have not been designed with this central insight in mind. Often, these tables will have a cross, a bunch of grapes, or words on the front, suggesting that such motifs need to be added in order to lend the Table "sanctity" or "theological meaning." In other cases, Christian symbols are applied to the altar frontal with the same purpose in mind. Worse still is the tendency to place sacred (or quasi-sacred) objects—an open Bible, a cross, or flowers—on top of the altar-table when it is not in use, ostensibly in order to make a "spiritual statement" about the ordinary function of the table. We have already seen how the introduction of such things can restrict the pastor's ability to move freely at the table.

But a much more significant problem is that the placement of these kinds of objects on top of the table sends a subliminal message that something needs to be added to the table to give it religious meaning. This is in direct conflict with the renewed understanding of the altar-table—and, indeed, of the Lord's Supper itself. At this table the sacrifice of Christ is remembered, and Christian obedience to Christ's invitation to "do this in memory of [him]" is realized. This is the table at which the covenant with God and with one another is renewed.

CONCLUSION

As United Methodist congregations begin to be drawn into and shaped by the theology of the services of Word and Table, it may well be the case that additional questions about the adequacy of their church building and furnishings will arise. But it is probably safe to say that if such a community has a lively sense of this richly textured symbolic meaning of the Table, most questions about the architectural setting for the Lord's Supper will answer themselves. Form will, quite naturally, follow function.

Special care must be taken to avoid anything that detracts from the table's own symbolic significance.

FOR FURTHER READING

Architecture for Worship, by E. A. Sovik (Minneapolis, MN: Augsburg Fortress Publishers, 1973).

Church Architecture: Building and Renovating for Christian Worship, Second Edition, by James F. White and Susan J. White (Akron, OH: O.S.L. Publications, 1998).

Sacred Places and the Pilgrimage of Life (Meetinghouse Essays: Architecture and Art for Liturgy Series, Number 1), by Lawrence Hoffman (Chicago, IL: Liturgy Training Publications, 1991).

ENDNOTES

1 From "A Service of Word and Table I," copyright © 1972, 1980, 1985, 1989 by The United Methodist Publishing House; from *The United Methodist Hymnal,* p. 9. Used by permission.

2 From "An Order of Sunday Worship Using the Basic Pattern," copyright © 1985, 1989, 1992 by The United Methodist Publishing House; from *The United Methodist Book of Worship,* p. 29. Used by permission.

3 For an example of the use of the sacrificial motif, see the fourth stanza of Charles Wesley's Eucharistic hymn, "Come, Sinners, to the Gospel Feast" (*UMH,* 616): "See him set forth before your eyes; behold the bleeding sacrifice; his offered love make haste to embrace, and freely now be saved by grace."

4 From "A Service of Word and Table I," copyright © 1972 by The Methodist Publishing House; copyright © 1980, 1985, 1989, 1992 by The United Methodist Publishing House; from *The United Methodist Book of Worship,* p. 38. Used by permission.

Creating Space for Baptism and the Renewal of the Baptismal Covenant

LESTER RUTH

*Assistant Professor
of Liturgical Studies,
Yale Divinity School and
Institute of Sacred Music,
New Haven, Connecticut*

AFTER A MULTI-DENOMINATIONAL SERVICE MY CHURCH ONCE hosted, I heard a story about a Baptist visitor trying to decipher our sanctuary's furnishings. She was able to figure out everything except for one piece, guessing it was some sort of "little pulpit."

What our visitor was trying to decipher was a baptismal font. In her best guess, she ended up being half right and half wrong. She was right in that the font is a kind of pulpit. There the message of salvation, particularly as it emphasizes the extravagance of God's grace in Christ, is proclaimed in the "visible word" of baptism as a tangible declaration of grace. But she had the "little" part wrong. Because the message proclaimed there is so important, a baptismal space is a "pulpit" of large dimensions.

Consequently, time spent on considering baptismal space is time well spent. As a simple principle, the message of this space must reflect the importance of baptism itself. This is true whether a church can think of making only small changes or whether a church is planning a whole new structure. The suggestions offered here apply to either case.

Many sources shout out baptism's importance and meaning. Some of United Methodism's most recent statements on baptism are strong in their affirmation of its richness, as in the document "By Water and the Spirit: A United Methodist Understanding of Baptism," adopted by the 1996 General Conference.[1] That document clearly states that baptizing a person is nothing less than a sign of saving grace from God, a revelation of God's most important provisions for humankind.[2]

Indeed, baptismal symbolism is rich and deep. Historically, basic baptismal associations have clustered into some key meanings: cleansing, forgiveness, the coming of the Holy Spirit, consecration, birth, death, and union with Christ and the church. These descriptions are supplemented by a range of biblical associations with water: creation, deliverance through the Red Sea, provision in the wilderness, passage into the Promised Land, the baptism of Jesus, the stream flowing from the throne of God. These obviously are not peripheral matters.

How can a space for baptism help proclaim the meaning of baptism? What are the features of a well-designed baptismal space? How can baptism be performed in a manner that facilitates the experience of God's grace by those baptized?

CONSIDERING THE NEEDS OF THE BAPTISMAL SERVICE

Begin considering the space by examining the text of the baptismal service itself. Three assumptions are inherent in the United Methodist baptismal service: The space must be one for the gathering of people, the proper movement of people, and the various addresses and responses among the people.

With respect to the gathering of people, a church needs to make sure that the space is large enough. Given the number of people involved even in a single baptism, the space must comfortably hold a half dozen people. Multiple baptisms require even more space. This can be only a minimum standard, too, because some churches might want the baptismal space as a place where the entire congregation could assemble at one time.

The baptismal service also assumes some movement within the rite. At a minimum, a baptismal space must be readily accessible, easy to get to and return from. To make multiple baptisms easier, thought should also be given to the manner of moving from one candidate to the next. Some churches will also choose the option of providing symbolic objects (candles, new clothing) to the newly baptized immediately after the service of water. The baptismal space should be such that these are easily accessible and presented. Also notice that the service's rubrics provide for optional pouring of water into the font and anointing the newly baptized with oil (*UMH*, p. 36; *UMBOW*, pp. 90–91). Consider where pitchers and oil containers might be placed.

Finally, the service assumes certain spatial features to facilitate the spoken nature of the rite. Specifically, much of the baptismal service consists of questions posed by the presider and appropriate responses given by a variety of people. The baptismal service is an interactive conversation requiring spatial elements to assist this dimension. Can the presider be heard by all parties: those being baptized, parents, sponsors, the congregation? If a sound system is used, can it be used in the baptismal space? If a sound system is not used, are the acoustics proper to hear plain speech? Can the pledges of the candidates, parents, and sponsors be heard by the congregation, and vice versa?

CONSIDERING THE FONT

Perhaps the central focus of any baptismal space is the container for water, the font. With respect to the font, several considerations must be kept in mind in planning: the font's size, shape, relative placement, surrounding environment, and decoration.

SIZE

The size of the font should be determined by the mode of baptism that is used. In United Methodist practice, any of three modes is considered permissible: sprinkling, pouring, or immersion. The crucial question, however, is not one of permissibility but of *desirability*. What mode of baptism is most desirable?

A sound viewpoint is that more water rather than less best fits the generous sign that baptism is. Whether related to being a sign of God's grace, which surely is ample and generous, or to being a sign of God's great acts of salvation for us (new birth, thorough cleansing, burial with Christ), a baptism that is a full, rich sign is best achieved when water can be seen and felt in an ample dose. Let us avoid baptisms with a minuscule amount of water—"dry-cleaning," as I heard one scholar say.

Abundant water is not absolutely necessary for a valid baptism, nonetheless an individual's perception of an event like baptism is tied to the tangible dimensions of the experience. Consequently, my preference is for immersion or pouring where the water is quite evident. To put it quite simply, to get wet is the goal and the sign of baptism. A font needs to be of sufficient size to hold adequate water for this end. At a minimum, the baptismal space should facilitate the application of a generous amount. The safe route is to consider the adult baptism with ample water as the norm, with adequate provisions for baptizing children, too.

Even if a church is unable to change its font, a greater emphasis on water can still be achieved by some simple steps. One step is to pour the water into the font immediately prior to the prayer of thanksgiving in the rite. In addition, the presider can make sure she or he intentionally uses a more ample portion of water. If sprinkling, cupping one hand (rather than simply wetting it) or using both hands cupped together delivers more water. Similarly, use of a small container such as a bowl or a shell to gather the water and then apply it serves the same end.

If a church is able to modify its font or baptismal space some but cannot do major renovations, better possibilities exist for a more ample use of water. Even some rather small changes can help. For instance, if a congregation wants to emphasize the visual dimension of water and have a more generous supply present, then a large bowl (some have suggested a wok or an inverted skylight) could be placed on top of a secure pedestal. Perhaps an existing font could be modified to serve as this pedestal.

Another possibility is to use a portable receptacle, such as a nice galvanized washtub, that could be brought in for an adult candidate to stand in while a generous amount of water is poured over him or her. Or use a large landscaping container that is made of aggregate stone and is multisided and a couple feet deep.

Be creative about options. If there is a concern about maintaining the "niceness" of the indoor space, go outside to use a natural body of water or a pool. If full immersion is not possible even outside, find a place where a generous amount of water can be poured over the candidate. If inside, find some way for water to be poured in ample amounts without damaging the surrounding area. Consider removing a limited amount of carpet and replacing it with a more waterproof flooring. When considering options, do not limit your thought to church supply catalogs; visit a garden or farm supply store.

For churches that want to attempt a major renovation or design a completely new space, two aspects should be considered with respect to the size of a font, particularly if it is designed for immersions: depth and width. The font must be of sufficient depth and of sufficient width for at least two adults (the presider and the candidate) to get in the water. Churches are not limited to preformed baptistries as offered by church supplies companies, even though these are adequate. An increasing number of North-American churches have used specially made fonts. (Some examples are shown in the resources listed in "For Further Reading," on page 100.)

Such congregations handle the depth and width issues in one of three ways. One way is to have the font totally inlaid in the floor. The presider and the candidate walk to the font and then descend into the water by

More water rather than less best fits the generous sign that baptism is.

steps. Some fonts have a separate set of steps opposite those used to enter. In this way the candidate gets the sense of passing through the waters. The other two ways are to have the font raised totally above ground level or to have a combined approach, with the font partially sunken.

In considering the width and depth of the font, attention should be given to different requirements for children and adults. Obviously, it requires less water to immerse an infant (normally done partially, holding the baby upright and dunking her or him downward to shoulder level) than to fully immerse an adult.

Different options are possible for addressing these requirements. Some churches section off part of a larger font when baptizing children. For instance, one church, which has an in-ground font in the shape of a cross, uses glass panels to separate the inner square at the center of the cross, allowing immersion of children at the same spot as adults. (Consideration to the shape of the font is given below.) Another option, effective in above-ground fonts, is to stack different-sized fonts on each other. Some churches, for example, place a smaller font on one edge of the larger adult font. The effect, particularly when designed for water to flow from the top container to the lower, can be quite striking. This arrangement allows for the possibility of "living" (flowing) water—a desirable aspect of a font. Another option is to use different modes of baptism for different ages. Perhaps a large, raised pedestal font, which is placed on a tiled floor with a small lip around it, could be used for infant immersion or pouring. Adults will then have room to kneel next to the font while ample water is poured on them.

SHAPE

With respect to the shape of the font, several classic options exist. If a simple round shape or a commercially preformed font is not used, then the shape selected should be a direct sign of some symbolic aspect of baptism. These symbolic shapes tend to fall into several basic types. One possibility is a womb-shaped font to emphasize baptism as a moment of spiritual birth. A variation is to use a tub-shaped font to emphasize baptism's cleansing. Another common shape is cruciform (or cross-shaped). The symbolic connections are obvious: Baptism not only links us with the source of our salvation—the cross of Christ—but also unites us with Christ in his death. In a similar vein, some churches in the past have designed fonts to resemble tombs or sarcophagi to serve as a sign that in baptism we are buried with Christ (Romans 6).

More abstract symbolism has also inspired font shapes. A very common one is an eight-sided font, a symbolic number for resurrection. God raised Christ from the dead on Sunday, the first day of the week; or, if one wishes to emphasize the Resurrection as God's first act in a new creation, the eighth day of the week. Thus an eight-sided font is a symbolic reminder that in baptism we enjoy the resurrection power of Christ and are made part of his new creation. (Note that a six-sided font has been used when churches have wanted to emphasize the connection of baptism to Christ's death on a Friday.)

RELATIVE PLACEMENT

Churches should think also about the placement of the baptismal space, because they have more options than automatic placement "at the front." Indeed, there are two special concerns—both of a symbolic nature—that should be addressed regarding location. The first deals with the position of the font relative to other key worship areas, particularly the pulpit and the Communion table. All are central to the life of the church. By Word, water, bread and wine, the church is born, fed, and sustained; all of these should have prominent positions. This seems less of a problem for pulpit and tables. Thus, care should be given to balance and symmetry between these spaces. Avoid making the baptismal space an afterthought, something superfluous that is squeezed in somewhere. Some churches have tried successfully a symmetry where indeed all three—pulpit, font, and Table—are at the front of the worship space.

In one particular possibility, if a church is renovating the entire worship space, an apse is a good elevated location for the font if the Communion table has been moved from the back wall out closer to the congregation. Thus, as one faces the front of the worship space, the font and the table form a single axis of unity. Others have likewise beautifully used an arrangement with a different axis: Instead of a table/font balance in the front, the axis is extended so that the balance is between the table at the front and the font near the entrance of the church.

Churches have often chosen to place the font near the church entrance to emphasize a theological truth: Baptism is the "doorway" into the church. This type of thinking represents the second special concern for font placement: positioning the baptismal space to symbolize its role in the church's life. In this way, every entrance into the worship space serves as a reminder of baptism as entry into the church, as people pass the place where they were initiated into the church. One possible disadvantage to this placement is decreased or awkward visibility by the congregation. Of course, it could be possible to place the font at the entrance, either making sure that the gathering space around the font is sufficient for everyone (thus allowing the entire congregation to gather at the font) or providing some sort of temporary basin at the front of the congregation, to which water could be brought in pitchers from the permanent font.

Another placement for the baptismal space is in the midst of the congregation, in the center of the congregation's seating. This placement emphasizes the fact that, theologically, baptism is an act that takes place in the center of the church's life. In this arrangement, the congregation can literally enfold the newly baptized into it. Of course, a church would want to make sure that ample gathering space is provided and that movement space for funerals and weddings is not restricted. A congregation would also want to be careful that concerns for gathering and movement space do not force an undue limitation on the size of the font.

Of course, other symbolic font placements are possible. One church, for instance, has placed its sunken font toward the front of its worship space at the spot where caskets rest during funerals. In this way, this church hopes to make visible this truth: Eternal hope resides in having been joined with Christ through baptism in order to share in the power of his resurrection.

SURROUNDING ENVIRONMENT

Another consideration for the font is the surrounding environment. Attention to this concern can help a church go beyond thinking of the font merely as an isolated piece of furniture and instead consider the

Avoid making the baptismal space an afterthought, something superfluous that is squeezed in somewhere.

overall architectural context. The goals should be to define an area for baptism (thus highlighting its importance) and to provide reinforcement of baptism's meanings (thus reinforcing its sign value).

These goals can be accomplished in a variety of ways, some of which were considered above in talking about the font's relative placement. In addition, some specific measures can be taken. A church can design a separate alcove—still keeping in mind visibility and audibility—dedicated to the font. Furthermore, a church can give special attention to placing the font at the main entrance, not simply using the entrance as a spot for the font but carefully integrating the whole entrance as a baptismal space. Less expansive measures include using a decorative canopy of some sort, a skylight, or special flooring to designate the baptismal spot. This latter measure not only helps define the baptismal area but also serves a functional purpose if waterproof materials are chosen. Sloping the floor slightly toward the font or using a slightly sunken area likewise serves this dual purpose. A church can also heighten the baptismal environment by using a window or artwork as a backdrop. The books listed in "For Further Reading," on page 100, contain pictures of many fine examples of all these measures.

DECORATION

Finally, a church should also give some thought to the immediate decoration of the font and baptismal space. It is probably best to emphasize central biblical motifs concerning baptism, specifically, or water, generally. Many of these were discussed at the beginning of this chapter. Again, for pictures of fine examples, see the books listed on page 100.

CONSIDERING THE NEEDS OF RELATED SERVICES

Consideration should also be given to the worship services that surround baptism and are really part of it. These include any special services associated with a process of preparing for baptism, as well as renewal of the Baptismal Covenant celebrated among an entire congregation. *Come to the Waters: Baptism & Our Ministry of Welcoming Seekers & Making Disciples* contains a full explanation of the journey toward baptism as well as the texts for all the worship services in this process. (See the book listed in "For Further Reading," on page 100.)

Many spatial needs for these worship services are the same as the general requirements for any baptismal space: The space must be a good one for the gathering of people, their movement, and their different addresses and responses. All of the special catechumenate (adult initiation) services in *Come to the Waters*, for example, place a strong emphasis on a sponsor's presence with the candidate, answering questions to witness on the candidate's behalf and making symbolic gestures with him or her (*Come to the Waters*, pp. 109–21). Thus, the space used for these services must be carefully chosen to facilitate these important actions.

Perhaps most important, the space should have symbolic harmony with the purpose of each service. For instance, in *Come to the Waters* the service for welcoming hearers is about receiving catechumens into the transforming center of the church's life. Not surprisingly, the rubrics for this service (pp. 109–12) suggest that the candidates and sponsors gather outside the church or in an entry area and that the presiding and assisting ministers approach to conduct the service. In a like manner, the service for calling people to baptism (pp. 113–15)—because its focus is to have the church hear the sponsor's witness about the catechumen and then issue a specific call to baptism—should be performed in a space that emphasizes a greater proximity to baptism and the enveloping presence of the congregation.

Creative thought should be given to how the call, issued by the presider, can emerge from near the font while the congregation surrounds it. (In a sense, the congregation itself is the true font through which Christ pours his life-giving power.) Similarly, the space chosen for the service for the affirmation of ministry in daily life (*Come to the Waters*, pp. 120–21) can emphasize both the font as the source for our general ordination in baptism, and the congregation as all who share in the continuing ministry of Christ. Perhaps, to show that the catechumen's baptism has come full circle so that she or he is now charged to go into the world in ministry, this service could once again be held at the church's entry area.

Such a use of space for affirming ministry can serve to remind the whole church that one result of baptism is to bring us into a share of Christ's ministry oriented to the world. Baptism is an outward-looking sacrament. To hear this calling anew is one goal of conducting a congregational reaffirmation of the Baptismal Covenant (*UMBOW*, pp. 111–14). To conduct this service is to believe that baptism is the foundation of the Christian life and is actually a lifelong process of deeper immersion in the way of Jesus Christ.

CONSIDERING THE SPATIAL NEEDS FOR RENEWING THE BAPTISMAL COVENANT

Many of the general principles discussed above about gathering, movement, and direction of speech are applicable in the service of congregational reaffirmation of the Baptismal Covenant. In fact, this service repeats much of a baptismal service itself, except that care should be given so that the use of the water is not interpreted as baptism itself. Thus the important features are the congregation itself and the water (and by necessity its container). The instructions for this service suggest that people could be invited to touch the water; the presider could scoop up a handful and let it flow back into the font; a small evergreen branch could be used to sprinkle water toward (but not on) the congregation; or the presider may mark the sign of the cross on each person's forehead using water.

Obviously, the importance of the service of baptismal reaffirmation is to have the congregation sense the water. This action can be accentuated by creative use of space. As noted above, placement of the font at the entry into the church can serve as a continuing reminder of baptism's centrality. The service of reaffirmation can become a vivid demonstration of that. If the font is located elsewhere, it would be appropriate to have the congregation surround the font during the reaffirmation. Since the reaffirmation is a joint covenant rooted in a common means of grace, it is appropriate that the people see one another over the waters of the Savior. We have but one Lord, one faith, and one baptism.

Placement of the font at the entry into the church can serve as a continuing reminder of baptism's centrality.

CONCLUSION

According to many prominent theologians, a sacrament—including baptism—is a kind of "visible word." That is, baptism is an occasion when the message of God's saving love and actions should be proclaimed boldly to our eyes. As confidently as the verbal word of God's grace is given to our hearing, so should baptism as a testimony of grace be given to our sight. Careful design and use of baptismal spaces can greatly assist this sort of proclamation. May the abundance of baptism as a "visible word" in our midst match the abundance of love God has for us.

FOR FURTHER READING

A Place for Baptism, by Regina Keuhn (Chicago, IL: Liturgy Training Publications, 1992).

Come to the Waters: Baptism & Our Ministry of Welcoming Seekers & Making Disciples, by Daniel T. Benedict, Jr. (Nashville, TN: Discipleship Resources, 1996).

On Baptismal Fonts: Ancient and Modern, by S. Anita Stauffer (Bramcote: Grove Books Limited, 1994).

Re-Examining Baptismal Fonts: Baptismal Space for the Contemporary Church, by S. Anita Stauffer (Collegeville, MN: The Liturgical Press, 1991).

The Complete Library of Christian Worship: Volume 4, Music and the Arts in Christian Worship, Book 2, edited by Robert E. Webber (Peabody, MA: Hendrickson Publishers, 1996), pp. 562–71 and 604–15.

ENDNOTES

1 See "By Water and the Spirit: A United Methodist Understanding of Baptism" in *The Book of Resolutions of The United Methodist Church—1996* (Nashville, TN: The United Methodist Publishing House), pp. 716–35.

2 See "Reclaiming the Centrality of Baptism," on pages 51–57 in Volume I of *Worship Matters.*

Creating Space for Proclaiming the Word

RICHARD L. ESLINGER

Pastor,
Zion United Methodist Church,
Cincinnati, Ohio

MAKE A SURVEY OF THE PLACES FROM WHICH PREACHING occurs in the churches of your community. Among the more traditional Protestant churches, a pulpit will be very much in evidence, either located centrally to the axis of the worship space or, in the case of a "divided chancel," perched at one corner of the chancel-nave boundary. In some of these churches, however, that space is no longer used, left like the wall-altar as a monument of times past. In these churches, the place for preaching may well be a much more modest lectern that is located both nearer to the people and at a lower elevation. In a nearby "family-life-center" type of facility, it may be difficult to discern the place for preaching unless you attend worship there. Certainly, there is a platform for the "praise team," and perhaps a series of music stands—sometimes made of transparent acrylic—but nothing that is recognizably a pulpit. A visit to a Roman Catholic parish presents a somewhat familiar scene. There, the focal points of worship include a pulpit-like "ambo," which is also designed to display the Gospel Book, the chair for the presiding priest or the bishop, and the altar.

In all of these alternatives, however, the layout and design of the furniture related to proclamation may or may not have anything to do with the actual location of the preaching during the liturgy. The preacher may remain at the pulpit or lectern (or music stand or ambo), perhaps will move about the chancel or platform, or may even stroll up and down the aisle. Certainly, we have come to a time in which the space for preaching is "all over the place," reflecting a homiletic situation in which the methods and content of preaching are similarly all over the place.

Before any attempt to chart a course through the present disarray in preaching's spatial aspects, it is necessary to review the tradition. How did our Christian forebears locate space for the Word?

SPACE FOR THE WORD IN HISTORICAL PERSPECTIVE

THE HOUSE CHURCH

The meeting place for Christians in the New Testament period and in the post-apostolic age was the house church. As followers of "the Way" (Acts 9:2) gathered on the first day of the week for worship, they met in the homes of the more prosperous members of their community. It was

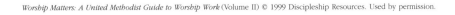

in just such a home that Paul preached far into the night in a crowded upper room lit by many lamps (Acts 20:7-12). The Lord's Day worship of Christians in the New Testament is sketched in this passage. There is a time for the Word—certainly including the reading of Scripture and preaching—and for the Eucharist. In these early gatherings of the domestic church, there was need only for a room for the gathering and a table for the Holy Meal. Most likely, the space for preaching was simply the preacher's location in the room.

As the church continued to grow and expand, the Christian community began gathering in houses fully dedicated to its meetings and worship, and altered to meet the needs of the expanding congregation. Significant among these changes are the enlargement of the meeting room for the assembly, which was achieved in one church by removing an internal wall, and the adaptation of another separate space for the baptistery. Two pieces of furniture would have been prominent in the enlarged worship space: a table for the Eucharist that was probably centered in the space, and a chair that perhaps was set on a small, elevated platform. It is from this chair that preaching would have occurred by the bishop or presbyter; the Jewish practice continued of standing for the reading of Scripture and sitting for its proclamation (Luke 4:14-21).

In the final stage of pre-Constantinian church architecture, certain Christian communities created specially built churches that remained strongly influenced by the house-church model. These "hall churches" were of a tripartite organization with a central worship space conforming to the house-church assembly room, only larger. The two halls on each side of the central assembly room were for Christian initiation, on the one hand, and for the honoring of martyrs, on the other. The focal points of the worship space, however, continued the house-church practice of having a raised chair and central table locating the space for the liturgy of Word and Table.

THE BASILICA

After the Peace of Constantine in 313 C.E. (Common Era), the church was free to move out into more public buildings. Rejecting the available form of religious buildings (the temples of the many deities and cults), the church adopted the more "neutral" public building: the basilica. It was devoted to an assortment of civic functions and easily adapted to the church's worship life. In a number of cases, these basilicas were donated or constructed by officers of the state.

Basilicas were built on a longitudinal axis, with an elongated nave for the faithful and a typically semicircular apse at one end. The seating around the apse, previously reserved for judicial functionaries when the basilicas were used for court procedures, included the bishop's central chair (or *cathedra*) and the benches occupied by the presbyters. An altar-table was placed at the end of the nave but before the apse. In this way, the presiding clergy faced the people at the Eucharist. Scripture was read from the ambo, a wood or masonry affair that was located somewhat out into the nave and to one side. Proclamation would have been from the cathedra and not from the ambo.

Augustine or Ambrose, for example, preached while seated in the cathedra, with the congregation standing for the sermon and for much of the service (the reversal of today's usual practice!). In some regions of the church, the ambo was later placed out in the midst of the nave and became the location for preaching as well as the reading of the Word.

MEDIEVAL ALTERATIONS

The essential idea of the basilican worship space persisted through the succession of architectural styles of the medieval period in the West. Whether in the early Romanesque style or the High Gothic, the longitudinal orientation of the church building remained evident, along with nave and apse. Under the pressure of increasingly sacrificial interpretations of the Mass, however, the altar became separated from the people, either by a rood screen or an actual wall. Driven by the needs of the monastic community for their daily office, the modest apse was lengthened into a chancel.

The diminution of preaching in the early medieval period was reflected in a loss of the space for proclamation in favor of a focus on altar and chancel. However, the emergence of the mendicant orders of religious men and women during the twelfth to fourteenth centuries worked to restore some balance to the liturgy and liturgical architecture. Pulpits were built for use by the Dominicans and other preaching orders. Typically, these pulpits were attached to a pillar or column somewhat out into the nave. Such pulpits were readily available for the preaching of the Reformers. (Recall the prints of Luther preaching from the pulpit of the Wittenburg Church.) More radical changes would be seen in other revisions of the existing Gothic churches and especially in new Protestant church construction.[1]

The Protestant Reformers approached the dilemma of existing church buildings with various degrees of iconoclastic zeal. Side altars, most statuary, reliquaries, and rood screens were eliminated. The high altar was singled out for demolition by the more radical reformers, and the chancel became a space without a function. Calvin was more modest in his reforms, but demolished the rood screen and relocated the pulpit from the first to the second pillar on the left of the nave.

The churches constructed following the first generation of the Reformers more fully expressed Reformation principles. The most significant shift was from a two-room worship space (nave and chancel) to a one-room *sanctuary*. This term itself expresses the core of the Reformation doctrine of church and sacraments: the shift from "house of God" to "house of the congregation," with the sanctuary now conceived as the entire church.[2]

These Reformation churches, whether elaborate structures designed by Christopher Wren in London or the simple meeting houses of the dissenters, reflected Reformation emphases on a people of covenant gathered for praise and on their attention to the proclaimed Word of God. The two focal points of worship became the congregation itself and the pulpit, an often massive structure built against the wall facing the people. Since these "auditoriums" functioned to gather the faithful and to proclaim the Word of God, galleries were often added above the first level of the building.

In its most pure (or severe) form, the Puritan meeting house of New England represented these Protestant principles without compromise. The pulpit is the singular piece of liturgical furniture and dominates the wall opposite the entry door to the church. A gallery is perched above, to the rear or on the three other sides of the room. The Communion table is either a very small piece of free-standing furniture beneath the pulpit or, in the case of one meeting house, a drop-leaf shelf hidden above the deacon's bench. In the meeting houses of New England, the dominant purpose of the church is to provide space for the elect to attend to the proclamation of the Word of God and to observe the Lord's Supper four times a year.

> We have come to a time in which the space for preaching is "all over the place," reflecting a homiletic situation in which the methods and content of preaching are similarly all over the place.

Reaction to these post-Reformation church buildings came in the form of the Cambridge Movement of the 1820–40's. These "ecclesiologists" critiqued the "rude" buildings of Protestant construction while championing a Gothic ideal as the most sublime and "catholick" in spirit.[3] Foremost among the characteristics of this Gothic norm was a restoration of the two-room (chancel and nave) worship. Since the newly opened or newly constructed chancels now had virtually no liturgical function, they provided the occasion for an innovation that remains dominant in most Protestant churches—they became the space for the choir!

Wall-altars were also restored and, at the meeting of the chancel and nave, a lectern was placed at the south corner and a pulpit at the north. The effect was to distance the place for the sacrament as much as possible from the place of proclamation. To this day, such a "divided chancel" layout remains the assumed norm of much of Protestant church architecture.[4]

RECENT TRENDS

Following upon the liturgical reforms of the Second Vatican Council (1962–1965) of the Roman Catholic Church, the ecumenical trend now evident in church design seeks to achieve at least two related goals. First, the recovery of the liturgy as the "work of the people" means that many recent worship spaces are designed in a semicircular or shallow arc pattern that invites a sense of community and reduces the sense of distance to the location for proclamation and the Lord's Table.

Second, these worship spaces attempt to emphasize and balance more adequately the focal points of worship, font, pulpit, and Table. Consequently, other features that before competed for visual attention—organ, choir, statuary, and so forth—tend now to be placed in less prominent locations. Most recently, the "contemporary worship" movement has retained the focus on the community's space, while deselecting many of the traditional forms and symbols for proclamation and the sacraments. In these worship spaces, the focal point of the assembly is a stage for the praise team and band, with ample space up front for dramatic offerings and the inevitable projection screen.

Before an adequate assessment can be made of these recent trends or any of the previous traditions, it is necessary to reflect upon the interplay between the church's theology of the Word and the ways in which the church provides for a space for proclamation.

THE SPATIAL ASPECTS OF PROCLAMATION

A close look at the history of the liturgy discloses four central considerations that govern how the space for proclamation shall be ordered. These four core elements include:
- the practical considerations of speaking and being heard;
- symbolic values that accrue to the place for proclamation;
- theological beliefs that undergird a community's preaching;
- ideologies that may exert constraint upon the space for proclamation.

PRACTICAL CONSIDERATIONS

Because preaching is "an acoustical affair," the primary consideration regarding its location is in being able to speak and be heard. It is obvious that the liturgical space will need to include a proclamation place that allows the distribution of sound from the preacher to the congregation. In other words, the assembled faithful will need to hear the voice of the one who preaches.

With regard to the spatial dimensions of preaching, form does follow function. As we saw in the preceding historical sketch, the shift from chair to ambo or pulpit was made when worship places grew beyond a certain size. Once a critical mass was exceeded, the community could no longer hear the seated preacher. Even with a raised platform for the cathedra, there was a limit to the distance a preacher could be heard. When congregations grew beyond that point, there was a shift to standing as the normal position for proclamation and a movement both closer to the congregation and to some elevated place. The elevated place—the ambo or pulpit—gave the human voice considerable audibility.

Other physical adjustments to the worship space included a sounding board placed over the head of the pulpit to reflect the sound out to the congregation and a desk designed to hold either the Bible itself or the preacher's notes or manuscript. More recently, a sound amplification system has become an essential element within these practical considerations in many worship spaces.

SYMBOLIC DIMENSIONS OF THE PREACHING PLACE

Each of the main focal points of worship—the font, pulpit, and Table—serve immediate and practical functions within the community of faith. However, while the practical aspects of these focal points remain, they come to be overlaid with symbolic meaning. These meanings are chiefly derived from the biblical stories that attend to proclamation and the sacraments, along with the images attendant to those stories. Central stories, along with their images related to water, bread, and wine, have now been recovered in prayers of thanksgiving found in the liturgies for baptism and Holy Communion. They are recounted in architectural designs, in fabric art, and, especially, in hymn texts on the sacraments.

The space for proclamation also gains symbolic meanings. We associate the place for preaching with the preaching of the prophets and with the teaching of Jesus. In contrast to the liturgical place for the sacraments, however, it is striking how few stories and images have come to name the place for preaching. The proclamation by Moses of the law of the Lord was as Moses descended from Mt. Sinai, while other proclamations by Moses and Aaron were mostly specified as being "in the wilderness." For the most part, the prophetic oracles are not specified with regard to place.

In the New Testament, places associated with proclamation include John the Baptist at the Jordan (Matthew 3:13-17) and Jesus' sermon on the mount (Matthew 5:1–7:27) or the plain (Luke 6:17-49). The synagogue is presented as the location for much of Jesus' teaching, and that location, though diminished in frequency, continues to be seen in The Acts of the Apostles. Also in the Book of Acts, a domestic location is specified for early apostolic preaching in the New Testament church. Such a location for early Christian preaching may echo more widely throughout the New Testament. Scholars have recently suggested that the Sermon on the Mount (or Plain) represents a collection of Jesus' "table talks" with his followers—a much more intimate setting than the public open-air scene. This domestic location for proclamation is a significant image for the church's preaching. It suggests that no matter how

Liturgical space will need to include a proclamation place that allows the distribution of sound from the preacher to the congregation.

imposing the liturgical space—cathedrals and all—there is an intimacy to proclaiming the Word, as if we are gathered around a table within a household of faith.

THE THEOLOGY OF PREACHING

Today, theologies of preaching span a huge spectrum, from a dialectical understanding of the Word of God to various liberation perspectives. The number of volumes in homiletics that begin "Preaching as..." seems to run into the hundreds. There is preaching as liberation, as pastoral care, as narrative—the list goes on. Yet David Greenhaw has suggested that most every approach to preaching may be located theologically within one of two chief groupings: "Preaching and Sanctification" or "Preaching and Justification."[5]

Within the former grouping, there is an emphasis on the formation of Christian character: "Preaching for sanctification aims at leading the Christian person and community toward a more fitting Christian life."[6] Moral guidance is a core theme of this approach, often related to the twin issues of preparation for receiving the sacrament and anticipation of the life of holiness in the world. On the other hand, "preaching and justification" collects various streams of Reformation theology that more recently have marched under the banner of "dialectical" or "neo-Reformation" theology. The constant within this theological grouping is the singular focus on proclaiming the Word of God, which comes to humanity directly "from above" (Karl Barth). So, as David Greenhaw observes: "If the word of God has such power, and if the word of God can be uttered by human preachers, then the preacher's voice can be God's voice."[7]

Clearly, the place for proclamation will be imagined differently within the groupings related to sanctification and justification. For example, in the "sanctification" grouping—here preaching is understood primarily as the ongoing task of delivering the faithful tradition of the church to a new generation of believers—the location from which the preaching happens may be closer to the place where the people sit.

The opposite may obtain for a model of preaching that sees the role of the preacher as not only that of speaking for God but also as having an authority that attends to the divine Word itself. The place for proclamation will, we assume, be more removed from and elevated above the place where the people sit. In actuality, however, faithful preaching week in and week out spans between these two polarities, especially if the diverse texts of the Lectionary are the basis for the sermon. Perhaps a thoughtful "middle ground" exists where preaching can speak both a sanctifying and justifying Word, and where space for preaching is therefore more tensive than constrained.[8]

IDEOLOGICAL CONSTRAINTS

It is the case from time to time in church tradition that the current ideology works to define and unbalance liturgical space in spite of practical, symbolic, and theological considerations. So, the iconoclastic movement of the post-Reformation period saw the destruction of many church altars in Europe even though the Reformers mostly held to a strong sacramental theology. We saw in the Puritan ideal of the New England meeting house a zeal both for diminishing any latent sacerdotalism and for elevating the ministry of preaching. Architecturally, this led to a rigid diminishment (if not elimination) of any Eucharistic space as well as a vigorous elevation—literally—of the place for preaching. In some recent architecture designed for "contemporary worship," spaces for the sacraments and for preaching are diminished in favor of a focus on the band, praise team, and projection screen.

When a more balanced theology of Word and Sacrament is recovered, it is frequently a challenge to pastors and congregational leaders to renovate the worship space accordingly. In cases where the existing wall-altar is far removed and prevents the pastor from presiding while facing the people, many churches have acquired a new table for the Holy Meal and have placed it closer to the people. Similarly, some churches with excessively high pulpits have moved the place for preaching both closer to the assembly and to a more modest height. Ironically, some new buildings constructed for contemporary worship will need serious renovation as the liturgical tradition is once more recovered and the focal points for baptism, preaching, and the Eucharist are restored. Incidentally, as contemporary worship's ideological excesses are reformed, the place of the people also needs to be reconsidered. The assembly could not do their work fully in those late-nineteenth-century "theater-style" churches; likewise, in some of the late-twentieth-century "cinemaplex-style" worship spaces, the people will find their liturgy hampered.

GUIDELINES FOR THE SPACE FOR PROCLAMATION

Within most Protestant traditions, the issue of the space for proclamation has focused on, and will continue to center on, the pulpit. Reviewing the practical concerns discussed above, perhaps the primary consideration for the location of the pulpit is the ability of the preacher to be heard. The sound systems available today certainly diffuse this issue as compared with the days before amplifiers, mixers, and loudspeakers. However, the oral and aural character of preaching needs to be reflected in the design of the pulpit. Even with the aid of a sophisticated sound system, the pulpit should be located in such a position that a sense of hearing the natural voice of the preacher is evoked within the congregation.

The pulpit also needs to be adequately elevated so that the speaker's voice can project throughout the worship space. Obviously, a space for proclamation that is too low relative to the congregation impedes both the ability to be heard and seen. However, an excessive elevation of the place for preaching runs into both practical and theological problems. Practically speaking, a pulpit that is too high may result in "an awkward head angle for those seated near the pulpit."[9] Theologically speaking, a balance needs to be struck between the authority of the Word and an appropriate view of the one who is called to preach. Harold Daniels states:

> The design of the pulpit should express a balance of intimacy between the preacher and people on the one hand, and the authority of the Word on the other. If too large and dominant, the pulpit will convey a sense of hierarchical structure, and an undue austerity. Preaching then tends to become oratory, formal and impersonal. On the other hand, an insignificant pulpit magnifies the preacher rather than the preacher's role as minister of the Word.[10]

A related value deals with the visible aspects of the event of preaching. The congregation needs to be able to see the preacher, but keep in mind Daniels' warning about seeing too much of him or her! Conversely,

As contemporary worship's ideological excesses are reformed, the place of the people also needs to be reconsidered.

the preacher needs to be able to see the congregation. Those of us called to preach understand the importance of visual cues from our listeners—the nod of recognition, the puzzled look, or even that dull, glazed-over expression. If at all possible, space for worship should be designed to make possible a lively nonverbal dialogue between preacher and people.

Proper lighting—both of the space for preaching and of the congregation—is an important concern. A lamentable byproduct of the Romantic Movement's impact on Protestant worship is the practice of dimming the light for the congregation while spotlighting the pulpit during the sermon. Theologically, this practice removes the congregation from its lively role in the dialogue of preaching. The focus is entirely on the preacher; and, consequently, the act of preaching becomes a "feat" of projecting the pulpit personality. Simply put, "the preacher should not be in the spotlight like an actor on a stage."[11]

The place for preaching is symbolically the place of the Word in worship. It is not the only place, but it remains the focal point of God's Word proclaimed within the liturgy. Given this core theological conviction, the location of the Bible within the space for proclamation is essential. Too often, our church architecture and liturgical practice have resulted in a separation of the Scriptures from preaching. Frequently, liturgical practice encourages such a casual relationship between the Bible and the sermon, particularly in the following ways:

1. *The distancing of the reading of the Scriptures from preaching.* Here, the problem originated in the ideal of a divided chancel promoted by the nineteenth-century Cambridge Movement. A lectern, attached to one corner of the chancel, became the place from which Scripture was read, while the pulpit was the location for the sermon. With the recovery of the reformed Sunday Service of Word and Table, the reading of Scripture and preaching are closely aligned elements in the service of proclamation. Both belong within the same space for proclamation. A lectern may be needed for other functions in the worship service, but the place for reading the Scriptures is also the place for preaching. James F. White and Susan J. White summarize the argument against splitting Scripture reading from preaching: "To read God's Word from one place (the lectern) and then go elsewhere (the pulpit) to open the Scriptures to our understanding is bad theology and a counterproductive effort."[12]

2. *The distancing of the Bible from the pulpit.* Nature abhors a vacuum, especially with regard to worship. Therefore, when God's people refrain from frequent celebration of the Lord's Supper, the altar-table will be used for purposes other than the focal point of the Holy Meal. Brassware multiplies, flower arrangements abound, and an open Bible is usually placed on altars in churches where Holy Communion is an infrequent occurrence. Meanwhile, churches with divided chancels may have a "pulpit Bible"—though it is placed not on the pulpit but on the lectern. In both of these examples, the symbol of the Word—the Bible—is separated from the place for proclamation. Moreover, in cases where an open Bible is placed on the altar, the purpose of the Scripture is more that of decoration than reading and hearing God's Word. The following comment from Frank Quinn is a welcome corrective to such abuses: "The authentic symbol of the word of God is the scripture itself."[13]

3. *The separation of the Bible from the reading of Scripture.* Even with the "pulpit Bible" lying in full view on the lectern or pulpit, it is remarkable how often the reading of Scripture is from another source: a "pocket Bible" taken out by the preacher, a sheet of paper containing the lectionary reading, and so forth.

Can we agree that the Bible needs to be seen within the space for proclamation and that the reading of Scriptures needs to be from that visible book? If so, our pulpits may need to be renovated so that the Bible is visible to the congregation throughout the worship service and that this symbolic, visible Word is also available for reading by lectors and preacher. The congregation should be able to both see a Bible when they look toward the space for proclamation and then watch and listen as that Bible is read during the service of the Word.

A final consideration regarding the space for proclamation is both immediately practical and highly symbolic. The pulpit should be moveable and removable—as the type of proclamation demands. If a drama or dance embodies the proclamation of the day, the pulpit may need to be removed from the space for proclaiming the Word. There will remain a space for proclamation, but the forms of that proclamation may vary. Mostly, however, the Word will be proclaimed through preaching and will occur mostly at and around the pulpit. And the people will be nearby, hearing the Word and seeing the one who brings good news.

CONCLUSION

Space for proclamation, then, is most effective in our churches when practical, symbolic, and theological aspects of preaching are aligned in harmony and when ideological issues do not override that alignment. Moreover, the created space for proclamation will hold in proximity the central liturgical acts of reading the Scriptures and preaching the Word. Therefore, the space for proclamation will be home to the Scriptures and habitat for the servant of the Word.

FOR FURTHER READING

Church Architecture: Building and Renovating for Christian Worship, Second Edition, by James F. White and Susan J. White (Akron, OH: O.S.L. Publications, 1998).

Concise Encyclopedia of Preaching, edited by William H. Willimon and Richard Lischer (Louisville, KY: Westminster John Knox Press, 1995).

Pitfalls in Preaching, by Richard L. Eslinger (Grand Rapids, MI: William B. Eerdmans Publishing Company, 1996).

"Pulpit, Font, and Table," by Harold M. Daniels, in *Reformed Liturgy & Music,* Volume XVI, Number 2, Spring 1982 (Louisville, KY: The Presbyterian Church, U.S.A.).

ENDNOTES

1 See "The Reformation of Liturgical Space," by Donald J. Bruggink, published in *Reformed Liturgy & Music* (Louisville, KY: The Presbyterian Church, U.S.A., A Corporation for Congregational Ministries Division, 1982), Volume XVI, Number 2, Spring 1982, pp. 53–54, for a discussion of these changes in liturgical space at the time of the Reformation.

2 From "The Reformation of Liturgical Space," by Donald J. Bruggink, published in *Reformed Liturgy & Music,* Volume XVI, Number 2, Spring 1982, p. 53. Copyright © 1982 by the Presbyterian Church (U.S.A.), A Corporation for Congregational Ministries Division.

The place for preaching is symbolically the place of the Word in worship.

3 See *The Cambridge Movement: The Ecclesiologists and the Gothic Revival,* by James F. White (Cambridge, England: Cambridge University Press, 1979).

4 During a recent sabbatical in residence at St. Meinrad School of Theology in southern Indiana, I served two rural United Methodist congregations. One church building was a turn-of-the-century clapboard structure. Its central pulpit design had been refurbished in the Cambridge pattern, with a wall-altar and a divided chancel. The other building dated from the 1970's and followed the Cambridge pattern consistently.

5 See "Theology of Preaching," by David M. Greenhaw, in *Concise Encyclopedia of Preaching,* edited by William H. Willimon and Richard Lischer (Louisville, KY: Westminster John Knox Press, 1995), p. 478.

6 Reproduced from *Concise Encyclopedia of Preaching* (p. 478), edited by William H. Willimon and Richard Lischer. Copyright © 1995 by Westminster John Knox Press. Used by permission.

7 Reproduced from *Concise Encyclopedia of Preaching* (p. 478), edited by William H. Willimon and Richard Lischer. Copyright © 1995 by Westminster John Knox Press. Used by permission.

8 See *Narrative & Imagination: Preaching the Worlds That Shape Us,* by Richard L. Eslinger (Minneapolis, MN: Augsburg Fortress Press, 1995), pp. 131–33, for a discussion of "imaginative stretch" and the spatial dimension of homiletic performance.

9 From "Pulpit, Font, and Table," by Harold M. Daniels, published in *Reformed Liturgy & Music,* Volume XVI, Number 2, Spring 1982, p. 66. Copyright © 1982 by the Presbyterian Church (U.S.A.), A Corporation for Congregational Ministries Division.

10 From "Pulpit, Font, and Table," by Harold M. Daniels, published in *Reformed Liturgy & Music,* Volume XVI, Number 2, Spring 1982, p. 66. Copyright © 1982 by the Presbyterian Church (U.S.A.), A Corporation for Congregational Ministries Division.

11 From "Pulpit, Font, and Table," by Harold M. Daniels, published in *Reformed Liturgy & Music,* Volume XVI, Number 2, Spring 1982, p. 66. Copyright © 1982 by the Presbyterian Church (U.S.A.), A Corporation for Congregational Ministries Division.

12 From *Church Architecture: Building and Renovating for Christian Worship,* Second Edition, by James F. White, University of Notre Dame, and Susan J. White, Brite Divinity School (Akron, OH: O.S.L. Publications, 1998), p. 26. For a further discussion of their perspective, see Chapter Two, "A Place for the Service of the Word," pp. 21–35.

13 From "Liturgy: Foundation and Context for Preaching," by Frank C. Quinn, O.P., in *In the Company of Preachers,* edited by Regina Siegfried and Edward Ruane (Collegeville, MN: The Liturgical Press, 1993), p. 22.

Creating Space for the Sacristy

TIMOTHY J. CROUCH, O.S.L.

Chaplain-General and Director of Publication, The Order of Saint Luke, Akron, Ohio

WITH THE ADOPTION OF *THE UNITED METHODIST HYMNAL* (1988) and *The United Methodist Book of Worship* (1992), The United Methodist Church has rediscovered patterns of worship used by the Christian church from the time of the apostles. According to the earliest documents found (second century C.E. [Common Era]), Jesus' followers have gathered regularly to read the Scriptures, to hear the Word proclaimed through preaching, and to celebrate the Holy Meal at the Table. It is in the breaking of the bread and the sharing of the cup—whether we call it "Eucharist," "Holy Communion," or "the Lord's Supper"—that the people of God continue to experience God's immediate and abiding presence in and with the gathered assembly.

We know from experience that we hear the Word more clearly if those who read from the Bible in the assembly have prepared for the task. Well-prepared sermons aid our understanding of what Scripture reveals. In the same way, making ready the things we use to aid in our celebration of the sacraments helps us to experience them as the means of grace that they are. To do this well, we need a proper space in which to make them ready and to provide for their care—that is, we need a sacristy. In this article, I offer a short history of the development of sacristies, an overview of their use, and some practical recommendations on how to create such a space.

A BRIEF HISTORY OF THE SACRISTY

ANCIENT IMAGES

Archaeologic explorations in ancient Greece, Persia, and Egypt have discovered numerous temples and places of religious worship. A consistent feature of such structures are side rooms in which were stored the hardware items used in the worship of the religious community. Separate facilities were designed for the use of the "clergy" for dressing in ceremonial clothing. A third space was often provided for the preparation of food that was consumed in the religious rites.

FROM THE SCRIPTURES

In his design for the Temple in Jerusalem, David laid out careful instructions for Solomon to follow. Treasuries for the storage of sacred vessels and ceremonial items were set in separate buildings in the complex

Worship Matters: A United Methodist Guide to Worship Work (Volume II) © 1999 Discipleship Resources. Used by permission.

(1 Chronicles 28:1-21). As Solomon followed his father's plan, the precious fixtures of gold and silver were delivered and given their place as part of the dedication (2 Chronicles 5:1).

When the Levites were designated as the priestly tribe, the various descendants of Levi's sons were assigned to various duties within the life of the Temple, including responsibility for the preparation of sacrifices and breads.

THE EVOLUTION OF CHURCH ARCHITECTURE

In early Christian times, before the religion was given legitimacy in the Roman Empire (313 C.E.), the job of the sacristan (keeper of the sacristy) was to bring the sacred items used by the gathered community to the place of worship and then return them to their hiding place until the next celebration. The writer Jerome (circa 400) referred to sacristans as "ministers of God." Until the latter part of the twentieth century, seminarians in the Roman Catholic Church were ordained to this ministry.

With the development of cathedrals and other large church buildings in the medieval period, an arrangement of rooms around the place of worship was designed carefully to support the work of worship. Sacristies in which the clergy dressed (vestries), for the storage of sacred vessels (treasuries), and for the preparation of the gifts of bread and wine *(prothesis)* were a regular feature of church architecture. In a time when the faithful stood in uncluttered naves, many churches provided for the presentation of the Eucharistic elements to be accomplished by a procession from the prothesis (located near the narthex), through the nave, and up to the sanctuary. The procession was led by the sacristans as the assembled congregation followed. Clearly, this architecture served well a church in which the celebration of the sacraments was a central part of its regular worship.

Although most of the Protestant Reformers sought to reclaim a balance between Word and Sacrament, their emphasis on preaching led to an unfortunate decline in sacramental worship. Many church structures in the post-Reformation era focused on the pulpit and reading desk (lectern), while the altar-table was relegated to an inferior position. Form followed function.

The American frontier presented a different set of problems, but with similar effect. When John Wesley sent his ministers to the colonies, he instructed them to celebrate "the Supper of the Lord on every Lord's Day."[1] The routes of the circuit rider often took three months to travel; therefore, while the circuit riders celebrated the "Supper of the Lord" each Sunday, the people received it only four times each year.

In charges under the care of lay preachers, the "preaching service" was the norm, and buildings were constructed accordingly. Again, with form following function, the majority of Protestant church buildings in this country were designed and built with little or no space allotted for the work of the sacristan. "Communion stewards" were relegated to church kitchens, classrooms, or their own homes as places to "attend to the mysteries of God."

With the publication of the Supplemental Worship Resources series in the 1970's, United Methodists began to rediscover the sacraments as means of grace and to understand the sacramental life as a norm for regular, weekly worship. This rediscovery brought a certain tension to buildings designed primarily for services of the Word. We need, once again, to create spaces to serve as sacristies.

HOW DOES A SACRISTY WORK?

The sacristy of today combines the traditional functions of the treasury and the prothesis. It is a place in which things are kept and in which people work on behalf of the worshiping community to prepare the things of worship.

The proper storage of the "things" used in worship is a matter of preserving the investment made to obtain them. An adequate sacristy promotes good order of the items used in worship and can set the tone for the rest of the building. Certainly, things such as altar cloths, linens, chalices, bread plates (patens), baptismal shells, and other equipment have a monetary value; but they have a sign value as well. While we do not think of these items as holy in and of themselves, they are the things we use to enhance our participation in holy acts such as the Eucharist and celebrations of the Baptismal Covenant, to name just two. Therefore, our care of them can help form our sense of care and awe that we offer to God.

We not only provide a fitting place for the storage of the things used in worship, but we also set aside a space for working with them. The sacristy is the space where we polish the brass furnishings, mend the torn fabric, and make preparation to uphold the celebrating community of faith. It is here that the Communion stewards (*sacristans,* in the traditional usage) prepare the bread and the wine for the communal feast. It is here that all the "tools" for sprinkling and pouring water in services of the Baptismal Covenant are made ready. And it is from here that the holy things, lovingly prepared, are set out for the assembly to use in worship.

CREATING A SPACE WHERE NONE EXISTS

When building a new church facility, the leadership could include a proper sacristy during the design phase. The best treatment for how to do this is found in *Church Architecture: Building and Renovating for Christian Worship.* (See "For Further Reading, on page 116.) However, few congregations have this luxury. The more likely case is the renovation of an older structure to meet the congregation's current needs. Given the limitations of existing walls, creating new space out of old requires thinking in new ways.

As a way to begin, it may be helpful to view an architectural floor plan of the church building, without the names of the rooms written on it. This helps to stimulate people to think about new uses for existing spaces. This approach may enable a planning committee to begin to think creatively about how many spaces in the church building can be put to new uses, thus not limiting the process to only the development of a sacristy.

The best location for a sacristy is as close to the worship space as possible. The three distinct areas of the worship space are the *narthex* (the gathering space generally between the front doors and the pews), the *nave* (the space where the congregation sits), and the *sanctuary* (the area immediately surrounding the altar-table.) The sanctuary may be situated in a *chancel*—a remnant from medieval times when the congregation was separated from the sanctuary by the choir seating. Since most of the sacristan's work addresses the sanctuary, finding a space nearby will parallel the historic location of this space.

Changing paraments (that is, altar and pulpit/lectern hangings) to mark the progression through the seasons of the Christian year means traveling between the place where they are stored and where they are

Making ready the things we use to aid in our celebration of the sacraments helps us to experience them as the means of grace that they are.

used. Likewise, placing the Communion vessels and other liturgical equipment where they may easily be taken up at the appointed time requires moving them from place to place. The shorter the distance, the more convenient for those who do the work.

One existing space to consider for a sacristy is a choir room, if it is appropriately located. These rooms are often larger spaces that afford closet facilities and room to add the necessary furniture. Making the decision to share space with other ministers of the service of worship (for example, the choir) can affirm for choristers their vital part in the worship life of the church while at the same time inviting them into a new ministry.

Unused or large Sunday school classrooms may well be converted to sacristy use without harm to the program of Christian education. Or perhaps there is an office nearby that is no longer being used by staff. The possibilities are many, if worship leaders will take the time to think beyond "the way we've always done it."

Congregations often make a significant investment in fabric and metalware for worship, only to have these show signs of wear because adequate places have not been provided for their storage. Altar cloths—frequently made of brocaded cloth purchased from church supply stores or lovingly made by hand by members of the congregation—are too often relegated to closets where they are left on the cheap hangers and plastic bags provided by the local dry cleaner. The result can be permanent creases (which weaken the cloth) and sagging ends; this is poor stewardship of the financial and personal investment made to produce them.

There are two ways to store paraments with little cost. One is to create a wide closet space with attachments for long dowel rods. Not unlike the wooden pieces on which public libraries hang newspapers, round wooden rods can permit paraments to hang while spread out to their full width. This prevents the creases that can develop when they are folded.

Another way is to obtain a cabinet with large, shallow drawers in which the paraments may be laid out at full length and shielded from dust and dirt at the same time. While cabinets for this purpose are available from church supply houses, a less expensive alternative may be as close as the local architect or engineer. As those professionals move into electronic drafting programs, the need for drawers in which to store large drawings has decreased. Such drawers are ideal for keeping paraments and linens.

In many ways, preparing a sacristy may well draw on issues encountered in the design of a kitchen. As in any well-designed kitchen, one cannot have too much counter space in a sacristy. Cabinets in modern kitchens are often wall-mounted and also afford plenty of countertop space, which provides excellent storage space for vessels such as cruets, flagons, chalices, and other altar-ware. The typical under-counter drawers found in such kitchen furniture allow ample space to store linens and small objects. If the church or the pastor owns items that are of particular value, a locked cabinet should be provided.

An alternative to locking cabinets could be a "tabernacle" converted into a safe storage space. Many Roman Catholic churches have an extra tabernacle or two stored away, which may be had for the asking. They are quite heavy (often made of cast bronze) and have sturdy locks. In many traditions, tabernacles are used to store the "reserved sacrament"—that is, the bread and wine left over from the Communion service to be taken to people who are sick or who are limited in their ability to leave home. United Methodists may use these tabernacles to store some of the items used in the celebration of Holy Communion, especially chalices and other items made of precious or semiprecious metals.

A sink is a must for the well-equipped sacristy. It permits for the washing of vessels and allows for the immediate soaking of wine-stained linens. (Any experienced altar-guild member knows the value of being able to quickly immerse stained linen in cold water as soon as the service ends.) There is a tradition of the *sacrarium* or *piscina* that might be considered. The sacrarium is an additional sink that drains directly into the earth without going through the sanitary system. This sink is for the initial rinsing of the Communion vessels and the soaking of the linens. Returning the consecrated elements and their remains directly into the ground reminds us that these are things of the earth that have been set aside for a holy purpose. For many, this device is a sign of respect for the holy things given into our care.

It bears repeating that there is no such thing as too much counter space in a sacristy. As more people share in this vital service to the congregation, the value of room in which to work will quickly be seen. Ample space for preparing bread and wine, for laying out the various fabrics, and for doing other necessary work makes the space functional and the experience pleasant. A refrigerator for storing fresh flowers (especially if the local florist makes the delivery on Friday) and wine or grape juice will enhance the convenience for all who work in and use this room.

If the pastor vests in the sacristy (another traditional function), tall closets with pullout hanging rods will be helpful. These closets should be tall enough to accommodate albs, cassocks, and other liturgical vestments, which are usually much longer than street clothes. An altar guild may even lay out the vestments for the pastor and other people who vest for the service; providing sufficient room for this purpose is one value of countertop space. A full-length mirror is a welcome addition for all who change clothing in the room.

In addition to the materials actually used in worship, adequate cleaning supplies are kept in the sacristy. Metal polishing creams and plenty of clean, soft rags will be used often. A dish-drying rack and drain board at the sink allow the vessels (for example, chalices and cruets) to air-dry after they are washed. Of course, dish towels help the process. An iron, ironing board, and spray bottle of distilled water can make last-minute touchups easy.

A calender of the liturgical year in the sacristy aids sacristans in choosing the proper colors and symbols for decorating the worship space. A cross hanging somewhere in the room can serve as a constant reminder that this is a place of work that is set aside for the glory of God. In my experience as a pastor, Martin Luther's "Sacristy Prayer" was essential. I prayed it before leading each service; it helped me keep a proper perspective.

> O Lord God, you have made me a pastor and teacher in the church. You see how unfit I am to administer rightly this great and responsible office; and had I been without your aid and counsel, I would surely have ruined it all long ago. Therefore, do I invoke you.
>
> How gladly do I desire to yield and consecrate my heart and mouth to this ministry! I desire to teach the congregation! I, too, desire ever to learn and to keep your Word my constant companion and to meditate thereon earnestly.
>
> Use me as your instrument in your service. Only do not forsake me, for if I am left to myself, I will certainly bring it all to destruction. Amen.[2]

Congregations often make a significant investment in fabric and metalware for worship, only to have these show signs of wear because adequate places have not been provided for their storage.

CONCLUSION

A well-thought-out sacristy can aid the congregation as it grows in its discipleship. Offering to God our best in preaching, in music, and in other artistic expressions, as well as in the sign-acts of baptism and Communion, requires that each element of the service of worship be carefully prepared. Seeking to bring congruence to what we say and do in worship (in its Old English root, *worship* means "ascribing worth to God"), and how we make our preparations for those acts, will be enhanced if we provide the people charged with that responsibility the proper space and tools with which to work.

FOR FURTHER READING

Altar Guild Handbook, by S. Anita Stauffer (Minneapolis, MN: Augsburg Fortress Press, 1985).

Church Architecture: Building and Renovating for Christian Worship, Second Edition, by James F. White and Susan J. White (Akron, OH: O.S.L. Publications, 1998).

United Methodist Altars: A Guide for the Congregation, by Hoyt L. Hickman (Nashville, TN: Abingdon Press, 1996).

ENDNOTES

1 See "Bristol, September 10, 1784," by John Wesley, in *The Letters of the Rev. John Wesley, A.M.: Sometime Fellow of Lincoln College, Oxford,* edited by John Telford, B.A. (London: The Epworth Press, 1931), p. 239.

2 From *Luther's Werke: Kritische Gesamtausgabe (Schriften),* by Martin Luther (Weimar: H. Böhlau, 1883), Volume 43, page 513. Translated by Timothy J. Crouch.

Part Three

PLANNING
AND GUIDING
WORSHIP

How to Welcome Children in Worship

MARYJANE PIERCE NORTON

Director, Family Ministries,
The General Board of Discipleship,
Nashville, Tennessee

I REMEMBER WELL ONE SUNDAY MORNING WHEN MY NIECE WAS three. We were running a few minutes late getting to worship and slipped as quietly as possible into the pew behind Jenny and her mother, Linda. Jenny turned around and waved, then settled back into the seat next to her mother. I couldn't help but notice her participation in the service that Sunday. Much of the time she sat playing with toys and items Linda had given her. When we sang hymns, she stood on the seat next to her mother and lustily added her own words here and there—whether they were the words of the hymn being sung or not. She joined in shaking hands and giving hugs when the congregation greeted one another. When we read the Scripture, Jenny looked on with her mother, pretending to read the Bible in just the way she pretended to read her storybooks at home. During the Lord's Prayer, I noticed her following along, saying correctly words and phrases as she remembered them, and ending with a loud, "Amen." At one point during the sermon, Jenny scooted past her mother and joined us, sitting quietly on my lap for a few minutes. Then just as quickly she scooted back to her mother and began another activity.

Would anyone watching Jenny say that she had worshiped that Sunday? I think most people would, because Jenny was indeed worshiping. In that hour on Sunday morning, Jenny participated fully with those who believe. Her participation was appropriate for a three-year-old. She sang and prayed and greeted. She "read" and she listened. Most of all, she joined with those around her in the acts of worship as part of the gathered community. Was Jenny welcome in that service of worship? Again, the answer is yes. She received hugs and smiles. No one reprimanded her or frowned at her mother when Jenny wiggled or drew.

Many times we hear arguments—some that sound pretty convincing—about why children should be excluded from worship. More often, what we hear is a justification for children participating in a parallel experience called "children's church." Those advocating children's church cite the obvious fact that much of what happens in worship is directed to adult rather than children's ways of thinking and acting. While this is the case, there are many good reasons for children to be present in worship. Consider the following:

• Under the doctrine of grace, we all are children of God. Chronological age is not relevant. None of us fully understand the miraculous power of God. We are all engaged in a lifelong pursuit of learning to respond to God and to live our lives out of that response.

Worship Matters: A United Methodist Guide to Worship Work (Volume II) © 1999 Discipleship Resources. Used by permission.

- Children remind us that people need not be mature, wise, or even able to leap tall buildings in a single bound to engage in the worship of God. When only adults gather to worship God, we are in danger of believing we can "think" ourselves closer to God. Children remind us that God's arms are open to all. We don't have to be able to think best or act best or perform best. God loves and accepts us all.
- The church is the body of Christ. If we are indeed the body of Christ, it takes all of us to be that Body. To exclude any one part of the Body means we worship not as a whole but only as a part. It takes all present to truly represent the body of Christ. Worship brings together the entire body—children, youth, adults.

ADVANTAGES OF INVOLVING CHILDREN IN WORSHIP

When I was growing up, Sunday was an all-day church commitment for my family. We attended Sunday school and morning worship, then were back at church for Sunday-night worship. Family members of every age went to Sunday school and to church. I didn't know there was any other way to "do church" on Sundays.

As an adult I discovered that not everyone did church this way. In fact, many congregations have worship and Sunday school simultaneously. In some cases, children attend worship for a portion of the time, then leave the gathered congregation for Sunday school. One of my colleagues noted that, after years of not attending worship in its entirety, the youth in her congregation did not know how to worship and really did not want to learn!

This helped me become aware of an important reason for involving children in worship: When involvement begins as early as possible, children learn to worship and become a people who worship. Keeping this point in mind, let us look at some of the other important reasons for involving children in worship:

- When children are included in worship, they feel accepted by the church. Sad to say, often children and youth express that they do not feel welcomed and are not included by adults in their congregation. Congregations that have separate children's or youth services are communicating that children and youth are not acceptable and must go to a place apart from the rest of the congregation. After all, we invite those we find acceptable to be with us and to participate in activities with us.
- When children are invited to participate in worship, they feel included in the church. They feel that they are the church and that all ages are welcomed by God. Remember, the church is the face of God to people.
- When children are included in worship, they learn that people of all ages can experience God's presence. Think of your most recent involvement in worship. When in worship did you sense God's presence? When was your spirit renewed? These experiences were most likely scattered throughout the service. Perhaps it was music sung by the choir. Perhaps it was a joy shared by another worshiper. Maybe it was through the reading of the Scripture. If you had not been present for the whole of worship, you might have missed God's presence weaving through the different parts of the service. This is true for children also. We cannot regulate when they will feel God's presence by proclaiming that they can be present only for the first fifteen minutes of the service!

If you watch children leave your service of worship for other activities, think to yourself: *Where might these children be missing the sense of God's presence because they are leaving the gathered body of believers?*

- Adults need to be with children. Children enrich our worship with the gifts of childhood. Children bring gifts of spontaneity, receptivity, thanksgiving, simplicity, hope, and honesty. These gifts can also be present in adults, but often as we grow we lose touch with some of these gifts. As we see a child move to the rhythm of a hymn, we who are afraid to move may find ourselves moving as well. As we see a child watch with awe as candles are lit, we see again the miracle of light replacing darkness. As we listen to an illustration made simple for children, we as adults catch new meaning in the simplicity of words.

- Children need to be with adults. Adults enrich worship with the gifts of understanding and perspective based on experience and years. Adults bring with them the ability to connect life within the sanctuary to life outside the sanctuary. Adults bring with them words to use to explore and explain God's presence in our lives. Children grow by being with adults and learning with adults. The gifts of child to adult and adult to child enrich the whole of the body of Christ.

HOW CAN CHILDREN WORSHIP?

Having established that children belong in worship, let's look at some of the barriers created by their age. Children do not sit still well for long periods of time. They are not patient with communication that involves only speaking and hearing. Children do not possess the ability to think abstractly. They think in ways that are different from an adult way of thinking and reasoning. Children respond to the repetition of simple psalm antiphons, to the color and pattern of banners, to the tangible taste and smell of bread and juice, and to the welcome embrace of parents as well as other adult friends.

PRESCHOOL CHILDREN

For children under the age of five, the most important people in their world are adults. Adults care for them, taking care of their needs often before they are even voiced. They love and respect adults. The most important adults in a child's life are those who care for them in their homes. These may include parents, stepparents, grandparents, aunts, uncles, and older siblings. Young children seek ways to be present with these adults and enjoy simply doing whatever task the adults are doing. Worship offers them the opportunity to participate in an important activity with the adults they love.

Children in early childhood mimic adults. If you need convincing, watch children at play. They speak the same words that adults they know speak. They try to walk and act in the same ways as adults they know. They are learning through acting what it means to be an adult. In the same way, when children are with adults in worship, they mimic the actions (or inaction) of these adults. They speak the worship words the adults speak. They use the prayer "actions" the adults use. They are learning what it means to worship God.

It is not necessary for a child to understand every act of worship to benefit from worship. After all, how many adults in the congregation truly understand Holy Communion? And yet, they still benefit from receiving

When only adults gather to worship God, we are in danger of believing we can "think" ourselves closer to God.

the bread and juice. They still enjoy remembering Jesus' love for all people. So, too, children receive the benefits of worship long before they understand any of the exact words or rituals of worship. Most important to young children is the feeling of being included. They love being a part of something with their families and with adults who care for them.

SCHOOL-AGE CHILDREN

Children in later childhood are beginning to formulate their own ideas of worship and God. They need the experience of hearing many ways to worship God and seeing many people express their faith in God. This helps them realize that people do not act out their faith in the same ways, but they are still part of the Christian community.

Although worship is not primarily an educational experience, school-age children are active learners in worship. They listen to the prayers and learn more ways of expressing their prayers to God. They participate in singing and receive words for praising God they might not have discovered on their own. They hear Scripture again and again and begin to store the verses and stories in their minds.

As they grow, children are capable of leading worship along with adults. I remember watching with pride one of the girls from my Sunday school class read the Scripture in worship. This child had practiced diligently for her part in worship. She read clearly and with meaning. She felt proud to be a part of the service.

Children form opinions about how much adults value the participation of children in worship. Children do this by observing the involvement of children in the worship service. A child who sees children involved in reading the Scripture, collecting the offering, greeting worshipers, or singing a solo receive the message that children are worthy contributors to the worship of the congregation. This feeling of being included by adults they know contributes to their faith that God includes them, too.

HOW CONGREGATIONS HELP CHILDREN FEEL INCLUDED IN WORSHIP

PRESCHOOL CHILDREN

Parents and those who sit with children in worship are primary guides for young children. It's not an easy job to sit in worship with a young child. A parent enters worship at the beginning of a new week, thinking about what's to come in the days ahead. They seek rest and worship to help them move with hope into the new week. They bow their heads and hear, "Mom, can I have some candy?" They stand to sing their favorite hymn and hear, "Daddy, I need to go potty." They open the Bible and settle back to enjoy the Scripture, and then hear, "Aunt Mary, read me a story, too."

However, one of the callings we respond to as a people of faith is to worship with and through our child in her or his younger years. To do this well, those who sit with children in worship need the support of the congregation. Here are ways the congregation can help:

- Provide times for caregivers of young children and the children to become familiar with the sanctuary. Some of us worship in very large spaces, which can be overwhelming for young children. Have an open house on a day other than Sunday. Invite young children and their families to come to your place of worship. Let them sit in different places. Let them touch the baptismal font, seeing and touching the water. Let them stand behind the pulpit and see what the pastor sees when she looks out over the congregation. Let them kneel at the altar and pray together. Encourage them to ask questions about what they see around the sanctuary.

- Encourage families with young children to sit near the front. The tendency for many people with young children is to sit near the back so they can slip out if the child becomes disruptive. However, unless the sanctuary has theater seating, it is hard for a child to see from the back. When children can't see, they are more likely to disengage from the action and be disruptive. By sitting toward the front, children will stay involved with the action taking place in worship.

- Recruit congregational members to be partners with families with young children. Encourage the partners to sit with the children on occasion. This helps support adults while helping the children form friendships with adults beyond their family.

- Provide worship packets for young children. Place these in the narthex or in the children's Sunday school classes, and encourage parents to pick these up prior to worship. Many congregations make these packets and include a variety of items. Consider including in each packet crayons, paper, a book marker, chenille sticks, a children's bulletin, and a *Pockets* magazine (available from the Upper Room).

- Notify families about upcoming worship events to enable adults to prepare children for what they'll see and experience in worship. Times for preparation include the first Sunday of each new season of the church year, baptisms, the confirmation of youth and adults, Holy Communion, special Sunday celebrations such as Native American Awareness Sunday, All Saints Sunday, and Student Sunday.

- Encourage worship planners to look at the sensory aspect of worship. Children experience life through the senses. Watch a young child explore a new kind of food. He will look at it, touch it, and smell it before eating it. What in worship can be seen, touched, smelled, and heard? What visually calls the congregation to worship? What allows children to tap into feelings of joy, sadness, quiet, or excitement?

- Include in the worship bulletin and in the church newsletter articles and inserts describing how children worship. Use the bulletin inserts and parent letters found in *Children Worship!* (See the book listed in "For Further Reading, on page 125.) While these were created to use as children take classes on worship, they can be used throughout the year to raise awareness and teach the whole congregation about worship.

- Provide learning times for parents and adults on how children worship and how to involve children in worship. We offer parenting classes on child development, on disciplining children, and on ways to increase our children's learning in school. What parenting classes do we offer for helping adults guide their children in worship and in faith?

Children receive the benefits of worship long before they understand any of the exact words or rituals of worship.

SCHOOL-AGE CHILDREN

By the time children begin reading, they benefit from additional experiences. It is hoped that the experiences we provide for preschoolers are still available for school-age children. However, in addition to what is mentioned previously, the following ideas help school-age children continue to grow as worship participants:

- Provide worship education classes for school-age children. *Children Worship!* provides material for a thirteen-week educational experience, particularly for children in first and second grade. It can also be used intergenerationally with parents and adults, as well as with children. Through these classes, children learn the movements of worship and something about those who lead us in worship. They learn some of the common response and prayers we use in worship. They learn about the tools of worship (the Bible and *Hymnal*), which help them participate more fully in worship.

- Include children in worship leadership. In the congregation I attend, we have been enriched as children have read Scripture, played bells, and served as greeters, ushers, and acolytes. Where are children leading in worship services?

- Provide times for children to create items to be used in worship. These could include bulletin covers, candleholders, containers for mission offerings, banners, and paraments. Let the children make palm leaves from green construction paper and distribute them for Palm Sunday. Use a litany written by a Sunday school class. Let the children act out the Scripture as it is read aloud to the congregation.

- Provide worship packets for school-age children. Talk to any elementary school teacher and she will tell you that children do not automatically grow out of some of the wiggles of the preschool years. Children continue to participate while involving more than their ears. It *is* possible for a school-age child to draw while listening to the sermon. In fact, many times that child will remember more from the sermon than the adult who was mentally going over the next week's schedule while appearing to be more attentive than the child. Worship packets for school-age children may include Bible-study games, paper for drawing or creating cards, suggested hymns for readings, and names of congregation members in need of prayers.

- Encourage worship planners to use hymns and Scripture the children are studying in Sunday school. We all learn from repetition. A child who sings a hymn in worship that he has learned in Sunday school has a better opportunity of remembering that hymn. And this helps the child feel that Sunday school is important, too! If a child hears Scripture in Sunday school, and then again in worship, she has a better opportunity to remember that Scripture. Similarly, encourage Sunday school teachers to use material from the worship service in Sunday school. Curriculum resources such as *The Whole People of God* and *The Inviting Word* that are based on the Revised Common Lectionary provide clear links between worship and Sunday school.

- Encourage those who preach to examine their sermons carefully. Are there illustrations that speak to the whole of the congregation? Are there times when a child's attention will be caught and held by the spoken word? Are there times of challenge for adults? Do youth hear through the sermon something that speaks of their fears and needs?

CONCLUSION

Worship is for the whole body of Christ. The whole of worship is for everyone present to be fed, to be in the presence of God, to rejoice as one of God's people. The whole of worship is for all of God's people to recommit to a life of loving God and loving neighbor, and to leave worship renewed and ready for life.

FOR FURTHER READING

Children Worship! by MaryJane Pierce Norton (Nashville, TN: Discipleship Resources, 1998).

Forbid Them Not: Involving Children in Sunday Worship (Based on the Revised Common Lectionary, Year A), by Carolyn C. Brown (Nashville, TN: Abingdon Press, 1992).

Forbid Them Not: Involving Children in Sunday Worship (Based on the Revised Common Lectionary, Year B), by Carolyn C. Brown (Nashville, TN: Abingdon Press, 1993).

Forbid Them Not: Involving Children in Sunday Worship (Based on the Revised Common Lectionary, Year C), by Carolyn C. Brown (Nashville, TN: Abingdon Press, 1994).

Hand in Hand: Growing Spiritually With Our Children, by Sue Downing (Nashville, TN: Discipleship Resources, 1998).

Helping Children Feel at Home in Church, by Margie Morris (Nashville, TN: Discipleship Resources, 1998).

Children continue to participate while involving more than their ears.

16

M. Anne Burnette Hook

Music Resources Director,
The General Board of Discipleship,
Nashville, Tennessee

How to Sing a New Song

T HE PASTOR OF A UNITED METHODIST CONGREGATION IN A suburb of Nashville was very unhappy. He had just been confronted by a group of women who were frustrated by the frequency of unfamiliar hymns in worship as well as the absence of hymns they know and love. He said rather forcefully, "These people do not understand how much effort I put into choosing hymns for worship. They have no idea how hard it is to find a hymn that really fits my sermon. All they do is complain that they don't know the hymns."

This is a rather common struggle between worship leaders and members of the congregation. Ask active worshipers in a given congregation what hymns they enjoy singing, and you will undoubtedly get this answer at least once: "I know what I like." In reality, that phrase often means, "I like what I know." Learning new music for worship can be uncomfortable for the average worshiper; so much so that some will stand stubbornly refusing to open their mouths when an unfamiliar hymn or song is included in the order of worship.

Worship leaders who are frustrated by such occurrences have three options:

1. Use only hymns the congregation knows well and loves unreservedly. This is a poor option, unless you are prepared to sing "Amazing Grace," "How Great Thou Art," and a handful of Christmas carols every Sunday for the rest of your life.

2. Quote (with great piety, if possible) a line from the familiar hymn "Come, We That Love the Lord" ("Marching to Zion"): "Let those refuse to sing who never knew our God" (*UMH,* 732). This tactic may shame some people into singing, but it will also drive some to the nearest church that sings the hymns they like.

3. Teach the congregation new hymns and songs, thus increasing the repertoire of hymns they know, and at the same time, adding new hymns to the list of songs they like. This is the best option, to be sure; but it is a difficult task to undertake. How does a worship leader carefully teach new hymns to a congregation in such a way that these songs are incorporated into the faith memory of the congregation?

It would be nice if all that worship leaders had to do was to present a clear argument for the learning of new hymns. Unfortunately, merely sharing this information is not enough to convince many people that

Worship Matters: A United Methodist Guide to Worship Work (Volume II) © 1999 Discipleship Resources. Used by permission.

learning new songs is a good thing. It is up to worship leaders to teach these songs with great care and intent if the songs are to become part of a congregation's singing repertoire.

PREPARING TO TEACH A NEW SONG

The first step in teaching the congregation a new song is for the worship leaders to select and learn the new song. The new song may reflect a variety of styles—a new praise chorus, a global song, a Taizé song prayer, or a new hymn.

After finding a new song, the worship team must decide if the song is appropriate for the congregation to sing. The church musician may be the best one to discern this, but certainly not the only one. If the song selected was first heard as a congregational song, then chances are good that most congregations could learn it. If it was a contemporary Christian song in a pop style or a song presented by trained singers, such as a choir, it may be more difficult to learn. In either case, careful analysis should take place:

1. *Check the vocal range of the melody line.* Most of the melody should fall between middle C and high C (an octave above). Most congregations can sing comfortably down to an A below middle C and up to an E-flat above high C on occasion, but songs that dwell in those extreme ranges will not be sung easily by most people in your congregation. The hymn "Amazing Grace" in the key of F stays between the two C notes.

2. *Check the contour of the melody.* Are there lots of skips and large intervals between notes? Or does the melody move step by step? As a rule, step-wise singing is easier for untrained singers, and some intervals are fairly easy as well. Intervals larger than a 6th (such as the opening interval in "It Came Upon the Midnight Clear") will be difficult for a congregation to learn easily.

3. *Check the different phrases of the melody.* Are some phrases the same? Are they all different? If some of the phrases are the same, the song will be easier to teach. Even if the notes are different but the shape of the melody is the same (as in a musical sequence), it will be easy for the congregation to pick up. For example, the hymn "Mantos y Palmas (Filled With Excitement)" (*UMH,* 279) opens with a two-measure phrase. The very next phrase echos the first phrase, using the very same rhythm on a pitch one step lower than the first phrase. The third and fourth phrases imitate exactly the first and second phrases. A congregation learning this hymn would become familiar with the melodic contour of the song very quickly because of the similarity of the phrases.

4. *Check the rhythms of the words.* Are the rhythms simple or complicated? Is there a lot of syncopation characteristic of popular music, or is it more of a classic hymn? Songs that are very syncopated are not impossible to teach, but it may be necessary to tone down the syncopation in order for the congregation as a whole to sing it. For example, the Scripture song "Thy Word Is a Lamp," which was made popular by Amy Grant, is very syncopated in its original recording. In the version that appears in the *Hymnal* (601), the rhythms are toned down to accommodate congregational singing. It may not be as exciting to those who are accustomed to the more syncopated version, but it does allow more people to enjoy singing the hymn. If you choose to keep

Ask active worshipers in a given congregation what hymns they enjoy singing, and you will undoubtedly get this answer at least once: "I know what I like." In reality, that phrase often means: "I like what I know."

the syncopation intact, be sure to teach the rhythm of the words first, and give the assembly plenty of time to become comfortable with the hymn.

If the song you want to teach the congregation is not really appropriate for the whole congregation, find a new tune for the text, preferably one that the people already know. Check the metrical index in the back of the *Hymnal* (pp. 926–31) for possibilities. Or write a new tune of your own. Keep the above characteristics in mind and test it with some church members before you try it in worship. The last resort is to have the choir or a soloist sing the song; however, if you really want the song to become part of the congregation's hymn memory, they need to sing it themselves, not hear it sung by someone else.

Once the worship team has determined that a song is appropriate for the congregation to learn, then whoever bears the primary responsibility for teaching the song needs to learn the song—backward and forward. If possible, this person should memorize the song; he or she should also know who sings what, and when they sing it. It is important to understand the flow and meaning of the song. Is it a prayer? Is it a praise song? What are the parts the congregation may have trouble singing, such as a difficult rhythm or an unusual and difficult skip in the melody? Only when the leader really knows the song well will she or he be able to teach the song with assurance and enthusiasm.

After learning the song, the leader should teach it to the worship music leadership. It is important to remember that the role of the choir or any ensemble who leads the congregation in worship is to help facilitate the congregation's song. If the congregation has a choir, praise band, or other ensemble, the leader should teach the new song to them so that they can help the leader with teaching and the congregation with learning. The song should be thoroughly practiced until all know it well. The congregation will learn faster and sing more comfortably if the leadership is confident in their knowledge of the song.

If the choir or ensemble who assists in teaching the new song is made up of children or youth, even the most resistant congregation is often more receptive to learning the song due to their delight at the presence of young people leading in worship. For example, in the last congregation I served, we initiated a year-long program to learn twelve new hymns. One of the hymns I wanted to include is "Cantemos al Señor (Let's Sing Unto the Lord)" (*UMH*, 149). Although committee members protested that our congregation was not ready to learn a Spanish song, they eventually agreed to include it. The leaders of the children's choirs taught the song to all of the children, who in turn taught the song to the congregation. That song became part of the congregation's hymn repertoire because the children introduced it.

Finally, the congregation needs to be prepared for learning a new song. Here are some ways to prepare the people:
- Introduce through a newsletter the story behind the song.
- If the song is tied to a specific theme or season, make clear the connection between the song and the theme or season; do not assume that the congregation will make the connection. (Too many times in the local church, people have expressed wonder at the "coincidence" that the closing hymn and the sermon actually went together!)
- Have the worship accompanist play the song, or have the choir or ensemble sing it as part of the service music. While the song is played

or sung, provide the text and invite the congregation to meditate on the words as the music is presented. Doing so will get the song in the congregation's ears and the text in their minds so that the song will not be as new when they are invited to sing it.

TEACHING A NEW SONG

Once the worship leaders have selected and learned the song, and have prepared the congregation, it is time to teach the new song. There are several ways to teach a new song to a congregation. Consider these two:

LINING OUT

The lining-out method has strong roots in the Methodist camp-meeting tradition. In a context where the congregation had no printed text, the song leader would simply sing a phrase, and the congregation would sing the phrase back. The assembly sang the entire song that way. This method is especially effective if the congregation does not have the music or text. It also works well in cases where the worship leader does not intend for the congregation to sing the whole song without the leader lining out the song.

Some examples of newer songs written to be sung in this manner include "Musical Setting B" of the Great Thanksgiving (*UMH*, pp. 18–20), by James A. Kriewald, and the second musical response to the Baptismal Covenant (*UMH*, p. 54), by Carlton R. Young.

ECHO METHOD

The echo method is very similar to lining out, except that the intent is to have the congregation learn the song and sing it on their own. The song leader sings a phrase and asks the congregation to echo it. After singing the whole song in that manner, the leader returns to the beginning of the song and invites the congregation to echo longer phrases until the congregation can sing a verse without echoing the leader. This method is more effective when the song leader sings the line unaccompanied, and the accompanist plays the melody only with the congregation. A simple harmony may be added as the congregation feels more comfortable with the song; the full accompaniment should be saved for the time when the congregation knows the song better.

It may also help for the song leader to use her or his hand to indicate the direction of the melody. If the notes go up, the hand moves higher; the hand moves lower if the melody moves down. A word of caution: For these hand movements to be effective, they must happen *before* the note sounds. If the hand moves at the same time as the note, the congregation will sing behind the leader. Also, it does not help for the leader to conduct congregational singing using a choral-beat pattern. Most congregations do not understand the relevance of the patterns. The tempo should be established by the voice of the song leader and the playing of the accompanist. This is especially true when the congregation is learning a new song. The leader should use a hand to indicate when the congregation is to sing and perhaps to outline the contour of the melody. Beat patterns are best left for the choir.

Some songs, especially the meditative Taizé choruses such as "Jesus, Remember Me" (*UMH*, 488) and praise choruses such as "Seek Ye First"

The role of the choir or any ensemble who leads the congregation in worship is to help facilitate the congregation's song.

(*UMH*, 405), are intended to be sung more than once. Many are also simple and require little teaching. The song leader sings the song through for the congregation and invites the congregation to join in singing the second time through. This method is most effective if the song is intended to be sung through more than twice, so that the congregation can become familiar with the song through singing it.

The echo method is also the most appropriate for use in the midst of worship, when spoken instructions may disrupt rather than enhance worship. This way of teaching works with fast and slow songs, and is best with short, repetitive songs. The method will also work with songs or hymns with several stanzas. The song leader sings a stanza or two and then invites the congregation to sing the remaining stanzas. The choir also might sing a stanza before the congregation sings, in order to give the congregation another hearing of the music before they are asked to sing.

FINDING THE RIGHT TIME TO TEACH A NEW SONG

When is it appropriate to teach a new song? Within most congregations several opportunities exist for the learning of new hymns. If the song is intended to be used in worship, then the time of gathering before worship is a great time to teach a hymn. The song leader can lead the people in a time of informal singing five to ten minutes before worship. As a way of warming up the heart, mind, and voice of the congregation for worship, this time of singing should include songs and hymns well loved by the congregation. Then the leader can introduce a new hymn using one of the methods suggested above. When the song comes up in the service, the same person leads the congregation in the singing, helping them remember what they have already learned.

Other times in the church calendar can provide prime opportunities for learning new hymns. If the congregation has a midweek evening program, a fun option is to introduce new material at a congregational hymn-sing. In some regions, the traditional hymn-sing or festival on fifth Sundays is a treasured event. Gathering before Sunday school, United Methodist Women's or United Methodist Men's meetings, family fellowship events, or any time the congregation gathers as a community present wonderful opportunities to teach a new song for the Lord.

Are there times when teaching a new song is inappropriate? The middle of worship, when the congregation is focused on hearing and responding to God's Word is not a good time to teach a new song that requires a good bit of instruction or practice. If a song requires such teaching and there is no time before worship to learn it, it serves the intent of worship better to use a song that is familiar to the congregation rather than to disrupt worship by teaching the hymn. Also, a funeral service is probably not the best place to introduce a new hymn, unless you use a song leader or choir to sing most of it and invite the congregation to join in as they feel led.

FROM OCCASIONAL TO INTENTIONAL

It is possible—and vital—to expand the hymn and song repertoire of even the most reluctant congregation. Sally Morgenthaler suggests that the work of the worship leader in developing a hymn repertoire is one of the most important and challenging tasks:

Few things you do as a contemporary worship leader will have as much impact on your congregation's worship life [as] developing a solid worship repertoire. That base of about 50 songs and hymns [should be] carefully scrutinized for both musical and textual quality. No easy assignment, especially when you consider that musical options now run into the thousands.[1]

Worship leaders should prepare an intentional plan for learning hymns and songs that reflects the whole range of Christian experience, not just selecting from a list that covers a variety of musical styles and tempos or focusing on what the congregation members (or worship leaders) like.

It is a daunting but exciting task to formulate a long-term congregational strategy for learning new hymns and songs. This task requires identifying the current hymn repertoire, seeing what gaps are apparent, and outlining a plan for adding new hymns and songs to that list of favorites.

1. *Identify the current hymn repertoire.* Unless a worship leader has been in a congregation since birth and the congregation is not prone to frequent membership shifts, he or she may not know fully which hymns and songs the congregation knows and enjoys singing. One way of determining this is for the leader to place in a prominent place the hymnal used in worship in that congregation. Invite congregation members to thumb through the hymnal, marking which hymns are favorites. Another way of learning which hymns the congregation knows is to conduct a favorite-hymn survey. Invite members to list their favorite hymns on a ballot. Tally the results and have a countdown of the congregation's top hymns and songs.

2. *Look for gaps in the hymn repertoire.* What types of songs or hymns are missing from the congregation's list? Does the congregation know the traditional, classic hymn literature, such as "Holy, Holy, Holy! Lord God Almighty" (*UMH*, 64), but not any of the praise choruses that are currently popular? Do they feel comfortable with hymns that speak of a personal relationship with Jesus, such as "Just as I Am, Without One Plea" (*UMH*, 357), but are not as familiar with hymns that speak of a corporate worship experience, such as "God Is Here" (*UMH*, 660)? Do they sing loudly when "Amazing Grace" (*UMH*, 378) is used, but stare mutely when any global music is used, especially when it is in a different language? These are the places where a congregation's hymn repertoire can be expanded.

3. *Outline a plan for teaching new hymns and songs to the congregation.* With the worship team or music committee, the leader develops a long-term plan for teaching new hymns to the congregation. They should select a reasonable number of new hymns to learn for the year. This number should depend on how and when the hymns will be taught and used, as well as the difficulty of the songs. For example, to teach the congregation the chorus of "Jesus, Remember Me" (*UMH*, 488), the leader may decide to sing that prayer song each time the congregation celebrates Communion. This song is easily assimilated into the hymn repertoire of the congregation. Or, the leader may wish to use part of a hymn as service music for a specific season. In the last congregation I served, we used the first stanza (without refrain) of "Spirit Song" (*UMH*, 347) as a congregational benediction response. Other hymns work better when used in their entirety. So, it may be helpful to choose a new hymn as a theme for a certain season, such as "Prepare the Way of the Lord" (*UMH*, 207) for Advent. Other hymns

> It is a daunting but exciting task to formulate a long-term congregational strategy for learning new hymns and songs.

can work in medleys with more familiar hymns, such as "There's Something About That Name" (*UMH*, 171) with "All Hail the Power of Jesus' Name" (*UMH*, 154).

In choosing new hymns, the leader needs to be sensitive to the congregation's saturation level of learning. A new hymn a month taught in the same way each month could become rather tedious; it also does not give the congregation adequate time to actually live with a song. Introducing and using new songs in a creative way will greatly reduce congregational resistance. Here are a few ways that are creative and can help prevent saturation and tedium:

- Vary the ways in which new songs in worship are taught and used.
- Teach a new hymn as a theme song for Lent.
- From Pentecost until Thanksgiving, use a prayer chorus in place of the spoken Prayer for Illumination.
- Use a Taizé song as one of the Communion hymns for a year.

It is important to develop a schedule for teaching new hymns. A hymn festival at the beginning of the year to introduce the hymns is an exciting way to get started. A second hymn festival, at the end of the year, allows the congregation to celebrate what they have learned throughout the year.

The leader should identify which hymns are more appropriate for specific seasons of the church year and keep those lists handy as he or she plans worship. Children and youth in the congregation should also learn these hymns. Sunday school teachers and choir leaders of these children could be asked to incorporate these hymns and songs into their curriculum, with the worship leader providing assistance as needed. These hymns should be taught in adult Sunday school classes as well. The worship leader should work with all who plan music for worship and other events to keep these new hymns before the congregation.

After implementation, progress should be evaluated frequently to make sure the intent of the worship leader's efforts is achieved. The leader may on occasion ask various members how they like learning new hymns. If they express some resistance, the leader should explore the issue further, with a view to discerning what changes can be made to increase the members' openness to learning new songs. This takes persistent effort, since it takes a while for a song to move from being new to being familiar to being well loved by a congregation.

Finally, as the worship team selects hymns for worship each week, it is important to remember that balance is the key. Many congregations are willing to give new songs a try when they know that the songs they know and love will also be sung with some frequency. Therefore, the leader should keep track of the hymns and songs that he or she uses by marking the dates in an office copy of the *Hymnal.*

CONCLUSION

There are few things more rewarding than teaching a new song to a congregation and seeing it become part of the faith story of those who sing it. Hymns and songs shape our understanding about God and offer us means by which to beautifully and musically express our faith experience. As we learn new hymns and songs, we join with all creation in singing praise to the God—the source of all that is, including our songs and our voices. Thanks be to God!

FOR FURTHER READING

Creative Hymn Singing, by Alice Parker (Chapel Hill, NC: Hinshaw Music, 1976).

You Can Lead Singing: A Song Leader's Manual, by Glenn Lehman (Harrisonburg, PA: Good Books, 1994).

Organizations you can contact include:

The Church Musician and the Copyright Law. Contact: Church Music Publishers Association, Inc., P.O. Box 158992, Nashville, TN 37215. Phone: 615-791-0273. Internet: *http://host.mpa.org/church.html*

Christian Copyright Licensing, International. Contact: CCLI, 17201 NE Sacramento Street, Portland, OR 97230. Phone: 800-234-2446. Internet: *http://www.ccli.com/unitedstates*

ENDNOTES

1 From "Exponential Repertoire: There Is More to Building a Repertoire Than Tempo or Theme, Mood or Mix," by Sally Morgenthaler, in *Worship Leader,* Volume 7, Number 2, March–April 1998, p. 14. Copyright © 1998 CCM Communications, Nashville, Tennessee.

There are few things more rewarding than teaching a new song to a congregation and seeing it become part of the faith story of those who sing it.

How to Introduce Baptism by Pouring or Immersion

DANIEL T. BENEDICT, JR.

*Worship Resources Director,
The General Board of Discipleship,
Nashville, Tennessee*

T HE THEOLOGICAL AND RITUAL RENEWAL IN THE UNITED Methodist Church invites and calls for revitalized celebrations of the Baptismal Covenant by the use of strong gestures and more lavish amounts of water. Consider the following scenarios.

In one church, with the people seated in the pews, a pastor holds a child in his left arm as he dips his right hand into the font, touches the head of the child with wet fingers, and says, "Peter Runyon, I baptize you in the name of the Father, and of the Son, and of the Holy Spirit." In another congregation in the same city, with the congregation standing close to the action, a pastor lowers a baby three times into a large pool of water, saying, "Maria Justine, I baptize you in the name of the Father…". The people say, "Amen" and "Thank you, Lord!" as the pastor holds the baby up before the people and the parents wrap her in a towel. In both baptisms God's promise can be trusted. As you imagine each baptism, which more strongly conveys the action of God for you? Which enactment, for you, "speaks" more clearly and powerfully of God's transforming grace offered without price and of incorporation into the body of Christ?

The question for pastoral leaders is how best to enact the power and grace of the triune God in the Baptismal Covenant service. The opening sentences of the service of the Baptismal Covenant reads: "Through the Sacrament of Baptism we are initiated into Christ's holy Church. We are incorporated into God's mighty acts of salvation and given new birth through water and the Spirit" (*UMBOW*, p. 87).[1]

Are there ways for this gracious action of the Holy Spirit to be more fully perceived and appreciated by both candidates and congregation? This article offers theological, liturgical, and pastoral reasons for increasing the amounts of water used in the rite of baptism and then gives specific guidance for introducing pouring and immersion. While this article does not address directly the use of oil and concluding the rites of initiation with Holy Communion, the reasoning used can be extended to these practices.[2]

STRENGTHENING GESTURES

The following questions may immediately present themselves: Why should we change from sprinkling? Isn't water, whatever the amount used, sufficient? The answer is: Yes, it is; and no, it is not. United Methodists have always honored three modes of baptism, as this paragraph from *The United Methodist Book of Worship* points out:

United Methodists may baptize by any of the modes used by Christians. Candidates or their parents have the choice of sprinkling, pouring, or immersion; and pastors and congregations should be prepared to honor requests for baptism in any of these modes. Each mode brings out part of the rich and diverse symbolism given to baptism by the Bible.

(*UMBOW*, p. 81)[3]

The text gives scriptural allusions and citations for the rich meaning of each mode of baptism. While sprinkling has been the predominant practice among United Methodists, particularly for infant baptism, the fresh recovery of a strong baptismal theology and the increasing frequency of adult baptism, is an opportunity for stronger sign-acts.

THEOLOGICAL, LITURGICAL, AND PASTORAL CLAIMS FOR STRONGER USE OF WATER AT BAPTISMS

We do not know the mode of baptism or the amounts of water used in the New Testament accounts of baptism (for example, Matthew 3:13-17 and Acts 2:37-42), so an appeal for strengthened gestures cannot be based on a claim to literal reenactment of Scripture.

There are several arguments for a more generous use of water in baptizing people. First, the theological significance of the rite of baptism calls for a corresponding generosity in the actions that conveys God's action. In baptism, God freely and lavishly incorporates people into the church and into the mighty acts of God. In the action, men, women, and children are born anew from above. Such momentous gifts call for enhancement of the symbolic context.

Second, we are recovering a strong sense of the paschal mystery through use of the calendar of the Christian Year and the Revised Common Lectionary. This attentiveness to the mystery of the dying and rising of Christ in every Sunday's worship draws the church into a continuing identification with the paschal mystery initiated in baptism.

Third, there is a profound cultural shift taking place in which the Enlightenment focus on thinking and words is fading in favor of experience, mystery, and symbol. This is not to say that words and thinking are unimportant; rather, it is to say that people are increasingly open to powerful experiences that convey more than words or rational and linear thinking alone can. Outward rites shape inner experience.

Fourth, the introduction of the reaffirmation of the Baptismal Covenant in the *Hymnal* (pp. 50–53) and *Book of Worship* (pp. 111–14) makes it necessary to distinguish carefully the ways we use water for baptism and the ways we use it in reaffirming the Baptismal Covenant. The rubric for confirmation and reaffirmation of baptism specifies that water is to be used "in ways that cannot be interpreted as baptism" (*UMBOW*, p. 92).[4] The problem is that if we already use minimal amounts of water for baptism, how do we use water in reaffirming baptism in such a way that it does not look like we are baptizing?

Effecting change successfully requires skill and compassion. While the focus of this article is on the actual use of water in the celebration of baptism, introducing a change in practice calls for leadership through teaching, preaching, and counseling sessions with candidates and parents, as well as with the congregation as a whole. The *Book of Worship* directs pastors and congregations to honor the mode of baptism that candidates or their parents choose (p. 81). The point is not to force change but to hold out the possibility of baptism by pouring or immersion. Most

The question for pastoral leaders is how best to enact the power and grace of the triune God in the Baptismal Covenant service.

congregations will accept and appreciate a more lavish use of water if they are helped to find the deeper meaning in the new practice. A man was asked if he believed in infant baptism. He replied, "Believe in it? I've even seen it!" Many of our people are aware of baptism by immersion, and may even have seen it; but they have thought that it was something United Methodists do not practice. Allusions to pouring and immersion in sermons related to scriptural passages (such as Romans 6; Acts 2:38; John 3:3-5) will help the people to see the biblical images for such actions.

A more general but essential aspect of preparing the congregation is cultivating a strong sense of hospitality and welcome for those being initiated into Christ and the church. *Come to the Waters: Baptism & Our Ministry of Welcoming Seekers & Making Disciples* [5] casts a vision of how congregational leaders and congregations can embody gospel hospitality in all aspects of their primary task of making disciples of Jesus Christ. Choosing, orienting, and assigning sponsors for baptismal candidates is very important. Their support and mentoring relationship prior to baptism will help candidates know that they will be accompanied and loved all the way—wet hair, soggy clothes, and all.

CREATING ALTERNATIVES FOR MORE AMPLE USE OF WATER

Few United Methodist church buildings are immediately suited for baptism by pouring or immersion. Most have a small bowl (slightly larger than a Communion chalice) or a font that holds no more than a quart of water. This, however, is no substantive obstacle to using water more lavishly for baptism. In his article, "Creating Space for Baptism and the Renewal of the Baptismal Covenant" (pp. 93–100 in this volume), Lester Ruth provides direction and help for creating adequate space for baptism by pouring or immersion. Here, I will point to alternatives without providing details, which must be worked out in each congregation's setting.

PREPARING FOR POURING OR IMMERSION: PRACTICE AND LITURGICAL PRESENCE

The most critical preparation for successfully introducing baptism by pouring or immersion is the preparation of the person or persons who will administer the baptism. The presider will communicate her or his comfort or discomfort with the practice through body language and liturgical presence. If the presider is able to administer the baptism with confidence, grace, warmth, and prayer, then the candidate and congregation will follow suit. It is dangerous for the presider to attempt baptism by pouring or immersion before she or he is ready in heart, mind, and experience.

The notion that worship leadership and presidential style should come naturally or should be spontaneous is detrimental to good presiding. No jazz musician worth her salt picks up an instrument without warming up. Jazz improvisations are possible only after a long process of learning the fundamentals. Why should those who preside in worship think that it is any different for them? So, if a presider is going to introduce baptism using a new mode, the key word is practice!

If one is self-conscious, it helps to "walk" through the baptism alone in front of a mirror. A next step is to get some people to assist in roleplaying the baptism. (Roleplaying is especially important in the case of the baptism of an older child or an adult-sized person.) Someone plays the candidate, while others observe the practice session and provide feedback. The presider should try the baptismal "sign-act" in several different ways, checking with the observers on issues of visibility, demeanor and confidence, and extraneous and inconsistent words or movements.

All of us are impressed with an actor or entertainer who has "presence." When we say a person has presence, we mean that that person holds him or herself "in character." Presiding at a baptism, particularly when baptizing a person in water, means enacting the gospel for the sake of the candidate and focusing the faith of the church on what God is doing in that action. To act in any way that belittles, diminishes, or compromises the sign-act undermines the sacrament. Poor liturgical presence hinders and foils the people who are present to worship. I strongly urge reading Robert Hovda's *Strong, Loving and Wise* and Chapter 9 of William Willimon's *Worship as Pastoral Care* as grounding for intentionally improving a sense of liturgical presence. (See "For Further Reading," on page 141.)

A final word about practicing the action of baptism: Practice is not only strongly urged in the case of preparing to introduce a new mode of administering baptism, but it should be done for all baptisms, particularly if there will be more than one candidate. The Baptismal Covenant I (*UMH*, pp. 33–39; *UMBOW*, pp. 86–94) is designed to be used with any combination of baptism, confirmation, reaffirmation of faith, reception into The United Methodist Church, or reception into a local congregation. In a way unlike any other rite of our church except for ordination, this service needs to be "choreographed" so that the presider and those assisting the presider are clear about what each is to do and when. Insisting on practice is not an admission that worship leaders don't know what they're doing. Rather, it is an act of stewardship of the mysteries of God and an act of care for those for whom this moment will be a liturgical and spiritual milestone.

BAPTIZING BY POURING

Baptism by pouring should be a lavish gesture that communicates God's outpouring of the Holy Spirit upon the candidate and allows the person to sense the reception of God's gracious gifts. Therefore, the use of water should be generous, gentle, and done with confidence. There are three basic approaches to pouring: (1) pouring over the head of a person bending over the font, (2) pouring over the head of an infant or a child in the presider's arms, and (3) pouring over the head of a person standing or kneeling.

POURING OVER THE HEAD OF A PERSON BENDING OVER THE FONT

The presider invites the candidate (a child, youth, or adult) to stand at the font and to bend over it. The assisting minister or acolyte offers the candidate a towel, and the presider pours water over the head of the candidate while addressing the candidate with the baptismal formula. Children may need a sturdy stool or small platform to stand on. Care should be taken to be as generous with the water as the font can accommodate. For example, if the font is quite small, the amount of water it can catch will be small. If the font is wide, a more generous stream of water can be poured. The floor surface should be adequately protected to prevent people from slipping or damage to the surface.

POURING OVER THE HEAD OF AN INFANT OR CHILD IN THE PRESIDER'S ARMS

This approach has several options. In choosing the best option, the age, wakefulness, and comfort level of the infant or child should be considered. If the candidate is an infant, the most common way is to hold the baby so that the head is cradled faceup over the presider's elbow. The water is then poured over the crown of the head while saying the baptismal address, allowing the effusion to fall into the font. If the candidate is a toddler and awake, the toddler's comfort level may be increased by holding the child with his or her face toward the water, permitting the child freedom to touch the font as the water is poured over the head with the address of the baptismal formula. If the child is asleep, then the first position (holding the child with the head faceup over the elbow) may be more comfortable and less awkward.

POURING OVER THE HEAD OF A PERSON STANDING OR KNEELING

With adequate preparation of the floor (using a large plastic sheet or a wading pool covered with appropriate cloth), this approach allows for more generous amounts of water. Here the presider invites the candidate to stand or kneel in the center of the space, and with a ewer (pitcher) the presider pours water generously over the head, addressing the candidate with the baptismal formula.

Pouring requires a nonporous receptacle or space where water poured over the head can be collected. If a font is large enough—say, eighteen to twenty-four inches in diameter—water can be poured from a pitcher over the head and collected without soaking the floor. If the pouring is over the head and shoulders of a person in a standing or kneeling position, then the nonporous space will need to be at least four to six feet in diameter. A small wading pool or large sheet of plastic will do.

BAPTIZING BY IMMERSION

Baptism by immersion is a lavish sign-act of dying and rising with Christ (Romans 6:3-11). The practice of immersion demands practiced action on the part of the presider and the assisting ministers.

There are two approaches to immersion, depending on the depth of water available and the size of the presider and the candidate. In one approach, the candidate stands or kneels in the pool and the presider immerses the candidate face forward. In the other approach, the candidate stands in the pool and the presider immerses the person backward into the water. In both cases, the person will need towels, dry clothes, and a place to change following the baptismal rite.

IMMERSION IN THE FACE-FORWARD POSITION

If the water is waist high or higher, the candidate should stand; if the water is thirty to twenty-four inches or less, it is best for the candidate to kneel. This approach has two advantages: First, this approach allows for a shallower depth of water—eighteen to twenty-four inches. Second, the height and weight of the candidate are much less of a factor than in immersion in deeper water.

The presider invites the candidate to enter the pool, and guides him or her to a kneeling position if the water level is less than waist high. With one hand on the candidate's shoulders and the other hand supporting the candidate's forehead, the presider dips the head, shoulders, and torso under the water, addressing the candidate with the formula so that she or he hears it just prior to entering the water. While not required, it is appropriate to dip the person three times, each time immersing the candidate with the successive names of the persons of the Trinity. If the candidate stands in water higher than waist high, the presider may dip the person forward as the person bends at the waist.

IMMERSION IN THE BACKWARD POSITION

With this approach, the presider may need the assistance of another person. The disadvantage of this approach is that if the presider is substantially smaller than the candidate, the candidate's size and weight may overwhelm the strength of the presider, resulting in an awkward and distracting sign-act. Here are some basic guidelines for the presider in considering this approach.

1. Prior to the baptism, tell the candidates that they can assist in the baptism by bending at the knees and holding their breath while going under the water.

2. At the time of immersion, stand at right angles to the candidate, with the candidate visible to the congregation. With an assisting minister on the opposite side mirroring your actions, support the person with one hand behind the shoulder blades and the other hand grasping the candidate's shoulder. With gentle pressure backward, lower the candidate's shoulders and head under the water after the address of the baptismal formula. Then, immediately raise the candidate's head and shoulders back up from the water.

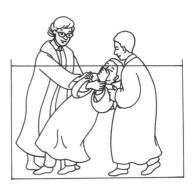

3. Some candidates tend to float up and their feet lose contact with the floor of the pool. In such cases, you and the assisting minister will need to grasp the person's upper arm and lift her or his head and shoulders above the water and ask the newly baptized to put her or his feet on the bottom of the pool. It is recommended that the candidate be directed to hold his or her breath and close the nasal passages with the hand when going under. In order to get the feel of this, practice with several different people of varying heights and weights is strongly recommended.

Immersion requires water at least eighteen to thirty inches deep and a pool no less than two-and-a-half by four feet. At its Easter Vigil service, one congregation introduced baptism by immersion using a hard plastic cattle drinking trough that had Easter lilies painted on it and that was banked with live Easter lilies. The advantage of starting with a temporary pool is that the cost is minimal and the installation is not permanent. This gives the congregation an opportunity to experiment with this mode without the expense of installing a permanent pool in the worship space.

Another way to introduce baptism by immersion is to hold the baptism at the ocean or at a nearby lake, stream, or swimming pool. Care needs to be taken to ensure that the water is not so cold or swift that discomfort or danger overwhelms the sacrament. A disadvantage of holding the service away from the congregation's normal worship space is that hymnals and other basic resources for worship are not available for the rite of baptism. The planners and presider must decide how the rest of the service that surrounds the rite (Gathering, Proclamation and Response, Thanksgiving and Communion, and Sending Forth) will be done.[6] The fullness of worship should not be weakened or diminished in order to strengthen the sign-act of baptism.

In most cases, the amount of water used in pouring and immersion will necessitate a space for people to change into dry clothes. Provision of baptismal gowns, towels, and space that accommodates privacy for changing will need the congregation's consideration and planning. In the case of immersion, it is very important that candidates wear a bathing suit of a dark color, since baptismal gowns stick and become translucent when wet.

While these suggestions for the sign-act of baptism are detailed, specific, and may seem mechanical, the rite should be enacted as an act of prayer. With practice and experience, the presider will find his or her own best ways to enact the initiating grace of God in the moment of baptism.

DEALING WITH OBJECTIONS

While most people in the congregation will respond positively to the introduction of baptism by pouring or immersion, there may be some who object to these changes. Generally, this calls for teaching and interpretation. In some cases, the objection may be rooted in an emotional wound in the past. Here are some possible objections:

1. *"This is the way the Baptists do it!"* A suitable response is to point the objector to page 81 of the *Book of Worship* while saying, "You may not be used to it, but United Methodists have always allowed for baptism by any of the modes used by Christians."

2. *"This is too messy."* The presider should listen carefully to find out what the real concern is. Is the person concerned about damage to the floor or carpet? Is she or he troubled by what seems to be a disruption in the otherwise orderly service? Does he or she feel self-conscious? It is important to explore what values are being stirred by the more lavish use of water.

3. *"I will look silly after I'm baptized. My hair will be a mess and my clothes will be wet!"* This objection is to be expected initially by youth and adult candidates. Once the practice is established, most people will have seen a baptism and will have felt the power of God and the joy and acceptance of the congregation. These realities usually overcome feelings of self-consciousness with anticipation of being the object of the congregation's care. When introducing pouring or immersion for the first time, the presider will need to reassure the candidate that he or she will be lovingly cared for and have opportunity to dry his or her hair and change into dry clothes.

CONCLUSION

The recovery and revitalization of our appreciation of baptism will come not only with transformed theology but with strong and grace-filled gesture and more plenteous use of water. This invites pastors and other leaders to pioneer the use of pouring and immersion in baptizing people in a church long at ease with sprinkling.

FOR FURTHER READING

Come to the Waters: Baptism & Our Ministry of Welcoming Seekers & Making Disciples, by Daniel T. Benedict, Jr. (Nashville, TN: Discipleship Resources, 1996).

Strong, Loving and Wise: Presiding in Liturgy, by Robert Hovda (Collegeville, MN: The Liturgical Press, 1983).

The Lord Be With You: A Visual Handbook for Presiding in Christian Worship, by Charles E. Hackett and Don E. Saliers (Akron, OH: O.S.L. Publications, 1990).

This Is the Night (videocassette), by Rev. Dan A. Neumann (Chicago, IL: Liturgy Training Publications, 1992). To order this videocassette, call: 800-933-1800.

Worship as Pastoral Care, by William H. Willimon (Nashville, TN: Abingdon Press, 1982).

ENDNOTES

1 From "The Baptismal Covenant I," copyright © 1976, 1980, 1985, 1989, 1992 by The United Methodist Publishing House; from *The United Methodist Book of Worship,* p. 87. Used by permission.

2 See *The United Methodist Book of Worship,* pp. 91 and 94, for the rubrics for using oil and for concluding the Baptismal Covenant with Holy Communion.

3 From *The United Methodist Book of Worship,* p. 81. Copyright © 1992 by The United Methodist Publishing House. Used by permission.

4 From "The Baptismal Covenant I," copyright © 1976, 1980, 1985, 1989, 1992 by The United Methodist Publishing House; from *The United Methodist Book of Worship,* p. 92. Used by permission.

5 *Come to the Waters: Baptism & Our Ministry of Welcoming Seekers & Making Disciples,* by Daniel T. Benedict, Jr. (Nashville, TN: Discipleship Resources, 1996).

6 See *The United Methodist Hymnal* (pp. 4 and 6) for placement of services of the Baptismal Covenant.

When introducing pouring or immersion for the first time, the presider will need to reassure the candidate that he or she will be lovingly cared for.

DIANA SANCHEZ-BUSHONG

*Director of Worship,
Music, and Outreach,
Westlake United
Methodist Church,
Austin, Texas*

How to Get Along Without a Choir

THROUGHOUT THE UNITED STATES OF AMERICA, CHURCHES gather for worship each Sunday morning. In each situation we find an array of styles of preaching and music; and yet, no matter what the situation or style of worship, worshipers and leaders are united in the single desire to connect with God.

Similarly, in The United Methodist Church we find congregations of all sizes worshiping in many different ways. Furthermore, in this decade we have seen the phenomenal growth of "alternative" worship services that are offered alongside "traditional" worship services in many churches, whether in urban, suburban, or rural locations. Thus, what used to be the standard worship service (or the standard by which we all measured our services)—one preacher, one choir (where available), one choir director (as needed), and one organist/pianist (or organist/choir director)—is now a complex configuration of song leaders, praise bands, and age-level choirs that offer specific styles of music for specific types of worship gatherings.

What we find is a pastor or team of pastors and other worship leaders who seem to undergo a metamorphosis between services so that they look and sound different at each service; or we see one group of leaders exiting while another group enters in preparation for the next service. The crisis arising from today's more complex approach to offering a variety of worship services has to do with how to find the appropriate music personnel and resources for each of these services.

Small-membership churches along with large-membership churches are having to decide on the best use of the talents and resources available in their congregations and geographical areas. Having a choir may not be a practical consideration for a church in a rural area that offers only one worship service. Likewise, a large church with multiple services may not be able to recruit enough musicians to have a choir present for each service. As a result, churches are having to rethink the issue of music leadership. They discover that they need to be willing to develop new approaches in order to have the musical leadership that not only enhances a worship service but that also leads people in an authentic expression of worship.

Whether your church has one worship service or several, this article helps you think about basic ways to provide musical leadership in cases where a choir does not exist. However, before we begin talking about

Worship Matters: A United Methodist Guide to Worship Work (Volume II) © 1999 Discipleship Resources. Used by permission.

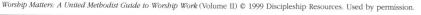

choirs, we look at how music and worship function as integrated parts of a whole experience in which leading worship as a team is essential.

WORSHIP AND MUSIC

The basic liturgical form that United Methodists use is a pattern that is both flexible and broadly structured. That is to say, Sunday morning worship services have some very specific actions—the Doxology, the Lord's Prayer, the hymn of praise, and so forth—that become "anchor points" for the congregation in the worship structure. On the other hand, most worship services are not identical week to week, and contain variations according to the Sunday in the Christian year, the Scripture readings, and the theme for the day. In such a flexible-yet-structured format, music becomes the cohesive element that often leads the congregation from one action to another, or it ties together several actions in a row.

The basic liturgical form provides opportunities for a congregation to gather, to pray, to hear Scripture and proclamation, and to respond to God both in worship and in ministry to the world. Within these opportunities are more specific actions, such as music during the gathering: the opening hymn, the unison prayer of the day, and prayers of the people. It is in these specific actions that we see the dynamic influence of music and its ability to bring a cohesive quality to a variety of actions. Here, too, we see that a worship service embodies a sense of rhythm between congregational actions (singing, unison prayers, responses, and so forth) and actions led by worship leaders. Whether we know it or not, a natural rhythm of *call and response* exists. Only when we acknowledge this rhythmic pattern do we find better ways to tap into it and allow it to provide shape to the worship service. Thus, when we talk about the integration of music in liturgy, we are speaking primarily about the use of music as both call and response.

In most worship settings in United Methodist churches, the role of the congregation is that of participant and active listener. This is liturgy at its best, since *liturgy* means "the work of the people." The congregation "works" by singing their praise of God, stating their beliefs, speaking aloud their joys and concerns, and sharing in Holy Communion. The congregation is not an audience—even in contemporary worship formats where words such as *audience* are used. Unlike an audience, a congregation has an active role to play. In some "informal" or "non-liturgical" worship settings, the congregation has a very active role; while in some more "formal" or "liturgical" worship services, the congregation has a less active role, with fewer responses and musical opportunities to join in singing. In both cases, people come together to be actively involved in worshiping God in community.

One of the most striking elements of informal worship is congregational song. While most of us can read Scripture on our own, pray on our own—even sing hymns on our own—such experiences cannot replace the unmistakable quality that is found when a community sings together. Furthermore, congregational singing is not about well-known hymns, perfect tempos, or even great harmonizations; it is about what we experience as Christians and how we give ourselves back to God. This is why, when we think about worship, the most important choir that comes to mind is the congregation. The congregation's song (the total repertoire and musical expression of a specific community of faith) is the most important because it is the one that is offered by everyone as a common action.

Music becomes the cohesive element that often leads the congregation from one action to another, or it ties together several actions in a row.

THE ROLE OF MUSICIANS IN WORSHIP

THE WORSHIP ACCOMPANIST

The musicians' role in worship is to enhance the congregation's song. All congregations and all worship services have a variety of musicians who support the congregation's song. The most obvious is the accompanist. The worship accompanist is the person or persons who provide instrumental support for congregational singing. Worship accompanists are usually organists or pianists, but now include praise bands, guitar choirs, and even taped music.

The role of the accompanist is to provide a firm musical foundation for the congregation so that the songs may be sung fully and confidently. A good accompanist takes a leadership role in congregational singing, but also remains flexible with regard to the congregation's needs (something taped music cannot do!). Most of all, a good accompanist listens for balance and "breathes" with the congregation in order to provide the appropriate time between phrases and stanzas.

THE CHOIR

A choir (where available) provides a dimension in addition to the worship accompanist. The choir's role is to enhance the worship service by supporting the congregation's participation in the singing of hymns and service music. Their role is, first, to lead in congregational singing, and second, to provide additional music that enhances the worship service. A choir offers music that provides a congregation with opportunities for reflection and prayer. Choirs have a definite advantage over congregational singing, in that choirs are a rehearsed body of singers who have experience singing and who often read music. While having experience in singing and reading music are helpful, having a weekly rehearsal seems to be the greatest benefit for a choir. Therefore, include the congregation in a "rehearsal" by having a mini-rehearsal each week before the worship service begins. Treat the congregation as a choir; have similar expectations, and you may be surprised at the kind of singing you will hear.

A choir is a vital part of the worship leadership, not an elite group of singers whose main concern is the morning "special music." All music in worship is special and offered humbly to God. The choir is a vocal instrument that supports the congregation in a way that is similar to the organ or piano, which provides a singing environment. Where a choir exists, the question of musical leadership is easily answered. Where a choir does not exist, the need for solid musical leadership from the accompanist (organ/piano) and a song leader is essential. The congregation then becomes the visible and audible choir in worship.

THE SONG LEADER

The presence of a song leader is still somewhat uncommon in the worship leadership in many regions of The United Methodist Church. We often think of a song leader as someone who stands and conducts the congregation while singing through a pasted smile. A true song leader is one who is in charge of the congregational singing. Quite often, the music director of a church is the song leader by virtue of her or his understanding of music and desire to lead singing. This person has input into what hymns will be sung, how many stanzas, and what style (meditative, upbeat, and so forth).

The role of the song leader is to be the congregation's musical facilitator, providing cues for singing while not becoming the focus of the song. A song leader is the "choir director" for the congregation, and is essential in situations where a formal choir does not exist.

Each one of these music leaders can help the congregation sing. When one leader is absent, the others need to compensate. The success of good congregational singing lies not in the choir alone, or the accompaniment alone, but in the overall leadership and vision of corporate music. Worship leaders should focus on what they have, not on what they don't have.

GUIDELINES FOR GETTING ALONG WITHOUT A CHOIR

Where a choir does not exist, the congregation (or groups within it) becomes the choir. Below are specific guidelines for helping a congregation's song leader (and other worship leaders) turn the congregation into a choir, develop short-term choirs, and find the resources to nurture new music leadership in the congregation.

THE CONGREGATION AS CHOIR

When congregations without a choir gather for worship—be it on Sunday mornings, Saturdays, or Wednesday evenings—the gatherings consist of rehearsal time as well as worship time. It is important to manage the rehearsal time properly. Consider these suggestions:

Find an appropriate rehearsal time, such as during the gathering time (before or after the announcements) to rehearse with the congregation the hymns and service music to be sung during the worship service. Use this time wisely. The accompanist and song leader should have a clear understanding of what is to be accomplished in the few minutes and must work together to achieve it. The rehearsal may begin with a historical sketch of the hymn, followed by a silent or oral reading of the hymn text as the accompanist plays the melody. The song leader may then sing a stanza alone or invite the congregation to hum along. A hymn with some difficult rhythms may be spoken in rhythm or clapped before trying to sing it. The song leader may share with the congregation a unique feature from each of the hymns being taught. This gives the people a deeper relationship to the music or text and a willingness to learn to sing it. Next, the song leader leads the people in singing a stanza, not the whole hymn, which comes later in the service. It is important to give positive reinforcement, such as, "Hey, that was great!" or, "You picked that up quickly!" If necessary, the stanza could be repeated; however, the rehearsal should not exceed five minutes. The song leader should have a goal in mind for how well a congregation should sing the new song or hymn. It is appropriate to set high expectations and to challenge the congregation to reach them.

Develop "singspiration" Sundays, on which the congregation gets to sing favorites and can truly experience the sound and sense of their uplifted voices. A variation on this is to have singspiration sing-alongs as the gathering music each Sunday or on special Sundays, such as Communion Sunday. This is a great way for the congregation to warm up their voices and focus on praising God from the moment they walk in the sanctuary.

> The success
> of good
> congregational
> singing lies...
> in the overall
> leadership
> and vision of
> corporate music.

SHORT-TERM CHOIRS

A different way to develop musical leadership is to use existing groups—Sunday school classes, Emmaus reunion groups, or even committees—and to encourage these groups to form an ad hoc choir to share music in worship. Groups that already meet regularly can easily make a short-term commitment to enhance the music ministry of the church. Often, the thought of making a long-term commitment, with rehearsal each Wednesday or Thursday evening, keeps many good singers from joining a choir. For some people, rehearsing in the evening will be difficult, because they do not drive after sundown. For others, frequent travel due to jobs or family obligations keeps them from making long-term commitments. For people such as these, short-term choirs are ideal. Choir participants make a short-term commitment, such as the six weeks prior to Christmas or Easter. Quite often this six-week commitment becomes a habit and leads to a desire to make longer commitments! Once this happens, one has the seed for an ongoing choral group, even if only in segments of a few weeks.

Another approach for short-term choirs are family or intergenerational choirs. Ask a family to prepare music for worship once or twice a year. If several families are willing to do this, they can all meet once or twice for a mass rehearsal, creating an extraordinary choir!

While congregations may either create short-term choirs by using existing small groups in the congregation or help the congregation become the choir, a combination of both choices is clearly the ideal.

MUSIC LEADERSHIP

In a case where there is no pianist or organist, the congregation may want to invest in piano lessons for a church member who is willing to give of her or his talents in exchange for lessons. Where no musical leadership exists, a congregation should look at cultivating leadership. This is part of the mission of the church.

There are a variety of resources that can help to develop musical leadership in a congregation. Publications from Discipleship Resources and The United Methodist Publishing House have numerous ideas about creating a vision for music leadership, obtaining easy hymn-anthems, and recruiting a choir. One can also call area churches or friends in ministry for some ideas and success stories.

Another idea is to develop the musical leadership in the congregation by surveying the membership. The members are the worship leader's greatest resource—along with his or her imagination and ingenuity. The worship leader can ask members about favorite hymns and styles of worship; he or she can also outline the opportunities for members to share their musical talents.

CONCLUSION

Regardless of whether a congregation is small (with few musical resources) or large and seeking to provide musical leadership for a variety of worship services, the leadership resources for experiencing vital worship are within the congregation. All that is needed is the desire, the vision, and the impetus to make it happen.

FOR FURTHER READING

Grace Noted, by Jane Marshall (Carol Stream, IL: Hope Publishing Company, 1992).

Melodious Accord: Good Singing in Church, by Alice Parker (Chicago, IL: Liturgy Training Publications, 1991).

A congregation should look at cultivating leadership. This is part of the mission of the church.

19

How to Make the Offering a Vital Part of Worship

VON W. UNRUH

Pastor, Kingston Springs United Methodist Church, Kingston Springs, Tennessee

IN THE LITURGY OF A SERVICE OF WORD AND TABLE I, THE words that govern the "taking of the offering" suggest that "as forgiven and reconciled people," we are to "offer ourselves and our gifts to God" (*UMH*, p. 8).[1] While the suggestion is a wonderful invitation to participate fully in the joy of our faith, I suspect that this is not how most of us view this particular response of the people. Instead of experiencing it as a legitimate and vital act of God's people that brings glory to God, we are much more apt to endure the offering as a necessary, yet "secular," intrusion into our "spiritual" worship.

As long as we think of the offering as simply the time-honored way we collect the money necessary to pay the bills incurred by our local churches, we should not be too surprised by our embarrassment surrounding the act. Indeed, we ought to be honest enough to admit to ourselves that until we are willing to reconceptualize both the function and the purpose of the offering, it will never again become a vital part of worship. We might as well turn completely utilitarian, put a collection box in a prominent site in the narthex, and remind people in worship to be sure they deposit their checks before they head home.

These days, we may be stymied as to what to do with the offering, but that doesn't mean the practice cannot be redeemed. When God is involved, all things are possible, even things we consider impossible (Luke 18:27)! Perhaps the best way to start is to realize that our reductionistic approach to the offering is a far cry from the missional sense it is capable of bearing. Even a summary study of Scripture or a cursory reading of our tradition reveals clearly that the offering we make is to be more than just a tithe of our money to the church. It is to be the gift of ourselves to God (Romans 12:1), a significant venture of faith that places our lives willingly in the strong hand of God.

Historically, participation in the offering has been one of the ways in which both Israel and the church have acknowledged the sovereign and providential care of God. By practicing the stewardship of our possessions, both Jews and Christians have learned to imitate God's dominion over (stewardship of) our world (Genesis 1:26). Similarly, when it harvested its crops every year, ancient Israel practiced being prodigal like God by leaving plenty of food in the fields "for the poor and the alien" (Leviticus 19:9-10). In the early days of the church, believers simplified their lifestyles, sold what they possessed, and distributed the funds to those they knew to be in need (Acts 2:45; 4:34-35).

Worship Matters: A United Methodist Guide to Worship Work (Volume II) © 1999 Discipleship Resources. Used by permission.

Just as Israel's ritualized offering of its first fruits made a statement about its faithfulness to God, so our approach to the offering today says something about the generosity of our character. It reminds us (and proclaims to others) that we are not a self-made people, but remain a providentially cared-for people. Thus our decision in worship to offer a tithe places us in direct conflict with the ideologies of greed and gluttony that pervade our culture under the guise of a consumerist mentality. Despite our reduction of the offering to money we "collect," it remains one of the primary ways by which we can still bear witness to our belief that God cares for us daily (Matthew 6:11, 33-34), supplying all our needs in Christ Jesus (Philippians 4:19).

If we are serious about wanting to restore the offering to a meaningful place in our worship, we must be willing to do more than play beautiful music while the ushers collect the money. Because effective gimmicks do not excuse bad theology, we must realize once again that *our offering to Christ needs to have something to do with Christ's offering for us.* The vitality of the offering we give of ourselves will be in direct proportion to our willingness to become transformed worshipers, a people ready to "offer ourselves in praise and thanksgiving as a holy and living sacrifice, in union with Christ's offering for us" (*UMH*, p. 10).[2] To be sure, this work is primarily the work of God's Spirit in our lives, but it is also a work we must be humble enough to respond to with obedience. Insofar as we are serious about restoring the offering to its place as a vital act of Christian worship, we will want to mimic the generosity of our Christ, who did not cling to his equality with God, but became as we are (Philippians 2:6-7). As we learn to imitate Christ, the Spirit of God will help us to become a more generous people who are truly willing to be sent "into the world in the strength of [the] Spirit, to give ourselves for others" (*UMH*, p. 11).[3]

All this sounds well and good, of course, but the very idea that the offering can be a liturgically appropriate and theologically valid expression of our faith remains so foreign to most of us that we need help achieving this goal. Thanks be to God, then, that the ritual structure of the services of Word and Table already provides us with the help and the kind of powerful form necessary to promote generous and repentant lives that are grounded in Christian worship.

At present, the offering may seem like a necessary intrusion into our service of worship, but there are steps we can implement in the order of worship that will return our churches to this "new" understanding of the offering. To this end, I offer six basic, yet transforming, proposals that honor the pattern of the services of Word and Table. In addition, they are proposals that any church—large or small, rich or poor, urban or rural, traditional or contemporary—can implement immediately.

- Reclaim the offering as a response of the people.
- Reestablish the connections between our offering and the Lord's Supper.
- Replace the prayer of consecration with the prayer of (Great) Thanksgiving.
- Encourage the participation of children.
- Rethink the purpose of the annual stewardship campaign.
- Live the generosity that the offering symbolizes.

Our offering to Christ needs to have something to do with Christ's offering for us.

RECLAIM THE OFFERING AS A RESPONSE OF THE PEOPLE

First, we must allow the offering to become once again what it truly is supposed to be: a response of the people. This means that, among other things, it will need to occur *after* the proclamation of Scripture and sermon, not *before.* Otherwise, to what is our offering a response? In fact, in light of Matthew 5:23-24, the offering needs to occur after the confession/absolution and subsequent kiss of peace, for we cannot even begin to offer ourselves to God and others—with integrity—until we are first reconciled to our brothers and sisters (*UMH*, pp. 7–8).

As long as we continue to take up the offering prior to the sermon, it will in practice function as little more than a preliminary act of worship we can dispense with prior to hearing the sermon. But acts of worship, by definition, are never "acts" we can dispense with. They are offerings of ourselves to God, lived expressions of our adoration of God, and thus ways we practice incarnational service to our world.

Waiting to take up the offering until after we have heard the proclamation of the Word enables us to know how to respond more appropriately to God. To be sure, there will probably be people in our churches who will "give" on the basis of what they think they have "gotten" out of the sermon. But this is a risk worth taking. Helping our congregations understand that there are a variety of ways we can respond to the Word proclaimed—the offering of our money being just one among many—will ultimately enable their relationships with God to mature and deepen. As the generosity of our character expands, so will the generosity of our offering.

RECONNECT THE OFFERING TO HOLY EUCHARIST

Second, the offering we give needs to be both physically and spiritually reconnected to the Holy Meal we eat. Practically speaking, this requires that pastors and congregations follow the rubrics already printed in the *The United Methodist Hymnal,* which instruct us that "the bread and wine are brought by representatives of the people to the Lord's Table *with the other gifts*" (*UMH*, p. 8; emphasis added).[4] Of course, many of our churches do not yet celebrate Holy Eucharist on a weekly basis, which forces us to raise the important question, How can we ever hope to reconnect the offering to the Meal if we do not begin to celebrate the Meal regularly?

The simple answer is that we probably cannot. Nevertheless, we can take some incremental steps in that direction. For instance, on days when the Lord's Supper is celebrated, bring the bread and wine to the altar-table along with "the other gifts," the money collected by the ushers. In other words, inform the stewards (or whoever prepares the altar in your church) that the bread and wine should no longer be placed on the altar before worship begins. Instead, it should be placed on a table at the back of the church (or in the narthex), where it will remain until "the other gifts" of the congregation are brought forward by the ushers. As members of the congregation see the bread and wine brought forward at the same time as the money that has been collected, they will intuitively begin to make the connection in their own minds between these two offerings.

Like the elements of the Meal, the empty offering plates should be placed at the back of the church at the beginning of worship, to be brought forward and placed on the altar only when they are full of the gifts we have given. Practically speaking, the altar-table should at no time be used as a storage site. Theologically speaking, no one in the church should ever place empty vessels on the altar. Why? On the altar, we place the gifts of our lives. At the altar, we receive from Christ the gift of his life.

To maintain the liturgical connection between the offering and the Meal on Sundays when the Eucharist is not celebrated, institute a missional drive to collect canned food that can be brought to the Table every Sunday along with the money collected. If adopted by our churches, this project will encourage people to think about mission (that is, going into the world) at the same time that they give their monetary gifts. In addition, if a large enough number of people in the congregation bring food, it will eventually become impossible for the ushers to carry it by themselves to the altar along with the offering plates. Thus, each person will find it necessary to carry forward the offering of food, an act that will (1) reinforce the notion that our offering is really an *act* of worship and (2) make it clear that our offering is not intended merely to pay bills we have incurred already, but is one of the ways we truly become the life-giving church in our life-denying world.

PRAY THE PRAYER OF (GREAT) THANKSGIVING

Third, we should stop offering a prayer of consecration prior to the taking of the offering. These prayers typically end up being little more than not-very-discrete reminders that we have reached that part of our worship when we are now supposed to reach into our pockets and pay an appropriate admission fee. The only prayer that we need to pray in regard to the offering is a prayer of thanksgiving, which should be prayed *after* the offering is brought to the altar, not *before*.

Of course, if our churches are celebrating Holy Eucharist every week, we will recognize immediately that this prayer of thanksgiving is, in fact, the Great Thanksgiving. If we are not celebrating the Eucharist weekly, we should notice once again how central the Meal is to making the offering vital. To bear witness to this connection, do as a friend of mine does: Use a shortened version of the Great Thanksgiving as the prayer of thanks every week. This act will reinforce the connection between our offering and the Meal and will continue the process of familiarizing our congregations to the words of the Great Thanksgiving—ultimately facilitating the process of increasing the frequency of sharing the Meal.[5]

ENCOURAGE CHILDREN TO PARTICIPATE IN THE OFFERING

Fourth, we can teach our children the importance of the offering we make of ourselves in worship by participating regularly in the various responsive offerings available to us each week. By always putting some money in the offering plate, we can encourage our children to follow our example, especially if we have prepared them ahead of time at home by helping them figure the tithe on their money. Similarly, when we bring a couple cans of food to place on the altar, we can invite our children to do the same. By eating the Meal of our Lord every chance we get and listening intently to the reading of Scripture and the sermon, we model the importance of these acts for our faith development. Whenever we sing the hymns with feeling and joy and pray with anticipation, our attitude becomes infectious and the joy of generosity fills our being.

A Prayer of Thanksgiving When Holy Communion Is Not Celebrated

All things come from you, O God, and with praise and thanksgiving we return to you what is yours.

You created all that is, and lovingly formed us in your image.

When our love failed, your love remained steadfast.

You gave your only Son Jesus Christ to be our Savior, that we might have abundant and eternal life.

All that we are, and all that we have, is a trust from you.

And so, in gratitude for all that you have done, we offer you ourselves and all that we have, in union with Christ's offering for us.

By your Holy Spirit make us one with Christ, one with one another, and one in ministry to all the world; through Jesus Christ our Lord. *Amen*.[6]

Since all social divisions in the church have been overcome in Christ (Galatians 3:28), there is no valid reason why the children in our churches cannot help take up the offering and the food we collect weekly. Indeed, they have as many gifts to offer to God as do the adults in our churches (1 Corinthians 12). We can invite children to serve as ushers alongside their parents, help the financial secretary count the monetary offering given each Sunday, and assist in bringing forward the elements of the bread and wine on Communion Sundays. As Scripture reminds us: "A little child shall lead [us]" (Isaiah 11:6); why not allow our children the wonderful privilege of leading us to the Table? In my church, children as young as three or four assist with the distribution of the elements—and do so with both dignity and joy! Already, they are learning to practice the kind of offering of themselves that we adults are still learning to make of ourselves!

RETHINK THE PURPOSE OF THE ANNUAL STEWARDSHIP CAMPAIGN

Fifth, we need to trust God enough to be willing to rethink our present approach to the annual stewardship campaign. It is quite appropriate for the church to encourage, even to expect, its members to finance the work of the church; but when the stewardship campaign is too narrowly focused simply on raising more money this year than last "to pay the preacher and the light bill," that is probably all it will raise. But as we have begun to see already, the offering is not so much about the money we raise as it is about the kind of character that develops in our congregations. Here is where a renewed understanding of the inner connections between the offering and our faith development is crucial. After all, where is the missional emphasis in a budget designed primarily to pay salaries and bills?

Instead of becoming more adept at the secular pursuit of fundraising, we need immediately to broaden our understanding of stewardship to include once again our prayers, presence, and service, too. To that end, stewardship forms should begin using covenantal, rather than contractual, language. Instead of compiling information about the vocational skills and work interests of our congregation, let's teach people to reflect upon their spiritual gifts, discerning what these are *and* how they intend to use them. And while we're at it, let's break the bad habit of asking for volunteers to do this or that project, and learn all over again how to extend a call to which faithful disciples can *offer* the obedient response of their lives.

Of course, on a practical level, if we really expect people to respond prayerfully to the stewardship forms we distribute, we cannot pass these out at the beginning of worship and then expect them to be turned in when the offering is collected. When we ask people to consider something prayerfully, but do not give them time to pray, we trivialize the very act of prayer. Indeed, we discourage people from acting with holy integrity. Offering the time of their lives is *not* something we want people making snap decisions about.

LIVE THE GENEROSITY WE ARE TALKING ABOUT

Finally, if the offering we make to God in worship is to have any vital connection to the self-offering God has made to us in Christ, then we must be willing to do the hard work necessary to embrace lifestyles of generosity like that displayed by Christ. Most of us have been trained all our lives by experts in the fine art of greed we call consumerism. We hardly know any other way to live. No wonder the ritualized vitality of the offering we give to Christ in our worship right now appears to us to lack vitality. It appears that way because we have become that way ourselves!

So, let's simply admit that the only way we are going to revitalize the offering is to move the church away from a money-based approach. That's why the underlying impetus of this entire article has been a plea for the church to stop playing around with gimmicks and get down to the hard work of conversion. For whether we reconnect the offering to Holy Eucharist, scrap the stewardship campaign, or encourage the participation of children is finally pointless if we don't at some point along the way become different ourselves. Or to say it a bit more plainly, there is no way the offering is going to be revitalized if all we do is tinker with the liturgical machinery. Or to say it even more plainly, the reason the offering is not more vital than it is has very little to do with the problems noted in the previous subsections of this article and everything to do with the kind of people we are.

It is time, then, to become a more generous people ourselves. The only way to do this is to learn some new habits from the faithful mentors in our midst. My parents, for instance, never forced me to give of either my time or money to the church when I was a child. They taught me how to give *by showing me how to live*, modeling for me a lifestyle of generosity. They lived simply, gave generously, loved prodigally. They taught me that loving God with my whole heart was a goal worthy of my devotion.

CONCLUSION

If worship truly matters—as we are claiming it does—then worship leaders need to be intentional when explaining what is happening in the liturgical forms that structure the worship we offer to God. However, the time for explanation is *not* in the midst of worship on Sunday mornings. Nothing puts a damper on the liturgy any more quickly than a worship leader who habitually explains what we are doing and why we are doing it—before allowing us actually to do it.

This is as true of the offering as it is of any other aspect of the liturgy. By all means, let's educate our congregations as to the vital role the offering can play in our worship, but let's do so one on one, or in small groups such as membership classes, confirmation classes, or Sunday school classes. Even church or administrative council meetings can provide an opportune time to discuss matters of worship. Indeed, if worship is to become once again the central priority of our churches, then the liturgical forms our offerings take ought to receive at least as much of our attention as the collection reports of the treasurer!

FOR FURTHER READING

A Peculiar People: The Church as Culture in a Post-Christian Society, by Rodney Clapp (Downers Grove, IL: InterVarsity Press, 1996).

For All God's Worth: True Worship and the Calling of the Church, by N. T. Wright (Grand Rapids, MI: William B. Eerdmans Publishing Company, 1997).

Reaching Out Without Dumbing Down: A Theology of Worship for the Turn-of-the-Century Culture, by Marva J. Dawn (Grand Rapids, MI: William B. Eerdmans Publishing Company, 1995).

We need immediately to broaden our understanding of stewardship to include once again our prayers, presence, and service.

Rediscovering Our Spiritual Gifts, Revised Edition, by Charles V. Bryant (Nashville, TN: Upper Room Books, 1991).

Selling Jesus: What's Wrong With Marketing the Church, by Douglas D. Webster (Downers Grove, IL: InterVarsity Press, 1993).

Selling Out the Church: The Dangers of Church Marketing, by Philip D. Kenneson, James L. Street, and Stanley Hauerwas (Nashville, TN: Abingdon Press, 1997).

ENDNOTES

1 From "A Service of Word and Table I," copyright © 1972, 1980, 1985, 1989 by The United Methodist Publishing House; from *The United Methodist Hymnal,* p. 8. Used by permission.

2 From "A Service of Word and Table I," copyright © 1972, 1980, 1985, 1989 by The United Methodist Publishing House; from *The United Methodist Hymnal,* p. 10. Used by permission.

3 From "A Service of Word and Table I," copyright © 1972, 1980, 1985, 1989 by The United Methodist Publishing House; from *The United Methodist Hymnal,* p. 11. Used by permission.

4 From "A Service of Word and Table I," copyright © 1972, 1980, 1985, 1989 by The United Methodist Publishing House; from *The United Methodist Hymnal,* p. 8. Used by permission.

5 See "Celebrating the Eucharist More Vitally and More Frequently," on pages 58–62 in Volume I of *Worship Matters.*

6 From *Worship Resources of The United Methodist Hymnal,* edited by Hoyt L. Hickman (Nashville, TN: Abingdon Press, 1989), p. 51.

How to Worship in Small-Membership Congregations

JULIA KUHN WALLACE

Director, Small-Membership Church and Shared Ministries, The General Board of Discipleship, Nashville, Tennessee

T HIS ARTICLE IS DESIGNED TO GIVE PRACTICAL IDEAS AND suggestions for celebrating the type of vital worship that is central to the life of the congregation. Worship in the small-membership congregation is the gathering of the family of faith to praise God—simply and honestly. Worship is not performance; it is the presence and a shared experience of the risen Lord. With this understanding in mind, let us examine worship in the small-membership congregation.

ANATOMY OF THE SMALL-MEMBERSHIP CONGREGATION

It is not always easy to understand the small-membership congregation, but it is possible to appreciate it and build on its uniqueness. In fact, the key to having vital worship in the context of the small-membership congregation is to know the three S's: *size, spirituality*, and *setting*.

SIZE

Let us consider size first. A small-membership congregation is more than numbers, but size counts. A small congregation is one that has fewer than 200 members (or fewer than 150 in worship). Actually, the small-membership congregation has two categories, each with its own distinct characteristics.

The *Family Church* has fewer than 60 worshiping members. It resembles a family, with a strong layperson providing leadership—a man or woman to whom the church looks for leadership. The pastor in this church functions as a chaplain who preaches, celebrates the sacraments, and officiates at marriages and funerals. Key decisions are made by the laypeople. A "bridge builder" introduces visitors to the congregation and eventually shares the church's history and tradition. When a newcomer joins the church, it usually takes a while for him or her to be adopted into the family and to be invited to share leadership and gifts. The congregation's leadership structure is small, and individuals often work on more than one specific task or area of ministry.

Worship Matters: A United Methodist Guide to Worship Work (Volume II) © 1999 Discipleship Resources. Used by permission.

The Family Church may be leery (even weary) of change. It is usually easier to focus on conserving what has been than to experiment with what could be. Change means conflict, which may mean losing people that one cannot afford to alienate. New ideas need to be introduced patiently and tested with key leaders. To make accepting them easier, new ideas need to be shaped by the past (traditions, values, and so forth) and guided by the hopes and gifts of people in the church today (pastor, leaders, and all members—even the newer ones).

The *Pastoral Church* has from 60 to 150 members in worship. In this size congregation, clergy are at the center, relating to different key leaders and groups—Sunday school classes, choir, and so forth. The pastor is expected to be at all meetings and to have a key role in decision-making. There is strong lay leadership, but power is diffused (or shared among key laity). Change is easier in the Pastoral Church than in the Family Church; however, change is sometimes resisted until the impact and opinions of key people surface. The members of the church value knowing one another. Churchwide activities exist (especially fellowship), but people gain a sense of belonging primarily in smaller groups. It is possible to have committees or leadership teams in this congregation.

Both the Family Church and the Pastoral Church tend to be people-focused. It is often difficult to draw up a vision statement or long-range planning guide that these congregations will actually follow. Small-membership congregations operate according to seasons and traditions, and to go by what people feel and think.

SPIRITUALITY

Another way to define the small-membership congregation is in terms of its *spiritual culture*. It is extremely helpful for a pastor to learn the congregation's shaping stories, traditions, culture, and honored methods for helping people grow spiritually. Some congregations favor revivals, altar calls, private and/or silent prayer time, and open sharing. One way to learn about the congregation's spirituality is to have a few people mark in the hymnal the hymns that the church knows and then to listen to the powerful stories associated with these hymns. Another way is to look at the congregation's worship bulletins over the last three to five years and to ask the question, Does our style of worship appeal to all the different generations who come here seeking to grow closer to God?

SETTING

The last way to define the small-membership congregation is *setting*. Here a few well-placed questions can help in understanding the setting of the small-membership congregation:

- Is the congregation new and growing?
- Is it adventurous and still forming its traditions?
- How open is it to trying new things?
- Is the congregation older? declining? stable?
- Where is the church located? In a rural area? suburban or urban setting?
- Who lives in the surrounding area?
- How does the church define community?
- How does the anatomy of the small-membership congregation outlined above relate to worship?

At least the following implications are clear: A pastor in a Family Church needs to consult with or involve the key layperson in any change or planning for worship. In a Pastoral Church, the pastor can work through a worship team or committee, even as people outside the group are also involved in key decisions.

THE IMPORTANCE OF WORSHIP IN THE SMALL-MEMBERSHIP CONGREGATION

Remember that the small-membership congregation pursues the same mission as the rest of the church: to make Christian disciples. Therefore, the means of grace—worship, reading Scripture, celebrating baptism and Communion, prayer, Bible study, fasting and abstinence, small-group participation, Christian conferencing, acts of mercy—as well as litanies, prayers of the people, and hymns are interwoven in the very fabric of a small-membership congregation's life together. It is in these experiences that vital worship and new life are found.

The best worship experiences in a small-membership congregation weave together the various facets of the congregation's life. The people who are in the pew on Sunday are the same ones who attend the administrative council meeting on Monday night, visit a sick neighbor on Tuesday, attend the Bible study on Wednesday, clean the church building on Thursday, work in the soup kitchen on Friday, and mow their lawns and do their laundry on Saturday. In a healthy small-membership congregation, the entire week is brought into focus during worship—it becomes the people's reason for being. (In a small-membership congregation, *being* is usually more important than *doing*.)

This connection between worship and daily life was brought home to me vividly through the experience of flying. To mask my fear of flying, I used to make a game out of flying in an airplane. As the plane would take off, I'd try to locate my church from the air. One time, I couldn't do it. I could see the State Capital where Jimmy worked, the elementary school where Mary taught, the newspaper office where Owen wrote, the house where Jean lived, but no steeple. Suddenly it hit me: I *did* see the church, only it was the church visible and present in everyday life. When we gather to worship on Sunday, it empowers us to move outward into the world as a renewed people to be about the business of making disciples even as we strive to live as disciples.

Despite the small numbers that gather, small-membership congregations represent the majority of congregations in Protestant denominations. But numbers can be deceiving. Large churches may offer more activities, but one should not disregard the deep level of caring and supportive relationships that happen in a small-membership congregation. Thus, it is easy to confuse quantity with quality in the small-membership congregation. The number of worshipers in the pews does not reflect the total number of people connected to the church. There are networks in a small-membership congregation that move out beyond the actual membership. We often fail to see the communion of saints that gather with the congregation in worship. These are men and women who were once a living part of the congregation and live on in people's hearts. People in the pews remember Aunt Massie and the West sisters long after they are no longer present in Sunday morning worship. There are also family connections that extend beyond the sanctuary to unchurched friends and to people who are limited in their ability to leave home. Each person sitting in a pew on Sunday carries the

Effective and faithful worship has nothing to do with the size of the congregation.

hurts and hopes of the people he or she lives with, works with, and learns with—it is the way things are in the small-membership congregation.

The small-membership congregation may not have the liturgical resources and leadership available for worship that larger churches have. But they do not have to compete! The small-membership congregation that tries to act like a big one will not only feel inferior but will also fail. Effective and faithful worship has nothing to do with the size of the congregation. Indeed, the small-membership congregation has a simplicity that is appealing in this high-tech, low-touch world. In the small-membership congregation, everyone has a place and a part in the worship service. Some prepare the worship space; others hand out bulletins or greet people as they arrive. Still others arrange the flowers, read the Scripture, share a children's message, or bake the bread for Communion.

VITAL WORSHIP IN THE SMALL-MEMBERSHIP CONGREGATION

Vital, meaningful worship in the small-membership congregation requires attention to two factors: *intimacy* and *involvement*.

INTIMACY

The small-membership congregation worships relationally. One of the strengths of the small-membership congregation is the family atmosphere, where everyone is important, needed, and wanted. Worship in the small-membership congregation is like a family reunion: News is exchanged, people are remembered, stories are told, new members are welcomed, departed people are mourned, and vital customs and rituals are observed. Such intimacy is displayed in a variety of ways: the usher who knows where every worshiper sits on Sunday morning; or the person who taps me on the shoulder, saying, "Julia, you left your car lights on."

In the small-membership congregation, everything depends on relationships. People connect with one another and interact as reminders of God's grace in their midst. A depth of caring surrounds the worshiper in a small-membership congregation. The congregation celebrates being the people of God by honoring each person and her or his place in the kingdom of God. People of all ages are accepted and differences are forgotten. A young person can read the Scripture; an older member can light the candles.

This strong family closeness extends into the congregation's prayer life. Sometimes it is shown in the humble request of a farmer asking those gathered to remember in prayer the delay in planting because of the heavy rain. Sometimes during the passing of the peace, a young couple ask the congregation to pray for their troubled marriage. In the small-membership congregation, these moments are sacred. They imply a profound level of trust and an intimate connection of life with the holy.

Sometimes the small-membership congregation can seem informal or even spontaneous in the nature of its worship. This is an advantage because people in these congregations want worship to be inviting and accepting of people and also open to the Spirit. Of course, there are also small-membership congregations that are more formal in their style of worship. However, these churches succeed because they respect the congregation's need for connection. In the small-membership congregation, it is not the style of worship that matters, but rather what worship says about the congregation's understanding of God, community, and its core values.

INVOLVEMENT

Worship in the small-membership congregation is more like a folk dance than a carefully choreographed ballet. Each person participates with his or her own personality and gifts. Moving with others in a spiritual dance as the people of God, small-membership congregations praise the Holy One, who creates, redeems, and sustains them.

In the small-membership congregation, everyone participates; there are no passive observers. The limited number of people and resources available makes it imperative for people to help one another discover their God-given gifts and use these in the community (both in the church and outside). Larry now serves as an usher because a long-time member noticed how well he greeted people when he entered the sanctuary. Larry says that had he stayed in a larger church, he may never have been noticed and asked to serve in this meaningful way. He claims hospitality as his spiritual gift. If liturgy is truly the work of the people, then it makes sense that worship in the small-membership congregation should seek to involve as many people as possible.

There are many ways to involve people in worship. Someone who is artistically gifted can draw a bulletin cover, construct a banner, make a stole or paraments, or design chrismons. People who enjoy acting can produce a drama. If there is a dancer in the congregation, he or she can be invited to interpret a passage of Scripture or a hymn through sacred movement.

Small-membership congregations sometimes reach beyond their membership to connect with a need or celebration in the community. This happens when civic leaders from outside the church (the sheriff, doctor, postal worker, or healthcare nurse) are invited and recognized for their service in the community at a special celebration. During times of crisis or tragedy, the small-membership congregation is able to bring people together for healing and hope.

PLANNING WORSHIP IN THE SMALL-MEMBERSHIP CONGREGATION

As in churches of any size, worship in the small-membership congregation must be planned with care. Consider the following guidelines for planning vital worship in your small-membership congregation.

1. *Begin with the worship setting.* The condition, design, and decoration of the worship space say a lot about the possibilities for renovation and improvement. Does the worship setting look drab, or does it "shine"? Are the symbols living symbols of faith, or do they represent days gone by? Is the room light or dark? How comfortable are the pews? Are contributions from the current generation prominently displayed, or are only accomplishments of the past honored? Does the worship environment say to a visitor, "Welcome"?

These questions may be hard for small-membership congregations to answer. They may have lived with the same worship space for so long that they have become blind to its need for improvement. Church members don't notice the cobwebs on the light fixtures anymore; nor do they see the peeling paint in the narthex.

To learn more about how the congregation understands its worship life, take a walk around the sanctuary with a group of members. Ask people what they see. Inquire about the meaning of pictures or items and the significance of their placement. Find out where people sit and why. Ask what is valued, by whom, and what can be improved. The

It is not the style of worship that matters, but rather what worship says about the congregation's understanding of God, community, and its core values.

goal is not to completely remodel the sanctuary, but to appreciate the worship setting and find ways to renovate it economically, if necessary. Sometimes a fresh, lighter coat of paint does wonders. Pulling up frayed carpet, sanding splintering pews, polishing brass, or adding a banner or two helps immensely.

2. *Plan special worship services in advance.* The small-membership congregation tends to be event oriented. Rather than trying to celebrate the whole season of Advent, it may be easier to plan celebrations that have special meaning for the congregation, such as a special candlelight service or an annual Christmas Eve celebration. If the congregation does celebrate the liturgical seasons, find out how much time is required to prepare adequately for the upcoming season. Some churches meet quarterly to look at what is ahead. Scheduling a specific amount of time for planning is more important than the length of time itself. Poor planning leads to poor preparation and low participation. Always involve laypeople in planning!

3. *Make minor changes before tackling major problems.* Remember to make small but significant steps! Some innovations in worship can be done simply because of who is doing them. Sometimes it is the little things in a small-membership congregation that make the biggest difference. Here are a few ideas:

• During the gathering time in worship, make sure that all people are welcomed warmly. This sets the stage for whatever else happens. Recognize by name the man who is back in church after recovering from surgery; announce the name of the new baby born to a young couple present; sing a birthday song to a member. Some churches make their announcements during the gathering. Others have a "Mission Moment" in which to talk about how the church has been in ministry during the past week, or will be soon. A Mission Moment may involve a brief statement about feeding the homeless, vacation Bible school, collecting baby quilts for the battered women's shelter, or commissioning people going on a mission trip. Encourage worshipers to make the passing of the peace a meaningful time of connecting with and supporting one another (other than exchanging pleasantries). Invite a layperson to pray an invocation; this signals the continuation of worship as the people gather.

• Examine the content of the sermon carefully. Most people in small-membership congregations tend to think in concrete, relational terms.[1] Therefore, sermon illustrations should relate to the people's experience. The sermon itself may take the form of a shared message, a dialogue, or a story narrated by different people. It is quite acceptable to involve people in the sermon. Consider the following options as variations upon the "standard" sermon:

—Use an object lesson, especially an object that is a part of the congregation's culture. (Jesus did this with the mustard seed, remember?)

—Have a question-and-answer session that relates to the Scripture reading. Invite questions or even doubts raised by members of the congregation, and seek the answer together.

—Ask a member of the congregation to give a testimony (or witness) in response to the Gospel reading for the day or the message of the Gospel.

—Interview members of the congregation on a specific topic. As the sermon, have a conversation with one or two people around a specific focus relating to the Scripture reading for the day. (Give individuals advance notice of the question or focus. Be specific in what you are asking them to share and how much time is available.)

—Use gifts of people to assist in presenting the sermon. For example, a photographer can illustrate the Scripture reading with slides; a dancer can interpret the Bible text with sacred movement; a potter may shape clay on a wheel as you preach on spiritual formation.

- Allow prayer to be a time in which the whole worshiping congregation participates. Pause to hear the joys and concerns or prayers of the gathered community. Pray for the ministry of the congregation and those involved—even for yourself! Pray for those in the community who do not know Christ. Remember to recognize unspoken prayer requests.

- Continually assess and evaluate the worship experience of the congregation. Occasionally, the small-membership congregation should look at how and why it worships, asking: "What are the traditions we value?" "Why are they important to us?" "How do we start new traditions?" "Are people motivated and energized during worship? Are people engaged in the movement of the service?" Evaluate carefully the responses to these questions in order to consider new possibilities.

- Involve others in planning and leading worship, considering the following possibilities:

—Use Bible study as a worship-planning activity. If the congregation meets regularly during the week for fellowship and study, it could look at the next Sunday's lectionary readings (or the Scripture passage the pastor chooses). Small groups could paraphrase the text, write a prayer, or even select hymns.

—Provide opportunities to talk about worship or a particular sermon series. This can be an informative and formative time for those who want to talk about the worship experience or their response to God's call on their lives.

—Hold a four- to six-week class to study worship. Invite laypeople to be teaching partners. Consider having a youth or children's service.

—Train laypeople as worship leaders. Recruit people to read Scripture, prepare the elements for Holy Communion, light candles, greet, and so forth. Always offer training.

IMPROVING THE QUALITY OF WORSHIP

In the small-membership congregation, the quality of worship depends on intimacy and involvement. Therefore, it is important to personally recruit people to help plan worship. In deciding when to meet for planning, the pastor should respect the calendars of the people he or she serves. In a rural setting, for example, the meeting should not be scheduled during busy planting and harvesting times.

The planning team may initially consist of only a small core of respected laity. Some of these people may be the people who lead the music, prepare the altar, or serve as head usher. It is important to include recent members as well as people of a variety of age groups. Before the group gets down to the work of planning, they should spend time praying and getting to know one another. Team spirit is important.

Key leaders in the congregation should be aware in advance what the worship team is planning. A member of the worship team could share the team's ideas at a church or administrative council meeting, listening to council members' questions and taking their concerns seriously. Patience and perseverance are important. Clear communication is essential.

Sometimes it is the little things in a small-membership congregation that make the biggest difference.

It is possible to make a change in the way a group worships, especially if the change is well-thought-out and the people are given time to understand it. Despite possible tension, the easiest place to implement change may be in the congregation's music (especially if new hymns are chosen and taught with faith experiences in mind). Change should always be done with care, since favorite hymns often have a great deal of sentimental value. The hymns that are chosen should fit the theme and mood for worship, but should also respect the feelings and history of the people in the congregation. Changes in the worship life of the small-membership congregation are possible only when the people are confident that a change respects the culture and rich heritage of the congregation.

The first thing a new pastor should do is to ask the lay leader to take a hymnal and mark in pencil each hymn the congregation knows, and then to pass the hymnal around to other key leaders. Each of these leaders should write where she or he learned a particular hymn, or why the hymn is important. The marked hymnal could eventually be circulated to newer members to mark their favorite selections and record remarks in the margin of the text. The pastor can then use the remarks to introduce the hymn in worship.

It is helpful to schedule learning new hymns in the formative times of the year. These times include liturgical holy days, such as Christmas and Easter, as well as special celebrations in the life of the church, such as homecoming and revival. People should have the opportunity two or three times during the year to choose hymns in the worship service and to tell where they learned the hymn and why it is important to them. Also, on occasion, hymns can be sung *a cappella.* Men and women can be invited to sing different stanzas of the hymn; or the choir and congregation can echo each other in singing. Where there is no choir, the congregation can serve in this role. Organizing special musical groups— a children's choir, short-term or seasonal choir, family choir, or men's chorus—to sing for special celebrations is very effective.[2] On occasion, a special guest singer, or a small choir or quartet from another church, could be invited to sing in worship.

Don't forget that not all music needs to be sung. Instrumental music provided by a piano, guitar, or hammer dulcimer can be just as effective as a four-part choir! *The United Methodist Hymnal on CD: Accompaniment Edition,* which contains piano and organ accompaniment for all hymns in the *Hymnal,* can be effective. God listens to all types of music and instruments.

Creativity in worship is possible in the small-membership congregation. If done in the right way, liturgical and annual seasons and holidays especially lend themselves to trying new traditions and ideas. In planning new, creative ways to worship, it is crucial to involve a variety of church members. Consider the following guidelines and suggestions:

• Gather a group to study the Scripture and other worship resources. Invite members of the group to help write prayers, to write alternate lyrics to a hymn, or to prepare a drama.

• Prepare the congregation sensitively. Give advanced notice of the special service, as well as the time and the reasons for the service.

• After the experience, provide worshipers and the planning team with an opportunity to reflect on the experience and to learn from it: What went well? What could have been done better? What should have been left out?

Small-membership congregations can also plan worship services that go beyond the traditional Sunday worship service. Such services should fit the location and needs of a particular congregation and community. Here are some examples:

- A congregation in a rural setting can plan a fall harvest service to honor God's goodness, while affirming their role as stewards of the environment.
- A suburban congregation can host a "Parents' Blessing" service that recognizes new parents who have had a baby in the last year. This celebration of new birth is an opportunity for a congregation to listen to new parents and their concerns and joys, then offer guidance and support for raising children spiritually in the community.
- A congregation in an urban setting may have a "Shalom in the City" worship service in response to a community cause or crisis. This service may take the form of a candlelight vigil, honoring those who live and work in the midst of the situation (civic, community, and church leadership).
- "Shared Ministries" can bring together in worship a number of congregations that share a special relationship—cooperative parishes, yoked or federated parishes, clusters, or even a shared focus. This can be done annually (for example, at charge conference) or during special occasions. A church that works in partnership with an agency or organization (such as United Way or the Boy or Girl Scouts) may join for worship in which people give thanks for the positive difference the partnership is making in their community.

CELEBRATING THE SACRAMENTS

Baptism is the moment in a small-membership congregation where hope blossoms. It is a reminder that God loves us, regardless of age or maturity; and that God loves the congregation, regardless of size. Baptism brings a sense of hope for the future. The baptismal vows, lighting a Christ candle during the baptismal service, giving a hand-smocked cap to the baby, or having a reception after worship to welcome the family are symbols of an ongoing relationship. For a congregation that does not celebrate baptism often, a service for congregational reaffirmation of the Baptismal Covenant (*UMH*, pp. 50–53) can be a vivid reminder of God's grace and goodness.

Holy Communion is a remembrance of Christ's life, death, and resurrection. It reminds the congregation of their oneness in the body of Christ. Both the preparation for and celebration of Holy Communion can be a special time in the small-membership congregation. Different people or groups—a children's Sunday school class, a new member, a woman's prayer group, a young family, even the men's prayer-breakfast group—could be invited to bake the bread for Communion. Preparing bread together provides an opportunity to talk about the meaning of the sacrament, both for the congregation as a whole and for individuals. It can also be a time for sharing faith stories.

CONCLUSION

Worship is at the heart of the small-membership congregation. Worship that builds intentionally on the intimacy and involvement of people helps provide vital and living experiences, as well as shaping the faith

Small-membership congregations can also plan worship services that go beyond the traditional Sunday worship service.

community. Worship leaders can develop or enhance the current style of worship so that it is sensitive to the people who worship as well as to the purpose and vision of the congregation. By doing this, not only will the worship be dynamic, but the congregation will be also.

FOR FURTHER READING

O For a Dozen Tongues to Sing: Music Ministry With Small Choirs, by Deborah K. Cronin (Nashville, TN: Abingdon Press, 1996).

Preaching and Worship in the Small Church, by William H. Willimon and Robert L. Wilson (Nashville, TN: Abingdon Press, 1980).

Small Churches Can Make a Big Difference!: A Resource for Small-Membership Church Leaders, videocassette and guide (Nashville, TN: Discipleship Resources, 1998). To order this videocassette, call: 800-685-4370.

ENDNOTES

1 See "How to Plan Worship in an Oral Context," on pages 172–76 in this volume.

2 See "How to Get Along Without a Choir," on pages 142–47 in this volume.

How to Worship in Multicultural Congregations

DAVID H. MARCELO

Pastor of the Filipino Congregation, Wilshire United Methodist Church, Los Angeles, California

A MULTICULTURAL WORSHIP SERVICE IS A COMBINATION OF different languages, features, symbolisms, and cultural distinctives. One chief characteristic of multicultural worship is variety—of music, format, participants, style, visuals, and languages. Variety is unavoidable, for there must be a mixture and a proper blending of these qualities in a worship experience that seeks to cater to people who come from various countries and cultural backgrounds.

As a pastor in a multicultural church, I am often asked these questions: Why do you have multicultural worship? How do you put together and conduct a multicultural worship service? How difficult or easy is it to plan, prepare, and conduct multicultural worship? This article explores these and other questions about multicultural worship.

WHY MULTICULTURAL WORSHIP?

A close look reveals that our world is becoming an increasingly interrelated community. Churches in metropolitan areas, especially, notice people from various countries and cultural backgrounds attending worship and becoming a part of the church community.

Immigration continues to increase. Immigrants come to our churches with something uniquely theirs: their culture. The common thinking is that immigrants should learn the ways and adapt to the culture of the country they immigrate to; however, this does not necessarily happen. Culture is an integral part of the life of an individual. Therefore, once immigrants become a part of a congregation, the congregation becomes multicultural (whether members recognize it or not).

When worship leaders accept the fact that many United Methodist congregations are fast becoming multicultural, they should want to become more inclusive in the formulation of worship experiences. Multicultural worship is the only alternative if a congregation wants to include immigrant people and their culture in its life. Multicultural worship is also an excellent opportunity for worshipers to bond together.

A positive trait of The United Methodist Church is its emphasis on inclusiveness. It makes a deliberate effort to recognize, affirm, and include in the life of the church people from every cultural background. This is definitely one positive way of embodying the gospel. Since

Worship Matters: A United Methodist Guide to Worship Work (Volume II) © 1999 Discipleship Resources. Used by permission.

worship is a vital part of a congregation's life, making the worship experience as multicultural as possible is not only right, it is also living out who we are called to be—God's people.

BASIC ELEMENTS OF MULTICULTURAL WORSHIP

Multicultural worship is hard but very rewarding work. To make successful multicultural worship happen, three basic elements require attention. They are language, cultural distinctives, and symbols and visuals. Without deviating from the guidelines of *The United Methodist Book of Worship*, it is possible to have a meaningful multicultural worship service simply by keeping these elements in mind. Let us look at each in turn.

LANGUAGE

Imagine worshiping in a foreign country in a language that is not your own. Your comfort level would certainly be very low. Now imagine worshiping in a setting where you can speak, or at least understand, the language. The comfort level will be higher. Last, imagine a worship setting in which your mother tongue is being used in small portions of the service. In this last scenario, you are likely to feel a deep sense of acceptance, and your comfort level will be much higher.

The first step to achieving a multicultural worship service, then, is to be as multilingual as possible. This is hard work. Providing translation is not simple, but the effort will make the service more meaningful to those worshipers whose native language is being spoken and heard.

CULTURAL DISTINCTIVES

Each culture has distinctive ways of doing things in worship. This could be anything from standing during Scripture readings to praying out loud during the time of prayer. In some cultures, standing up during the Scripture reading is very important as a gesture of reverence and respect. This may seem small and unimportant, but the inclusion of this small feature in a service gives it a touch of multiculturalism. People coming from a cultural background in which standing for the reading of Scripture is a feature of worship will feel affirmed and respected.

SYMBOLS AND VISUALS

Symbols and visuals include everything from flags to the kind of bread used for Holy Communion. I have observed that the hanging of flags can be a powerful means of showing respect and affirming the people the flags represent. Other symbols or visuals include the cross, banners, and pictures or objects that are distinctly important visuals or symbols for a specific cultural group.

With the three basic elements of multicultural worship in mind, let us explore in a step-by-step fashion how to put together a multicultural worship service. This process has worked well over the last few years in the multicultural context in which I minister.

CREATING MULTICULTURAL WORSHIP

Multicultural worship services do not just happen. A considerable amount of time and effort are needed to put together a successful and meaningful multicultural worship service. The process can be lengthy and tedious, but the rewards far outweigh the efforts.

STEP 1: FORM A COMMITTEE

The first step is to form a committee that will work on the service. Committee members should come from as many cultural and language backgrounds as possible. Bear in mind that the more languages one includes, the more work there will be for all members of the committee; but it will be a rewarding experience.

Each member of the committee must share the vision of being inclusive. Each must be sensitive to the needs and preferences of the other cultural groups represented. A coordinator should be appointed whose task it is to head up the entire process, from the preparation stage to the actual worship service.

STEP 2: GATHER IDEAS

Using the *Book of Worship* as the basic guideline, the coordinator asks each committee member to offer insights about how the kind of worship service the committee is planning is conducted in his or her culture. The member describes the entire worship service—the format, the music, the preaching, and other features. It is important for the person to provide as much detail as possible, because this gives the committee a better sense of the overall scope and functioning of the service in the member's culture. A deeper understanding of worship in a particular cultural setting enables the committee to discern better how to plan the multicultural worship service. The ideas each member describes become the basic ingredients of the multicultural worship service.

STEP 3: SELECT THE FEATURES OF THE SERVICE

After ideas have been gathered, the committee uses these insights to identify which features to include in the multicultural worship service under discussion; the remaining ideas are recorded for future use.

Committee members accept the fact that not all of the ideas put forward by any one member can be included in the worship service being planned. However, in selecting ideas to use in the worship service, the committee should ensure that each cultural group in the congregation is equally represented. For example, music for the service could be chosen in such a way that all of the cultural and language groups have an active part by presenting a special musical number, anthem, praise chorus, or hymn drawn from their culture. For a Communion service, one of the best ways to display a cultural symbol is to use breads representing the different cultures of those in worship. This may seem a small and insignificant gesture, but it is very meaningful to the person who sees the bread from his or her culture used in the worship service.

The theme, format, music, Scripture readings, preachers, and participants are also chosen at this stage of preparation. The theme for the service should relate to the needs of the congregation. The format should be as sensitive to each cultural preference as possible. Try to choose hymns that are used in as many language groups as possible. If a specific

The United Methodist Church...makes a deliberate effort to recognize, affirm, and include in the life of the church people from every cultural background.

hymn is not found in the hymnbook of a particular language group, ask the committee member representing that language group to translate the words of the hymn so that it can also be included in the service.

As mentioned earlier, each language group is asked to participate in the music component of the service. One effective way for language groups to participate together in providing the music for the service is to have a joint choir, composed of singers from different language or cultural groups. To make the choir even more multicultural, they could sing a song in a language different from their own. In the multicultural congregation I serve, we once had a joint choir—composed of Korean-speaking, Filipino-speaking, and English-speaking members—sing the "Hallelujah Chorus" in Spanish! Imagine the excitement and the special touch this brought to the rendition of this well-known anthem. Creativity is an important characteristic in the entire process of preparation.

At this point in the preparation process, all those who will provide leadership in the worship service are also selected. A rather large number of participants are needed in a multicultural worship. The participants include choirs, musicians, Scripture readers, liturgists, acolytes, Communion servers (during Communion services), ushers, greeters, flag bearers, preachers, and translators. The Scripture readings are determined either by the Lectionary or by the preference of the preacher.

The involvement of so many people in the service not only adds to the much-needed visual aspect of the service but also encourages a spirit of participation and inclusion. Even in multicultural worship done on a smaller scale, the need to involve many participants is important. One feature of such participation is that more people are given the opportunity to become actively involved in the life of the congregation. A guest preacher could be invited to come. He or she must have a commitment to be culturally sensitive and must be willing to prepare the sermon manuscript ahead of time for translation purposes.

The committee must also decide which languages will be used in the worship service. In the congregation in which I serve, we identified four languages that represent all the people in the congregation. We committed ourselves to preparing a bulletin written in four languages, so that everyone could benefit from the worship experience.

It is also at this point that the committee must decide which items in the service should be read together (read simultaneously by worshipers in different languages) and which items should be read in just one language. Experience shows that items such as the call to worship, the opening prayer, the prayer of confession, and community responses are best read together. Scripture readings can be done in a particular language. There are two ways to do this: One is to choose a short passage that can be read in different languages at different times during the service; another way is to choose several passages, with each passage read in one language. Since each worshiper has a copy of the multi-language bulletin, either way works well.

STEP 4: COMPOSE THE FORMAT OF THE SERVICE

After all the features have been selected, the next step is to compose the format for the worship service. This involves placing each item or feature of the service in logical sequence. In some cultures, it is very important for the sermon to be toward the end of the service. In other cultures, this may not be so. To avoid conflict, it is helpful to alternate where the sermon is placed from service to service: In one service, the sermon may be placed toward the end to affirm the preference of one cultural group; in the next service, a different format may be used to accommodate another group. This is not always an easy task, but the commitment to give and take makes the process go more smoothly. Bear in mind that multicultural worship is not the worship of just one culture with the other groups serving as spectators; rather, in a multicultural service, every cultural group is involved and represented. Having said this, the reality is that not every aspect of a specific culture's worship life will be represented in any one service; therefore, the congregation needs to be flexible and patient.

Multicultural worship experiences are more successful and more interesting when they are as musical and visual as possible. The more music there is in such a worship service, the more enjoyable and meaningful the worship becomes. Music is indeed a universal language.

Symbols and visuals are other important tools; for these, too, are universal. Imagine being in a service where you see a lot of objects and symbols and hear a lot of music. Even if the language is somewhat unfamiliar—or altogether foreign—a good dose of music and visuals still provides a sense of connection and appreciation. Making the service more musical and visual is not only enjoyable but also encourages participation and involvement. For obvious reasons, sermons in such services tend to be short!

STEP 5: PREPARE TO TRANSLATE THE BULLETIN

I said earlier that multicultural worship is a lot of work. Translation alone requires a lot of time and effort; however, it is very important to have a multi-language worship bulletin.

In my experience, it is relatively easy to translate spoken words. Written items, such as the call to worship, Communion liturgy, and prayers are not always easy to translate. The same is true for hymns and anthems. The rhythms and rhymes of music pieces can be a big challenge to translators, but with patience and perseverance translation is possible. (This is where commitment comes in.)

Cultural groups have Bibles and hymnbooks, so Scripture passages and common hymns do not present problems for translation. The most practical way to proceed is to prepare the bulletin in English first; then, different committee members can translate the bulletin into the languages needed.

STEP 6: PREPARE THE FINAL LAYOUT

Committee members give their translations of the bulletin to the coordinator, who does the layout. Preparing the bulletin is a big part of planning the multicultural worship. As I mentioned, the congregation in which I serve has a four-language bulletin. Each page in the bulletin has four columns, one for each language. The goal is to make the content of the bulletin align properly in each of the languages. The same content translated in one language may require more words than in another language; therefore, aligning the sections of the bulletin in the different languages requires proficiency in a good word-processing program.

Aside from the actual liturgy, each column in the bulletin also has instructions to help the worshiper know which sections of the liturgy are

Multicultural worship services do not just happen.

to be read together and which sections are to be read in one language only. Needless to say, a multi-language bulletin complete with instructions is a must.

STEP 7: PREPARE THE WORSHIP PLACE

Preparation includes decorating the place of worship with the different cultural symbols and visuals the committee members have agreed to display. Each culture should be equally and properly represented. For example, if flags are displayed in the service, care should be taken that the flags are of the same size and that they are positioned in such a way that no one flag appears superior or inferior.

The final preparation requires a lot of people. A strong feature of having a large group of people work together is that they tend to bond. The time of preparation is actually an excellent occasion for fellowship and bonding. The individuals involved in the preparation share precious moments with one another.

STEP 8: REHEARSE THE SERVICE

Because of the complexity and the nature of the service, rehearsing is a must. It is helpful to have the rehearsal after the place of worship has been decorated. This provides the worship team with a better sense of how the place will look during the actual worship service. Everyone providing leadership in the worship service should be urged to attend the rehearsal. Again, this is another opportunity for the people from various cultural backgrounds to share moments of bonding.

The coordinator prepares a guide, or notes, for the participants of the service to follow. It works best for the coordinator to write the notes and instructions in the bulletin each participant will use in the service. The coordinator then gives each participant his or her marked bulletin, making sure that the participant understands what his or her role is in the service.

Another helpful item is a schematic diagram of the place of worship. The diagram indicates where each participant should sit or stand, and how he or she should move during the service.

The key is to prepare rehearsal notes that are detailed and yet simple to follow. The goal of the rehearsal is to make the participants knowledgeable and comfortable as to what they are supposed to do, when they are supposed to do it, and where.

CONDUCTING THE MULTICULTURAL WORSHIP SERVICE

When it comes to conducting the actual worship service, excitement is always in the air. Different symbols decorate the place of worship; different people are eagerly waiting for the service to start; choirs are warming up; participants are in their costumes or beautiful dresses; and music is playing. There is a deep sense of excitement everywhere. Right away, the worship leadership feels that its efforts have been rewarded.

The moment the service starts with the first item—whether it be the call to worship, the introit, or the organ music—a sense of excitement is evident. That excitement is sustained throughout the service. To be sure, the sound of people reading and singing in different languages can be annoying to some, but overall it is a powerful experience. As mentioned earlier, some languages require more words than others; so the sound of people reading when others have finished becomes commonplace. Again, for some people this may be tantamount to chaos, but, overall, the experience of worshiping together and hearing different languages can be a powerful tool to help people from different cultures relate to one another and experience worship together.

The preaching could be done in at least two ways: giving direct verbal translation from the pulpit or providing worshipers with a written translation. The advantage of direct verbal translation is that the worshiper's attention is focused on the preacher; the disadvantage is that this process can be time consuming. The advantage of a written translation is that the sermon tends to be less time consuming; the disadvantage is that people tend to focus on their translation notes and not on the preacher. Again, the key here is to make the sermon as short and direct as possible.

As an extension of the worship experience, it is invaluable to host a fellowship meal following the service. The fellowship meal does not just serve to feed the people, although this is necessary; it also provides an excellent opportunity for the people to get to know one another. With this in mind, it is important to make sure that people from different cultural and language groups are represented at every table. There is a natural tendency for cultural groups to band together at one or more tables.

Multicultural worship is best complemented by a multicultural meal. Therefore, the fellowship meal should consist of a variety of foods from different cultural groups. On occasion, the different cultural groups can take turns hosting the meal. Each cultural group then has an opportunity to participate in a meaningful way.

CONCLUSION

At the end of a multicultural worship service and a fellowship meal, the worship committee and worship leaders have time to reflect. They realize that everything worked out well and that people were blessed because the entire planning process was followed faithfully. They recognize that the process was not easy but that everyone gave it their best. With this realization comes a deep sense of satisfaction: Through the worship service not just one group of people, but the whole worshiping community, was served. Then, in his or her own language and from whatever cultural background he or she comes, each worship leader can say, "Hallelujah!" (By the way, that word is the same in every language and culture. Others may spell it differently, but it is basically the same.)

FOR FURTHER READING

We Are the Church Together: Cultural Diversity in Congregational Life, by Charles R. Foster and Theodore Brelsford (Harrisonburg, PA: Trinity Press International, 1996).

Worship Across Cultures: A Handbook, by Kathy Black (Nashville, TN: Abingdon Press, 1998).

Multicultural worship is not the worship of just one culture with the other groups serving as spectators.

22

How to Plan Worship in an Oral Context

TEX SAMPLE

Robert B. and Kathleen Rogers Professor of Church and Society, Saint Paul School of Theology, Kansas City, Missouri

THE UNITED METHODIST CHURCH SUFFERS FROM AN ENORMOUS literate bias in a great many of its forms of worship. While literate forms of worship are appropriate for congregations that are made up of literate people, it is a form of imperial activity when imposed on people who are oral. In these cases, a bias becomes a bigotry. Hardly anything more important could be done to lift the authentic character of worship for oral people in the church than to make their worship indigenous.

By "literate" I mean people who engage the world in terms of theory, conceptualization, and discourse. Such worship typically includes a long, "printy" bulletin or extended readings from *The United Methodist Hymnal* or the *Book of Worship.* By "oral" I refer to people who engage the world through proverb, story, and communal relationships.[1] Such folk do not "do" theory, but rather relate to life through proverbs that convey a wisdom that is often implicit and tacit in its understanding. For oral people, stories do not make "points" as in literate discourse; rather, the stories *are* the point. Thus, when engaging in conversation with oral people regarding social questions, it is typically not helpful to develop theoretical perspectives on the issues. It is better to deal with these questions in terms of someone the people know—that is, as Anthony Pappas says, to "put a face on [it]."[2]

When worship is done in this way, it makes use of practices that are basic to the lives of oral people. My purpose in this article is to suggest ways in which worship, when done in an oral context, can be liturgy; that is, the work of the people.

In planning and conducting worship in an oral context, three things need to be taken seriously. First, we hear a great deal about "globalization." If such language means anything more than the pretensions of academic and ecclesiastic striving for status, it suggests that the church needs to become adept at oral practices. Two-thirds of the world is oral. To be global in worship means to be able to do liturgy in these oral forms. Moreover, my guesstimate is that in the United States of America, forty to fifty percent of people in The United Methodist Church are oral. In saying this I do not mean to suggest that these people are illiterate (though some are), but that they basically engage the world through oral practices. Worship should not be a "sideline" or a "backstreet" practice, either in the United States of America or in the rest of the world; rather, it should be one of the major forms of liturgical expression in the church.

Worship Matters: A United Methodist Guide to Worship Work (Volume II) © 1999 Discipleship Resources. Used by permission.

Second, if The United Methodist Church wishes to be a racially and ethnically inclusive church, it must face up to the fact that rich oral traditions are found among African Americans, Anglo-European Americans, Asian Americans, Hispanic and Latino/Latina Americans, and Native Americans. To be diverse and inclusive is to be able to do oral worship.

Third, I take seriously the Incarnation, especially John 1:14, which says that "the Word became flesh and [dwelt] among us." *Dwelt* is a translation of the Greek *skeenoon,* which means "pitched tent." Pitching tent is a basic practice in Jesus' time and is a central metaphor for expressing the Incarnation. I take this to mean that Christ joined the indigenous practices of his time. Such an indigenous move is central to the work of the church as it reaches out to people in the cultures where they are formed. Such a claim does not deny that the church has distinctive practices of its own, but rather that such practices will engage the context of the cultures of the world. The church cannot simply do what the church did in Jerusalem, but must take seriously the culture of the Gentiles, as Paul did in the first century.

A FAITH LANGUAGE OF THE HEART

Basic to an oral culture is an approach to faith that can be described as "a faith language of the heart." By this I mean that such faith is more oriented to believing and feeling than to thinking and knowing. Although oral people think and know a great deal, it does not typically take literate forms. Rather, this faith language of the heart is oriented toward religious commitment as "a way of life" more than "a view of life."[3] It is oriented toward coping and survival and to gaining and sustaining a sense of identity and belonging.

These insights are crucial to the importance of oral worship. If the worship does not engage believing and feeling, does not help such people make it through difficult times, and does not enable them to identify who they are and Whose they are, it is simply unrelated to their lives. Hence, oral worship will take forms that express trust more than explanation, assurance more than coherence, and the capacity to cope more than the consistent statement of a literate *tour de force*. At this point, the Wesleyan emphasis on assurance is central to oral worship. Such an approach is especially germane to prayer, preaching, and other oral/verbal expressions.

THE PRACTICES OF ORAL WORSHIP

How, then, do we plan and practice oral worship? First, oral worship can be fully practiced in a setting in which the Christian Year, the Lectionary, and classical worship resources are fully engaged—but not in literate forms. Moreover, such worship can be structured in terms of the Basic Pattern: Entrance, Proclamation and Response, Thanksgiving and Communion, and Sending Forth (*UMH*, p. 2). The point here is that tradition is not lost in oral practices.

How do worship leaders plan oral worship? The first step is to do away with print in the worship service, or to use it predominantly through oral practices. Reading by the congregation in the service should be kept to a minimum.

Oral people enjoy gathering; hence, worship is more like a gathering. It is informal in character, emphasizing personal connections that can be conveyed in handshakes, passing of the peace, hugs, and, in some

While literate forms of worship are appropriate for congregations that are made up of literate people, it is a form of imperial activity when imposed on people who are oral.

contexts, a holy kiss. There is often an "insider's knowledge" in these settings, so that worshipers are more like a family than an organization—focused more on events than on programs, and far more communal than associational.

A basic practice in oral worship is call and response. The call to worship, for example, can be done this way—that is, the liturgist speaks a line and the congregation is instructed to respond with yet another line indicated by the liturgist. Call and response can be used at any number of points in a service: in litanies or prayer, in singing, in the affirmation of faith, in the Eucharist, and so forth. A variation of the call-and-response pattern is when the choir or soloist sings the stanza of a song and the congregation sings the chorus.

The practice of "lining out" is also common in oral worship. Here a leader states or sings a line of the hymn and the congregation speaks or sings this same line in return. Lining out thus can be done in spoken and in sung forms. In lections where a psalm is read, lining out reduces the problem of lection-reading as the work of a "talking head." Such a practice can also be used as a way of doing the Great Thanksgiving during the Eucharist.

Music is crucial to oral worship. An important form of music is called "soul music." Soul music means two things. First, it is the music with which one is "encoded" and that shapes a person over the course of his or her life. Second, it is the music that tells a person's story. Ruth Finnegan reports in her research that popular music today provides the "social pathways" and "urban passageways" of most people's lives.[4] And Simon Frith, the British rock critic, supports and substantially extends her point by claiming that most people today find the "convincing narratives" of their lives in popular music.[5]

This means that the worship of the church needs to "pitch tent" with the soul music of people in oral cultures. The use of soul music engages the basic narratives of people's lives. In worship the use of soul music is basic to placing the story of the people into God's story. A great variety of soul music abounds: country, rock, rap, jazz, blues, and others. Worship leaders in oral congregations must learn what is the soul music of a congregation and make use of it.

Oral people in The United Methodist Church have perhaps suffered most from the colonial activity of classical-music purists, who often insist on imposing a "high-culture" genre of music on popular-culture people. It is a violation of the first order to refuse a people the language and music not only of their culture but also of their hearts and of their spiritual lives. In such cases, we need a notion of *liturgical abuse* to name not only the imperialism of liturgical forms externally imposed but also that of alien forms of music. Such activities by these purists need to be so named.

Memorization is a key practice in oral culture, although today it may seem to be absent. Yet when one looks at the capacity of people—especially young people—to know hundreds of lines from rap music or country music, it is clear that memorization is still strong. For example, quite usable renditions of the prodigal son are available in rap, as are other well-known scriptural passages. These can be used initially in solo performances, but could also be extended for congregational use as these songs are learned. This would be especially meaningful to many younger people for whom rap is soul music.

Another way to employ memorization in worship is to use verses of Scripture in oral form. Take, for example, Psalm 23. (This is often the best-known passage of Scripture.) This psalm could be used as an affirmation of faith. Other worship resources that are first learned through lining out and call and response can later become expressions of memorized worship resources by the congregation. I think here of Scripture passages such as Matthew 22:37-39; Luke 4:18-19; Micah 4:6-8; or selections from the Sermon on the Mount.

Movement, dance, swaying, marching, and other forms of embodied participation are significant in worship in many oral traditions. The place of indigenous forms of music and dance in worship is important. In the West, print culture has historically been far too disembodied. The notion in most United Methodist congregations that worship should be "physically restrained" serves to disable the participation of oral people. The exclusion of dance and the drum from so much of Native-American worship in United Methodist services is a case in point.[6]

Testimony is yet another basic practice in oral culture. While we tend to hear more about its abuses, testimony can be done well. Worship leaders can surely place limits on those brothers and sisters who get up and tell the same story every time, never seeming to tire of the same old lines. By planning ahead and asking a person or two to give a testimony in a worship service, it is not difficult to place time boundaries on witnesses and to make sure that the opportunity is shared by a large number of people in the congregation. In my experience, such testimonies are not abused and play an important role in informing the congregation of the impact of the faith on people they know.

In the literate world, the *visual* metaphor is pervasive in referring to knowing. For example, we talk about someone's "point of view" or "perspective" or "angle of vision." When one is used to print and the visual metaphor as media of knowing, it is easy to forget how important *sound* is in an oral culture—indeed, sound is central. If something doesn't sound right, it isn't real, isn't authentic, isn't true. Thus in worship, making the right sound is crucial to the worship experience. For example, an oral congregation will greatly appreciate a "ministerial tone." That is, a preacher who speaks in rich, round tones. That preacher will be quite in tune with the congregation. In a literate congregation, however, such a style of speaking may seem phony and exaggerated; hence, a more conversational style of speaking may be appropriate.

The emphasis on the right sound may apply to a host of practices in oral worship, including the singing of hymns; the kinds of musical instruments chosen and the ways they are played; the rhythmic cadence of congregational vocal participation; the use of repetition; and the style of testimonies. In planning worship in an oral congregation, it is crucial for the worship leaders to get in touch with the character of sounds by which the truth is presented, enacted, and made known.

Obviously, in an oral culture, preaching is not a literate endeavor. That is, the pastor does not preach from a manuscript—unless she or he can read a sermon and make it *sound* for the world like an oral effort! Sermons in an oral context will use the perceptive story or the crystallizing proverb and work with the communal knowing and the relational thinking of a local context; that is, being able to tell a story that *is* a point is central. Oral people think in stories. Such preaching is comfortable with the biblical stories and finds it necessary to relate the more heavily discursive material in the Bible through story and proverb, and through "putting faces" on the more literate passages of Scripture.

It is easy to forget how important *sound* is in an oral culture.

CONCLUSION

The worship practices as outlined in this article are but a beginning, and yet they are crucial if the church is to be truly inclusive and global. In their worship, The United Methodist Church and other mainline denominations have generally neglected oral culture as found all over the world and among a very large section of people in the United States of America.

Even with the third millennium approaching and with the increasing encroachment of electronic culture, oral culture will remain for some time—even as it is influenced by the impact of television, computers, digitalization, virtual reality, and the popularity of electronic media. What is emerging is not a world without oral culture but an *electronically influenced* orality; this is also the destiny of literality. Clergy and lay leadership in worship will not learn oral practices in their heads alone; they will learn these practices by doing them.

FOR FURTHER READING

Entering the World of the Small Church: A Guide for Leaders, by Antony G. Pappas (Bethesda, MD: The Alban Institute, Inc., 1989).

Ministry in an Oral Culture: Living With Will Rogers, Uncle Remus, and Minnie Pearl, by Tex Sample (Louisville, KY: Westminster John Knox Press, 1994).

The Interface Between the Written and the Oral: Studies in Literacy, Family Culture, and the State, by Jack Goody (New York, NY: Cambridge University Press, 1987).

White Soul: Country Music, the Church, and Working Americans, by Tex Sample (Nashville, TN: Abingdon Press, 1996).

ENDNOTES

1 Regarding the difference between oral and literate cultures, see the two books by Walter J. Ong, *Orality and Literacy: The Technologizing of the Word* (New York, NY: Routledge, 1991) and *The Presence of the Word: Some Prolegomena for Cultural and Religious History* (Minneapolis, MN: University of Minnesota Press, 1981). See also Jack Goody, *The Interface Between the Written and the Oral: Studies in Literacy, Family, Culture, and the State* (New York, NY: Cambridge University Press, 1987). I offer a more extended treatment of oral culture in *Ministry in an Oral Culture: Living With Will Rogers, Uncle Remus, and Minnie Pearl* (Louisville, KY: Westminster John Knox Press, 1994).

2 See *Entering the World of the Small Church: A Guide for Leaders,* by Anthony G. Pappas, (Bethesda, MD: The Alban Institute, Inc., 1988), p. 80.

3 See *Constructing Local Theologies,* by Robert J. Schreiter (New York, NY: Orbis Books, 1985), p. 126.

4 See *The Hidden Musicians,* by Ruth Finnegan (Cambridge, MA: Cambridge University Press, 1989), pp. 323–25

5 See *Performing Rites: On the Value of Popular Music,* by Simon Frith (Cambridge, MA: Harvard University Press, 1996), p. 276.

6 I am indebted to Donna Allen, instructor in worship and preaching at Saint Paul School of Theology, for her helpful comments on the importance of movement in oral worship.

How to Plan Worship for People Who Are Deaf, Deafened, or Hard of Hearing

KATHY BLACK

Gerald Kennedy Chair of Homiletics and Liturgics, Claremont School of Theology, Claremont, California

PLANNING WORSHIP FOR PEOPLE WHO ARE DEAF, DEAFENED, or hard of hearing requires a visual orientation on the part of the worship planners. Most "hearing" worship services tend to be orally and aurally oriented. Speech and hearing are the primary modes of communication. Music not only signals the opening and closing of worship but also sets the mood and tone for various aspects of the worship service. We are not always conscious of how important speech and hearing are to being a full participant in worship.

When people who are deaf, deafened, or hard of hearing are members of our congregations, certain adjustments need to be made so that these individuals have full access to the worshiping life of the community. It would be easy to say that each group—those born deaf; those who became deaf in adulthood (deafened); and those who are hard of hearing—has different needs in terms of access to worship. However, the issues are not that clearly defined. Several factors play a role in what accommodations are most appropriate for any individual. The severity of one's hearing loss is not always the determining factor.

For example, Sally is audiologically profoundly deaf, but her hearing loss occurred in retirement years. Though she is considered deaf, she is culturally hearing and communicates most comfortably in English. She is trying to learn sign language, but communicates best by speaking for herself and learning to speech read (lip read) what others are saying. She is highly dependent on printed materials.

On the other hand, David is mildly hard of hearing. He was raised in the Deaf culture by parents who were deaf, so American Sign Language (ASL) is his first language. He is more comfortable in the Deaf community using sign language to communicate. (Deaf children with deaf parents are born into the Deaf culture. ASL is their first language; and the values, mores, and history are passed down to them from birth. The Deaf community, on the other hand, is comprised of people who are deaf, deafened, and hard of hearing, most of whom have hearing parents. Their language ranges from manual codes of the English language to Sign-Supported Speech to American Sign Language. People who are deaf who have hearing parents have to be enculturated into the Deaf culture—often through schools for the deaf—to be become full participants.)

Worship Matters: A United Methodist Guide to Worship Work (Volume II) © 1999 Discipleship Resources. Used by permission.

The age of the person when the hearing loss occurred, the culture the person identifies with (Deaf culture or hearing culture of whatever ethnicity), and the preferred method of communication (speaking and speech reading English or their native spoken language, American Sign Language, or an English-based sign language) are all factors that need to be taken into consideration when adapting worship for people who are deaf, deafened, or hard of hearing.

While the diversity among these people is great, they do have one thing in common: Some form of hearing loss requires them to be visually oriented and visually dependent on the world around them. For people who are deaf, deafened, or hard of hearing who are fluent in English (or the written language of the worship service), any print material that can be provided is always helpful (words to the choir anthem printed in the bulletin, an outline or copy of the sermon so they can "fill in the blanks" of what they missed, or page numbers printed in the bulletin to tell where the Scripture texts are located).

In recognizing the uniqueness of each individual's needs in relation to how worship may be adapted, there are several general guidelines that can be identified for people who are deaf, deafened, or hard of hearing.

DESIGNING WORSHIP FOR THOSE WHO ARE HARD OF HEARING

Almost every congregation in the country has members who are hard of hearing. While we tend to identify hearing loss with an older population, studies show that rock music, boom boxes, earphones for tape recorders, and an increasingly noisy environment are causing hearing loss in people of much younger ages. Don't limit yourself to those with gray hair when asking, "Who's hard of hearing in our congregation?"

Besides including more printed materials in the worship bulletin, the most common adjustment made to the worship space for those who are hard of hearing is the installation of an Assistive-Listening System, which includes devices that transmit sound through space in a variety of ways. They range in price and effectiveness. The three most common systems are FM, infrared, and audio-loop. When using any of these systems, it is important to remember that whoever speaks or sings must use a microphone. Otherwise, the Assistive-Listening System will not pick up the sound.

FM Systems

FM systems use a radio wave to transmit sound from the microphone directly to a small transistor radio. The person with the hearing loss holds the radio and puts earphones into her or his ears. Because the sound goes directly from the microphone into the person's ear, background noise is diminished and the sound does not get distorted traveling through the air to the person in the pew.

If a person is in denial about his or her hearing loss, holding the receiver and wearing the earphones may make him or her feel conspicuous. If a person has taken steps to correct a hearing loss by getting a hearing aid, an adaptation needs to be made to the FM system so that the person can use the system without removing the hearing aid. (See the section "Audio-Loop Systems," on pages 179–80.)

The benefit of the FM system is that it can be used for worship services that are held outdoors as well as in the sanctuary. The problem with this system is that the sound can travel through walls and ceilings; therefore, the church cannot have two FM systems operating at the same time. For example, it may not work to have one system operating in a children's Sunday school room while another system is on in the sanctuary because the signals may get mixed.

The church purchases one transmitter per room and a separate receiver (the transistor radio) for each person with a hearing loss. These receivers need to be checked periodically to make sure the batteries are working properly.

INFRARED SYSTEMS

Infrared systems operate using light waves instead of radio waves. The church purchases as many infrared boxes as are necessary to blanket the worship space with light waves. Only one box is required in many church facilities. In addition, each person must wear her or his own receiver. These receivers have built-in ear pieces so the device actually hangs under the person's chin. The "glass bubble" on the receiver picks up the light waves and transfers these into sound. People who are still in denial about their hearing loss may resist using an infrared system because, like the FM system, they may feel conspicuous wearing a receiver.

Infrared systems cannot transmit light through walls or ceilings, so two systems can operate at the same time. The batteries are easier to maintain because the receivers come in a briefcase that can be kept plugged into an electrical socket. The batteries are removed from the receivers after each use and are placed in their proper place to be constantly recharged so that they are always ready. An infrared system is often the most expensive, but it provides excellent sound quality.

AUDIO-LOOP SYSTEMS

Audio-loop systems operate using the same electromagnetic field that allows sound to travel through the telephone. Phone wire is placed along the floorboards or in the ceiling around the sanctuary space. The wire creates an electromagnetic field within its bounds (with a little spillover outside the bounds). A person with his or her own hearing aids can turn on the "T" switch (telephone switch), which is built into the hearing aid. The person then eliminates background noise and picks up the sound directly into the hearing aid.

Audio-loop systems are the least expensive, but they do have drawbacks. There can be "holes" in the electromagnetic field where the sound quality is not very good. It all depends on the angle at which the telecoil is placed in a person's hearing aid. Sometimes a person can move her or his head up or down or side to side in order to get better reception, but that is awkward at best. Hearing-aid manufacturers can install two telecoils at right angles to each other, which seems to take care of this problem. However, the modification must be requested by the owner of the hearing aid.

A person wearing hearing aids should move around the sanctuary and sit in different pews/chairs until he or she gets the best reception of sound. But once the right area of the sanctuary has been found, tilting one's head in different directions may improve reception even more. Since not all hearing aids come with a "T" switch, it is important when educating people about hearing loss to encourage them to get a

Almost every congregation in the country has members who are hard of hearing.

hearing aid that has a switch built in. Without the "T" switch in the hearing aid, the person cannot access an audio-loop system.

A person who has his or her own hearing aids, but whose church is using either an infrared or FM system, can buy a telecoil adapter. This consists of a phone-wire loop that goes around the person's neck like a large necklace. The "necklace" can plug into either an FM or an infrared receiver. The radio waves or light waves are transformed into an electromagnetic field that can be picked up by the telephone switch on the person's hearing aid. This allows people with their own hearing aids to use any of the systems described above.

DESIGNING WORSHIP FOR THOSE WHO ARE DEAFENED

People who become deaf in adulthood find themselves caught between two worlds. They are audiologically deaf but, because they were hearing up to that point, they "think" as a hearing person would. With practice, they can often maintain their speech for expressing themselves. Since they are competent in the spoken and written language of the culture, this tends to be their primary mode of receiving communication. Learning sign language may be difficult. If sign language is learned, it is usually a manual code of the English language rather than American Sign Language. Learning how to speech read, however, is essential as an auxiliary tool to facilitate one-on-one communication.

Adapting worship for people who are deafened requires not only additional printed materials but also a more complete form of communication. This includes Computer-Assisted Notetaking (C.A.N.) and the use of oral interpreters.

COMPUTER-ASSISTED NOTETAKING

A screen is set up on one side of the sanctuary, or a white wall in the chancel area can be used. Someone types into a computer everything that is said in the worship service that is not printed in the bulletin (or at least the basic meaning of what is said, depending on how fast the person types). The words are projected from the computer monitor onto the screen. Or, to avoid looking at the screen, then at the bulletin, then back at the screen again, the liturgy and sermon or sermon outline (received from the preacher) can be typed into the computer in advance. During the worship service, all that needs to be typed into the computer are those parts of the service that are given extemporaneously.

This adaptation requires a computer, large screen (or white wall), one or more typists, and the software and hardware technology for projecting the words from the computer monitor onto the screen. This technology is rather common today and can be achieved with different programs and equipment. It is the large-room equivalent of open captioning.

The implementation of this communication method is not extremely expensive, and one can usually find people who will take turns typing what is said during worship. The biggest difficulty with this means of communication seems to be the resistance some people (both clergy and laity) have to a large screen with constantly changing words that is placed in the front of the sanctuary (even if it is off to one side). This equipment and technology seem, in the minds of some, to "profane" the sanctuary. Other people just find the visible words distracting. On the other hand, many people who are still in denial about their hearing loss find this a tremendous help.

Education is crucial to overcome these attitudinal barriers. Despite the resistance, it is worth the undertaking. Computer-Assisted Notetaking can really make the entire worship service fully accessible to people who are deafened or severely hard of hearing.

ORAL INTERPRETERS

Another means of assisting communication during worship for those who are deafened is to provide an oral interpreter for those who can receive communication through speech reading (lip reading). Some people who are deafened are skilled at speech reading, but have difficulty speech reading the worship service because of the distances and odd visual angles between the person sitting in the pew and the leaders of worship.

An oral interpreter sits on the same level and opposite the people who are deafened. The interpreter repeats (lip-synchs) everything that is said during the worship service but without voice. The members of the congregation who are deafened read the interpreter's lips (speech read) to understand what is being said.

While there are professional oral interpreters, it is also possible to use volunteers from the congregation. They should be individuals whom the people who are deafened know and can speech read well. Not everyone speaks in a way that can be easily understood in speech reading. Beards, mustaches, verbal accents, and other characteristics can make speech reading almost impossible. If volunteers from the congregation are to be used, those who are deafened should have a part in choosing the most adequate oral interpreters.

Speech reading is a viable means of one-on-one communication, but keep in mind that only forty percent of spoken English is distinguishable on the lips. Sixty percent is still guesswork. Therefore, even with oral interpreters, the printed material is still crucial for full participation to take place.

DESIGNING WORSHIP FOR PEOPLE WHO ARE DEAF

In this section, I focus on those people who consider themselves part of the Deaf community and who communicate primarily in one or more form of sign language—American Sign Language or one of the sign languages based on the English language. The use of any sign language is important because participation in worship requires signing the words of the prayers and liturgies, which precludes holding hymnals or bulletins while participating in corporate acts of worship.

Those whose primary mode of communication is sign language appreciate various aspects of the Deaf culture, such as storytelling, drama, American Sign Language poetry, and other visual art forms rather than the various uses of music that are common in most hearing churches. The more visual worship can be, the more accessible it is to people who are part of the Deaf culture and/or community.

Because of the linguistic and cultural differences, as well as the need for a truly visual worship experience, many people who are deaf prefer a church for people who are deaf, where worship can be designed specifically for the Deaf community and conducted in sign language. In

People who become deaf in adulthood find themselves caught between two worlds.

this country, there aren't many churches for people who are deaf outside major metropolitan areas. This means that if people who are deaf choose to attend church, they often attend a hearing worship service with an interpreter.

It is not surprising that there are few people from the Deaf community in our churches today. For the most part, Sunday schools were not accessible to them as children. That lack of access over the decades has communicated a very clear message: People who are deaf are not welcome here. Despite the exclusive nature of most hearing churches today, God is still able to move in the lives of people who are deaf and to instill a need for a worshiping community. Those who want to establish a ministry with people who are deaf need to take seriously how their worship includes or excludes those who are deaf.

VISUAL WORSHIP

In ministering with people who are deaf, the first step is to try to think visually, keeping in mind that in order to sign, people who are deaf need their hands. Therefore, the prelude, which establishes the tone of the worship service and signals its beginning, needs to be replaced by something visual. The liturgical tradition provides just such a visual counterpart, which is called the procession. For people who are deaf, the procession creates the tone and signifies the beginning of worship. Worship leaders should give attention to the visual nature of processionals and recessionals.

In many congregations, a call to worship, prayer(s), a responsive reading, hymns, and other liturgical elements are often components of the liturgy. The entire congregation participates in these components, either through singing or reading aloud. Since people who are deaf cannot "read aloud" with their hands while holding a hymnal, Bible, or bulletin, alternative methods need to be used to ensure their full participation.

One adaptation is to project the words to hymns, Scripture readings, calls to worship, prayers, and so forth, onto a screen or white wall in the front of the church by means of an overhead or opaque projector or a computer. (See "Computer-Assisted Notetaking," on pages 180–81.) In this way, people can see the words and sign collectively with the rest of the congregation. This works only if the worshipers who are deaf are fluent in the English (written) language used in worship.

Another method requires a sign-language interpreter. Basically, the members of the congregation who are deaf copy what the interpreter signs. The interpreter signs the corporate elements with the congregation, and people who are deaf copy. This puts people who are deaf a little behind the rest of the congregation in timing, but the problems this causes can be alleviated if there is a slight pause before the next speaker begins.

Any use of visual arts in worship is often appreciated by people who are deaf. Visual assistance, such as drama (scriptural or contemporary), liturgical dance, mime/clowning, or slides, gives people who are deaf fuller access to the worship service.

Many hearing churches with ministries with people who are deaf also have sign-language choirs. These choirs take various forms. Sometimes they are made up only of the members who are deaf, using no music for accompaniment. They may sign to the beat of a drum (since they can feel that vibration), or they may sign in total silence while copying a director. In other churches, the sign-language choir is a way for hearing people to be involved in ministry with people who are deaf and to learn sign language. The choir consists of people who are deaf and people who can hear, using either live or taped music during their performances. In some cases, this choir exists in addition to the hearing choir; in other cases, the sign-language choir signs whatever the hearing choir sings for the anthem that week.

SIGN-LANGUAGE INTERPRETERS

Providing a sign-language interpreter is another important step in making worship accessible for people in the Deaf community. This is not as easy as it sounds because several issues need to be resolved. Should the interpreter be a professionally trained and certified interpreter, or a volunteer from the congregation? What sign language will be used in worship, American Sign Language or a sign language that is more dependent on the English language? Will the interpreter be expected to lip-synch simultaneously for the benefit of members of the congregation who are hard of hearing or deafened?

Although somewhat expensive, it is better to use certified interpreters, provided they are knowledgeable about religious vocabulary (in English and in sign language). Theological vocabulary is not easily interpreted by someone who has not been personally active in a faith community. Since interpretation is not transliteration (exact translation), the interpreter has to make many instant decisions as to what certain words and phrases mean and how to interpret them into sign language.

On the other hand, a volunteer interpreter may have a deep theological understanding and fluency in religious vocabulary and their meanings but be inadequate at basic sign-language or interpreting skills. For example, a person who is a teacher of children who are deaf may or may not know religious sign vocabulary and may or may not be skilled in interpreting. The decision about which sign language to use will depend on who the constituency is. Worship leaders should make these decisions in consultation with members in the church or community who are deaf.

CONCLUSION

Almost every congregation in the nation has a member who is living with hearing loss. Unfortunately, because our worship services are not accessible, many of these people have withdrawn from the faith community. Since they are not physically present and making demands, it is easy to say that the cost for adapting the worship service to the needs of people who are deaf, deafened, or hard of hearing would outweigh the number of people served.

But hearing loss is not going away. It will become a major health crisis as people begin losing their hearing during their working years, rather than during their retirement years. Various forms of adaptation can make a big difference in people's lives and keep them active in the life of the church for years to come.

When designing worship for people who are deaf, deafened, or hard of hearing, these people should be included as consultants at every step of the process. They are the worship leaders' teachers and guides. It is very important that the congregation be brought on board as well.

As we make our churches more accessible, education and preparation go a long way to alleviating backlash when changes are made to the Sunday liturgy or to the sanctuary space.

The more visual worship can be, the more accessible it is to people who are part of the Deaf culture and/or community.

FOR FURTHER READING

Deaf in America: Voices From a Culture, by Tom Humphries and Carol Paddon (Cambridge, MA: Harvard University Press, 1990).

Eye Centered: A Study on the Spirituality of Deaf People With Implications for Pastoral Ministry, by William Key and Ann Albrecht (Landover Hills, MD: National Catholic Office for the Deaf, 1992).

Religious Signing, by Elaine Costello (New York, NY: Bantam Books, 1997).

Signs of Solidarity: Ministry With Persons Who Are Deaf, Deafened, or Hard of Hearing, by Kathy Black (Cincinnati, OH: General Board of Global Ministries, UMC, Health and Welfare Ministries Program Department, 1994). Contact: Service Center, General Board of Global Ministries, The United Methodist Church, 7820 Reading Road, Caller #1800, Cincinnati, OH 45222-1800. Phone: 513-701-2100.